Father Dearest

Neelima Dalmia Adhar was educated in a convent school and a reputed college in Delhi and has a Master's in Psychology with a specialisation in 'Personality'. Her first and only job was to teach Psychology to undergraduate students of Delhi University. A passionate 'people-watcher', she is drawn to oddities and thrives on writing about personalities and human behaviour, from the quirky to the mysterious to the bizarre, a subject she does chillingly close to the bone.

She lives in Delhi with her husband, children and two grandchildren.

Other books by the author

Merchants of Death
The Secret Diary of Kasturba
Radha: The Princess of Barsana

NEELIMA DALMIA ADHAR

Father Dearest

the life and times of

R. K. DALMIA

WESTLAND
NON-FICTION

First published by Namita Gokhale Editions, an imprint of Roli Books Pvt. Ltd, in 2003

Published by westland ltd in 2017

Published by Westland Non-Fiction, an imprint of Westland Books, a division of Nasadiya Technologies Private Limited, in 2024

No. 269/2B, First Floor, 'Irai Arul', Vimalraj Street, Nethaji Nagar, Alapakkam Main Road, Maduravoyal, Chennai 600095

Westland, the Westland logo, Westland Non-Fiction and the Westland Non-Fiction logo are the trademarks of Nasadiya Technologies Private Limited, or its affiliates.

ISBN: 9788196011833

10 9 8 7 6 5 4 3 2 1

Typeset by Newgen KnowledgeWorks (P) Ltd, Chennai
Printed at Nutech Print Services, India

This book is dedicated with love and humility to Dineshnandini, my mother, and to the omnipresent energy source that guided me during my writing and exorcised the ghosts from within my soul.

Contents

Acknowledgements · viii
Preface · xix

PART I

Me Neelima Dalmia Adhar · 3
(21 May 1951)

PART II

My Father Ramkrishna Dalmia · · · · · · · · · · · · · · · · · 39
(7 April 1893–26 September 1978)

PART III

My Mother Dineshnandini Chordia Dalmia · · · · · · 167
(16 February 1925)

Epilogue · 302
Who Lives Where · 305
Glossary · 309
Bibliography · 316

Acknowledgements

I thank

My father who forms the focal point of this story and the seed of my being;

My mother from whom I inherited the chromosomes that impart the ability to write;

My brothers and sisters with whom I grew up, and without whom I would not have been 'me', especially Raja who provided me with the photographs, documents, newspaper clippings and letters that contributed to the making of this book;

My husband and soulmate of many lives, Amitabh, who has patiently endured my 'Dalmia eccentricities';

My two children Mrinali and Yameer who are the pulse of my being;

and

My first publishers, Roli Books, for letting me tell this story.

Ramkrishna Dalmia in the mandir at *Teen Number* during a special puja performed on his birthday. He was a deeply religious man.

The family man, Ramkrishna Dalmia with his sixth wife, Dineshnandini on Babu's third birthday. From left to right: Laxmana, Babu, Ramkrishna Dalmia, Padma, Dineshnandini and Neelima.

Ramkrishna Dalmia and Dineshnandini during his One World
Mission.

In New York during his One World Mission. From left to right: Rakeshnandini (Dineshnandini's sister) Mrs. Margolin, Dineshnandini, Ramkrishna Dalmia, Mr. Margolin (Press Secretary) Sharma (Private Secretary to Ramkrishna Dalmia).

Ramkrishna Dalmia and Dineshnandini in London with Lord Pethic Lawrence and the Chinese Ambassador during the One World Mission.

Ramkrishna Dalmia arriving in Rome on his One World Mission.

Ramkrishna Dalmia with his close friend Mohammad Ali Jinnah. It was believed that if there was one man who could have prevented the Partition, it was Ramkrishna Dalmia.

Ramkrishna Dalmia performing the *kanyadaan* at Neelima and Amitabh's wedding.

Today on the heights I stand
Where God's winds sing lullaby
And no more I reach for the gleam
Of the baubles for which men die
For I reach to the heart of God
And Master of fate am I.

(From A *Guide to Bliss* by
Ramkrishna Dalmia, January 1962)

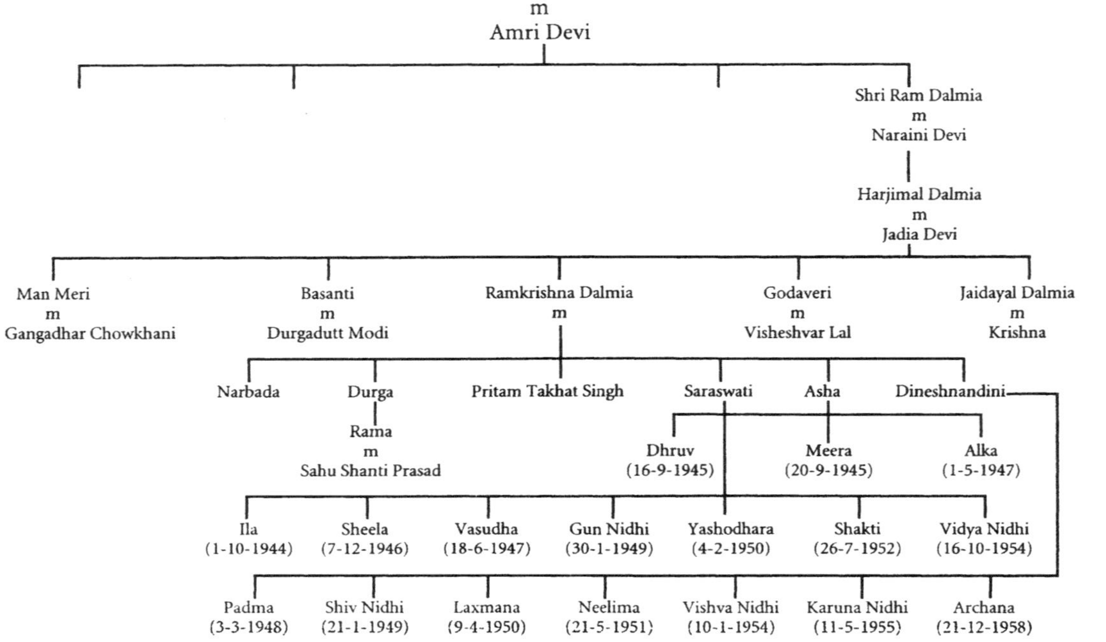

Kashi Ram Dalmia
m
Amri Devi

Shri Ram Dalmia
m
Naraini Devi

Harjimal Dalmia
m
Jadia Devi

Man Meri
m
Gangadhar Chowkhani

Basanti
m
Durgadutt Modi

Ramkrishna Dalmia
m

Godaveri
m
Visheshvar Lal

Jaidayal Dalmia
m
Krishna

Narbada

Durga
Rama
m
Sahu Shanti Prasad

Pritam Takhat Singh

Saraswati

Asha

Dineshnandini

Dhruv
(16-9-1945)

Meera
(20-9-1945)

Alka
(1-5-1947)

Ila
(1-10-1944)

Sheela
(7-12-1946)

Vasudha
(18-6-1947)

Gun Nidhi
(30-1-1949)

Yashodhara
(4-2-1950)

Shakti
(26-7-1952)

Vidya Nidhi
(16-10-1954)

Padma
(3-3-1948)

Shiv Nidhi
(21-1-1949)

Laxmana
(9-4-1950)

Neelima
(21-5-1951)

Vishva Nidhi
(10-1-1954)

Karuna Nidhi
(11-5-1955)

Archana
(21-12-1958)

Preface

This narrative is an endeavour to resurrect the memory of a grand and forgotten man—my father. I will not trivialise him by claiming that I have accomplished an all-comprehensive survey of his life. Nor have I forayed extensively into his world of commerce and finance because those do not constitute the subject of this book. I have only attempted to enter the mind of a multifaceted person who evoked sharply conflicting reactions ranging from derision, anger and sympathy to curiosity, amusement, perplexity and admiration. A man who has been largely viewed as carnal and depraved owing to his polygamous lifestyle. I have arrived at the conclusion that his persona defies the insular boundaries of words.

During my research and writing, I have rid myself of many angers and fears and have exorcised many phantoms from my soul. For me the journey has been both cathartic and liberating. I have learnt to recognise the frailty and impermanence of human life. I have learnt that the mind follows its own logic and can make a heaven of hell or a hell of heaven!

I am proud to have undertaken this journey unto neutrality, and even more so of being a part of the genealogy that makes me the daughter of this exceptionally charismatic man.

My intent is not to injure the sensitivities of those innumerable others who shared his life with greater or lesser intensities—I only shared with him a time span of twenty-six years (he was fifty-eight when I was born)! I may be accused of an underlying personal bias but to the best of my ability I have tried to divorce the daughter from the writer.

The perceivable gaps in my narrative remain because of the practical limitations of accessibility to more factual material. However, on an emotional level, I have said it all and set myself free in the knowledge of truth!

Neelima Dalmia Adhar
New Delhi, July 2002

Part I

Me
Neelima Dalmia Adhar
(21 May 1951)

It was claustrophobic and suffocating. I was immersed in a pool of pale fluid, a mixture of plasma and blood. I was being pushed upside down towards a small opening at the end of a narrow tunnel. Something closed in around me and propelled me forward. I could not move nor breathe. I wanted to break out. It was dark and I felt afraid. I wanted to scream but there was liquid inside my throat. My head was fixated at a tiny opening that was too small to let me out. I screamed but no sound came out from my throat.

I had been in my mother's womb for over ten months. Against all odds she had conceived me in an effort to produce a male child ten months and eleven days before 21 May 1951. That was the year my father was embroiled in a bitter and losing battle with Jawaharlal Nehru. As the owner of Bharat Insurance Company, my father had been charged with conspiracy and fraud in the biggest scam of those times. It changed irrevocably the course of twenty-one lives: eighteen—those of his children, and three—those of his wives. All my life I bore the stigma of landmarking his downfall with my birth.

So, as ordained by karma, I was born to a screaming and disappointed mother on a hot, steamy Monday, after a night spent in painful labour, at 03.23 a.m. one morning in May. I broke out of the confines of her womb into the arms of a midwife who spanked my bottom as she held me upside down shouting, '*Ladki hui hai. Ladki hai* (A girl has been born. It's a girl).'

At birth, it seems I weighed nine and a half pounds and was 30 inches from head to toe. The moment my mother set her eyes on me, she had exclaimed, She looks just like him—hairless and cruel.

I was born on the first floor of a sprawling forty-room mansion set amidst lush green surroundings of three acres of palm trees, magnolias, pines, gulmohars, neems, jacarandas, peepuls and a hundred-year-old shisham.

That was home *Teen Number* on Sikandra Road—the home that welcomed my mother as a newly-wed bride in the heart of Lutyen's Delhi.

My mother's was a womb that had borne three foetuses before me—four if you counted her first miscarriage. I had my earliest tryst with death or birth here, and the fear of closed, dark places has stayed with me ever since.

I was my mother's fourth child. My father waited impatiently outside the makeshift labour room with a wristwatch to mark the time of my birth. It was a ritual that he had performed twelve times earlier. To him each of his children was the harbinger of the good or bad that was to befall him. His three wives—my mother being the third living wife, the sixth and last all told—produced children continuously and simultaneously in the hope of giving him the perfect heir!

I was an unnaturally tall and a big baby, and my mother could not conceal her disappointment. I had let her down. She had desperately wanted a boy. The midwife rubbed the rest of the placenta from my mother's womb all over my body before handing me to her. This would make my skin soft like honey and glow like gold. It would never let hair grow on my body and make me the essential beauty described in the *Kama Sutra.*

The time of my birth was communicated to the family astrologer who drew up the birth-chart that would map the course of my life. My father hailed my birth as a divine blessing. 'Devi has come into our home,' he said. But my mother felt otherwise. Even though the astrologers predicted that I would be lucky for my father, be distinctive in my accomplishments, produce poetry of a novel kind like Dante's *La Divina Comedia,* excel in arts, show remarkable qualities of leadership and clairvoyance, have encounters with the spiritual world and bring fame to the family, my mother remained unconsolable, and never forgave me for the betrayal! I inherited this split in my persona from her right then, and the recklessness and restlessness from my father later.

My three elder siblings and I got woven inadvertently into the complex pattern of a fabric that was the product of many lifetimes of entangled karma. That marked the second stage of my struggle to be free. Right from the time of my conception, my primal desire was to be free. That was ingrained in me in that unique moment, during the act of copulation between a man and a woman, the moment when a mortal comes closest to being God. It was the DNA imprint shaped by my karma. It propelled me towards an unknown journey to an obscure destination. Therein began the shaping of my being in an unconventional but orthodox Marwari home of the third richest man in the country with his sixth and youngest wife—my mother. There, on the potter's wheel of life, in the hands of my frail mother, fraught with her own complexities, I began to take shape. Soon after my birth two brothers and a sister were born to my mother each consecutive year. My stepmother, Saraswati, also gave birth to two children—one boy and a girl simultaneously and consecutively. On 21 December 1958, my father's last child and my youngest sister was born, after which there were no more children.

There were eighteen of us in all. Each different, but the seminal link of our procreator tied us together, firmly and inexorably.

'You don't belong with us Neelima,' my mother said. 'You look like you are Saraswati's child. You have her thick nose, and Ila's smile. Look at your mouth. It is like Sheela's and your father's body is exactly like yours. You have nothing of me. I am certain you got changed with her child at birth!'

This never upset me. I approved my mirror-image wholeheartedly after fantasizing to be my stepsister Ila, whose syrupy voice and overwhelming sexual aura was legendary.

My father was fifty-eight when I was born.

In the same city, exactly eight months and six days earlier, not more than one mile away, a frail and petite woman had given birth to a male child on 15 September 1950. That male-child was also born in a karmic cycle that linked him to a soul that had not yet taken birth, and was still in search of a womb and a body.

He was to be my husband. We were to come together on a path of redemption of a karmic debt of many lifetimes, each oblivious of the other's existence till eighteen years later.

I was different from my brothers and sisters. My father believed I was the reincarnated daughter of Kuber, the God of Wealth. I never stopped thinking that he imagined he was Kuber himself, and, therefore, this parallel always made me smile. I loved the feeling.

I was taller than all my siblings. I was the only one of us who was born in a different room of the home on the first floor. I was anorexic-looking, not beautiful, with long spindly limbs, straight, long black hair and buck-teeth. I was understandably the most neglected child sandwiched somewhere between the eldest and the youngest. I had to fight to be heard or noticed. Nevertheless, the untiring energy that lay within me made me a fighter. Life was tough but I was tougher.

My father's life was at a dip. Business was bad. The government headed by Nehru had ruthlessly turned on the heat because it was Nehru's single agenda to destroy my father. Dalmia—the media baron, and the first Indian owner of *The Times of India* who dared to defy and oppose him! Dalmia, who every single day, savaged Nehru on the front pages of his daily.

My father's loyalists had deserted him. His younger brother Jaidayal and eldest son-in-law Shanti Prasad Jain, for fear of persecution from the government, had disassociated themselves from him. The family partition that followed left him with loads of liabilities and a handful of unmanageable business concerns that were threatening to go down. His flagship, the Bennett Coleman and Company that owned *The Times of India* and the Sawai Madhavpur Cement Works were still with him. His spirit never sagged. With this ammunition he was confident that he would make it to the top again. His battle with Nehru thereafter escalated out of control. But he was sure he would rise like a phoenix from its ashes all over again. Material or human loss was neither painful, nor was it permanent.

I grew up an ordinary child. I had my father's wide nose and brow. My deep-set eyes immediately connected me to the family tree and belied my mercurial temper.

My wide mouth, thin lips and crooked teeth made me a distinct Dalmia. My not-so-fair complexion condemned me to instant mediocrity on the beauty scale. But my maid Sunder Bai, who was also my surrogate mother, told me I was beautiful, like the *mogra* that bloomed on the bushes in the garden. While she combed my long hair, she sang songs in Telugu, pinning freshly made *gajras* on to my plaits.

She touched the countless beauty spots on my body every time she bathed me and very often while I lay on my cot on summer nights, in the large open-air court-yard, staring at the sky full of stars above, I recounted:

> The one on my throat will bring me pearl
>   necklaces,
> The two on my neck will bring me kisses,
> The twin-ones on my breast will bring me lovers,
> The one on my arm will bring me bangles of
>   gold,
> The one inside my palm—untold riches,
> The one on the soles of my feet will take me far
>   and ...

Dreaming of travels to distant exotic lands, flying on magic carpets, I would fall off to sleep till the whispers of my older sister awakened me.

'Neema, come into my bed—I'm feeling scared.'

Then I would climb into her bed, hug her tight and drift into the world of Enid Blyton's fairies and elves— comforted and secure.

Growing up with six brothers and sisters and a demanding mother was not easy. Although I spent many happy moments in the company of my siblings, life with, or most times, without my father was hard. My own early years were spent struggling to get out of the mould that I had been cast into—that of a girl. I was strong, independent and fearless, which Marwari girls were not supposed to be. It made my mother nervous. Early in my childhood I developed an attention problem. I learnt to laugh loudly and incessantly in a manner that reverberated in the home that I hated and loved, because I wanted to be seen and heard all the time. Being a female child didn't help. I felt I was being left out of everything I wanted to do. I wore my brother's shirts, climbed on trees, rode bicycles, swore like a vagabond and never played with dolls.

Playing in the garden one summer day, both my younger brothers pulled down their shorts and peed standing at the edge of the marble fountain, singing at the top of their voices, 'Pop goes the weasel...'

Their urine formed a pale yellow arch as it splashed on the sunken-in marble floor below. I stared at them wide-eyed in admiration, pulled my panties down and stood up tall.

'See, see...I can also do what you are doing...and better.'

The warm pee trickled down my legs in stinging rivulets making an untidy puddle around my ankles. The smell of ammonia hit my nostrils. Two of my sisters chorused in unison with one hand over their mouths in shock!

Shame! Shame!
Poppy Shame!
All the boys
Know your name!

Shame! Shame!
Poppy Shame!
All the boys
Know your name!

Their index fingers waved wildly at me, mocking and mean. Pulling up my dripping panties swiftly, I ran into the home, my shoes and socks soaking wet. My eyes brimmed with tears that stung my cheeks.

Sunder Bai came running up to me and chided me:

'What have you done Babyji? Baisahab (that is how she addressed my mother) will be very cross and you know that you will get a frog tied to your *Chi Chi* if you wet your panties... Come quick! Let me wash you before she comes!'

She huddled me into the bathroom. I was feeling very sorry for myself. She undressed me in front of the full-length mirror; the thought of a frog tied to the elastic of my panties terrified me.

'I'll never be born a girl,' I sobbed, 'I can do everything that those boys can do. You'll see Sunder Bai ... You'll see...' Tears streamed down my cheeks.

My thumb went into my mouth and I started sucking furiously. Dopey-eyed I leaned on Sunder Bai's shoulder muttering to myself: 'I will do it … You'll see Sunder Bai … I will do it!'

Receding echoes drummed in my ears …

Shame! Shame!
Poppy Shame!
Shame! Shame!
Poppy Shame!

The backyard of our garden had an enormous fig tree that had wide branches touching the grass below. That was our tree house. All seven of us had fixed places on the tree house. We spent hours and hours on it all day reading comics, singing, playing, joking, sitting around like a bunch of chimpanzees. Never could our places be changed nor could we sit higher than the seat we had been assigned. My sister Laxmana who was thirteen months older than me, had given us the places. Every once in a while I would climb onto the highest branch, hook my legs tightly around it slowly lowering my body like an agile acrobat on a high trapeze in a circus, waving my arms in the air, giggling gleefully.

I closed my eyes and heard a loud round of applause around me and revelled in the appreciation.

Me—the prima donna in a circus …

The crowd cheered and applauded …

I was taking a bow …

taking a bow …

taking a bow …

A huge Burma teak *takht* with legs carved in the shape of a tiger's paw lay along the east wall of my mother's bedroom. It was larger than king-size. All seven of us could sit on it comfortably with my mother and father. A wooden fireplace adorned the wall on the opposite side, over which hung a life-size oil portrait of my parents. Around my father's head was painted a faint halo!

On either side of the fireplace lay two humungous wing-chairs where Laxmana and I played. We spat bubblegum into the grate and drew boobies and blobs with crayons on the walls behind the fully upholstered sofa. We took positions on the arms of the wing-chairs, riding them vigorously. One day all of a sudden my whole body wracked with a new and strange sensation that shot up my spine from deep within the base of my pelvis. I stopped and then started riding again. It happened again. It was a sensation that I had never known. I rocked back and forth again and again feeling the waves of pleasure like a rolling tide! I shouted to my sister.

'Laxma see what I am doing! Watch me! Come on try it! You'll feel a funny tickle climb up your back from down below! Come on Na, try it...'

Laxmana climbed on to the other arm of the wing-chair. We rode away into the fantasy land of princes and ponies feeling the ticklish waves of pleasure that seemed like they would never stop!

That was my first brush with my own sexuality.

I was five years old.

I had a strong bond with my father. Unlike my friends' fathers, he rarely displayed affection physically. The time I spent with him was never enough. I shared him with two sets of step-siblings, a fact that I deeply resented. The internalised damage manifested itself much later in my life.

My father was a strict vegetarian. He was against cow-slaughter, a movement that he pursued feverishly till his last breath. He gave up eating cereals in keeping with the vow that he would never touch *anaj* until every cow in this world was safe. He began this penance the year I was born. The same year he also bought four brand new Chryslers, two each for my mother and Saraswati, but the stigma associated with my birth still stuck to me.

'*Iske paida hote he unhonne anaj chod diya* (As soon as she was born, he gave up eating cereal),' my mother said.

'*Aur usi saal se unka* downfall *bhi shuroo hua* (And from that very year started his downfall).'

For some reason I thought I had a special lien on the Chrysler.

My father was an emotional dwarf but an intellectual giant. His mind and libido defied all parameters of human logic. His attitude towards women was Vedic, his relationship with his children stormy, and that with his wives, the most enigmatic that modern India knew.

He spoke to us openly about sex and in a sense my early sex education which came from him was essentially different from the one I received from anyone else. I sat around him with my sisters and brothers on a *gol gadda* which occupied three quarters of the floor of his room. He ate from a special silver *thali* from which no one else could eat. The food was cooked by my mother (not the *maharaj)* as if it were an offering to the gods—reverently and religiously.

He regaled us with tales from the *Mahabharata,* the *Upanishads, Chandrakanta,* and recited slokas from the scriptures, like nursery rhymes—quite a sharp contrast from the fairy tales that our Christian nanny read to us at teatime or the *bhoot-ki-kahani* that Sunder Bai narrated at bedtime.

He described the process of childbirth in graphic detail. I listened in rapt attention, picturing myself hanging head downwards in my mother's womb like a blind, baby bat, drowned in a pool of blood, urine and faeces, begging God to set me free, promising to pursue a life of moral righteousness, praying to be rid of the painful cycles of birth and death. No one ever told me that children were brought by storks in blue bundles if they were boys and pink bundles if they were girls.

Sometimes we were allowed to sleep on the gol gadda in his room. On one such night a heavy foot crushed my chest as I lay on the mattress. I groaned loudly.

It was my father. He patted my head. 'Go back to sleep *Bachiya.* I stepped on you because I could not see in the dark.' Clutching my bruised breast in pain, with eyes half shut I saw him crawl under my mother's blanket. I thought nothing of it as I drifted back to sleep. I did not notice the fast rhythmic rise and fall of her blanket. But I heard her stifle a groan.

A little while later I saw her receding silhouette go into the bathroom but before the sound of running water fell on my ears, I was fast asleep.

While there existed a cardinal similarity in all seven of us, yet all seven of us were different. Our dissimilarities surfaced gradually like cross-currents in a static pool of water. Like a host of varying organisms that develop differently in the same ecosystem, we grew. And only the fittest survived!

Padma—my eldest sister, then Babu or Shiv Nidhi; then Laxmana—the reincarnation of the Rani of Jhansi, Laxmi Bai; then I—the daughter of Kuber, the God of Wealth (I still wonder why my mother named me Neelima which means moonlight) then Raja; Vishva Nidhi and Bunny, Karuna Nidhi, and Dolly who was called Archana. Padma was quiet and withdrawn. She was as stubborn as a mule and never talked to any of us. She was always seen carrying a kitten in her arms or chasing birds in the garden.

Babu was born club-footed. My father said he was a great yogi, sitting in the lotus position at birth. He was a fat child, wore his shorts pulled high up, right till his armpits and scratched his balls shamelessly all the time. He always had his 'letter-box' open. Laxmana and I even posted a letter in it once while he slept! He was a big bully. My mother had fed him special baby food from little glass jars that she had brought from America. She thought it would make him grow faster. It did—but laterally! He was my mother's favourite child.

Babu was obnoxious. He spat on every passer-by from the roof of the home and crouched behind the railing before the spit-bubble hit them. He loved the way it fell on their heads and the sound it made—*phachak!* It tickled him. Sometimes he peed from the parapet, standing atop the water tank and gleefully watched the trajectory fall down on the grass below. He did it in fits and starts. He poked his finger into Raja's eye and made him cry. Once he defecated on the roof in a cardboard box and told my mother it was the cat. My mother always believed his lies. She never scolded him.

Laxmana was short and dark. I looked older than her since I was taller. She was a chronic sulky-poo. At the slightest excuse she would stop talking to me and leave me out of her *pitthoo* team. She always locked up my toys in her drawer. She never ate her own vegetables and made sure I sat next to her at the dining table. She made me swallow all the horrible *tinda* and *karela* from her plate that she slyly passed on to me from under the table. I did it because I feared that she would 'Send me to Coventry.' She sucked on an orange bar slowly and teasingly till it turned white and called me a greedy glut when I begged her for a lick after having devoured my own.

Dolly was cute. She was very fair and plump. She always clung to Sunder Bai—her umbilical cord and surrogate mother. She licked the fresh cream that was kept in the bathroom to wash her face and carried back a piece of cake in her crushed handkerchief for Sunder Bai after any birthday party we attended. Dolly was a cry-baby. She looked cute when she curled up her nose, twisted her mouth to one side and cried. Her red cheeks contorted as her whimper rose and fell in a melodious crescendo. It was fun to watch her and very easy to make her cry. It became one of our favourite games.

Cry-baby cr–aa–aa–y,
Put your finger in your eye!
Cry-baby cr–aa–aa–y,
Put your finger in your eye!

We sang in chorus she never let us down.

Raja and Bunny were like Luv and Kush. They always stayed together. Raja collected creepy-crawlies with a hundred legs and beetles in an empty matchbox and set fire to them. He loved the crackling sounds they made as they roasted. He loved holding caterpillars and cockroaches and kept them in glass bottles, when he had finished playing with them.

He fed pieces of bread to the hawks in a daring show of strength. He ran around the garden in circles calling out to them: *'Cheelari, lelari … cheelari, lelari …'* and his chest filled with pride when they swooped down to snatch the morsels from his hands sometimes making them bleed. He also broke one new toy everyday and puked into the milk jug.

Bunny chased *girgits* up the *kathal* tree.

He swore that a girgit threw a *gola* at him because he counted its teeth. He made up his own nursery rhymes about them and claimed to have always spotted them changing colour.

He even defecated behind the kathal tree to spite the girgit!

I find it hard to say whether it was Dolly, Laxmana, Bunny or I who was loved the least. I suspect it was Dolly for she was the last, or perhaps Bunny for he was the farthest from my mother's care and father's affections.

My mother was snared in contradictions. She was a Mewari born in Udaipur, completely unaware of the ways of my father. Her own father was a professor of English at the Maurice College in Nagpur and had tutored some of the most outstanding achievers of his time.

My mother was initiated into writing at an early age. She created 'Poetry-Prose' like that of Mahadevi Varma. Right from the age of ten she began seeing her name in print. Her writings were rich with sensuous descriptions of pain felt by separated lovers. Profusely colourful poems on beauty and love earned her the laurels that she thrived on. It was those very laurels that threw her across my father's path almost two decades later. Catapulted into his world of riches and power, she was to play the role of a slave to him, and mother to his progeny. She could never adjust to his demands. Thereafter the layers of her life began to unearth in front of her. Misery, stress, tears, tribulations, unfulfilment and pain.

Her writings were prophetic!

She imbibed my father's orthodox ways. From being the first woman graduate from Rajasthan in the early 1930s, she transformed into a backward and repressed woman who never succeeded in pleasing her whimsical husband—a process which was as self-destructive as it was impossible. The transition was stormy albeit complete. However the schism could never really be wiped out.

Why is it that men destroy the very attribute in a woman that draws them to her in the first place?

My own early memories of them as a couple are faint and I only remember stray but sharp, vivid incidents that are permanently embedded on the screen of my mind like shards of glass.

My father built mandirs in each of his homes. Our mandir was a fully marbled, sparkling white room in the southeast. It housed larger-than-life-sized statues of Bhagwan Vishnu lying on the *shesh-nag* with the Goddess Laxmi pressing his feet. The *saptrishis* sat around them in a lotus position. Bhrigu Rishi stood beside him on his *nag shaiyya*. One leg was lifted in a *roudra mudra* as if he were about to kick Bhagwan Vishnu with great force. Bhagwan Vishnu epitomises forgiveness and his wife Laxmi, the eternal and perfect woman.

My father often recited:

Kshama badan ko chahiye
Chotan ko utpaat
Ka Krishna ka ghat gaya
Jo Bhrigu maari laat!
[Legend has it that Bhagwan Vishnu was put to the test by the gods. When he was kicked by Bhrigu Rishi, he rubbed Bhrigu Rishi's feet in apology gently asking if he had been injured by the impact. Thereafter, he was declared the greatest of all gods.]

My father believed that his own virtue of forgiveness was as great as that of Bhagwan Vishnu and even greater than that of Christ.

There was another room right above the mandir. A glass cabin rose from the centre of the mandir that enclosed the statues of the gods. It had a glass roof that extended towards the ceiling of the room above. The room above had a floor that stopped just short of the glass cabin so that no one could walk over the cabin of the gods. The floor-to-ceiling windows of this room allowed a view of the *sanctum sanctorum* from the top. This room was meant for the women, if they did not want to sit with the men in the mandir.

On the walls were painted pictures that depicted tales from the lives of Radha-Krishna, Meera Bai, the *Ramayana* and the *Mahabharata*. All around were inscribed slokas from the *Vedas* and the *Bhagwad Gita*.

Very prominently placed was a life-size oil painting of a beautiful Durga riding a tiger, and at the highest level in blatant blasphemy, hung an oil-portrait of my father with a golden halo around his head!

Dividing the mandir into two was a pair of sliding-doors that had tall panels of stained glass which reflected shades of red, maroon, yellow and flaming orange when light fell on them. On one side was the meditation room.

One afternoon all seven of us were playing in the room above the mandir. In a swift sequence of events that I vividly remember I pushed open the window above the *sanctum sanctorum* to peep into the mandir below. I leaned over to look.

Then I found myself floating downwards like a feather into the most beautiful pair of dove-like, milky-white hands that were covered with black-silk at the wrists. They placed me down gently at the foot of the glass cabin on the floor of the mandir. After what seemed like a deep, long slumber, I heard my father's voice chanting *Om*, followed by a Sanskrit sloka echoing far away, getting louder and louder... then the sound of my name... *'Utho Naliya... utho bachiya... aankhen kholo... aankhen kholo beta* (Get up baby... get up little one... open your eyes... open your eyes child).

I felt my head in his lap, opened my eyes and sat up slowly. The whole family was gathered around, staring down at me, fear written large on their faces.

'She's all right... no bones broken...'

A bitter mixture of *haldi* and warm milk was pushed towards my mouth roughly. I gulped it down holding my breath. I wanted to puke.

From the corner of my eyes I could see the jealousy on the faces of my brothers and sisters. I knew all of them were secretly wishing it had been them!

Two of my *mamas* were standing behind them looking anxious—but smiling at me.

I smiled in slow motion and closed my eyes tightly to freeze that moment into eternity.

'She's God's child…'

'It is a miracle…'

'She is unhurt and unscathed…'

'Even the glass she fell on did not break…'

'*Naliya, meri bachiya*…You are my own child…'

'It is a miracle…'

But only I knew that I had never fallen on any glass—that I had floated down like a feather, and those beautiful hands had placed me gently, ever so gently on the cold marble floor.

No glass broke. I was not hurt. Those beautiful, fair, hands…that shining soft black silk…the echoes of the chants of *Om*…and the *Maha Mritunjaya Mantra*…

Om Trayam Vakam
Yaja Mahe Sugandhim Pushti Vardhanam;
Urva Rukamiv Bandhanat
Mrityor Mukshir Mamritat…

Sometimes, many times—those hands and then the sounds of that mantra and the long drawn reverberating chants of *Om* haunt me.

I curled into a foetal position and dreamt that I was back in my mother's womb.

I started to menstruate at the age of fifteen. Late by normal standards. Padma had started her periods at ten. It was a matter of grave concern. My mother thought Padma was too young to manage her sanitary napkins, but my father was not perturbed. Laxmana started at thirteen. I remember she cried a lot. Sunder Bai held her close all night. Her sobs wracked my senses.

Menstruating women were unclean. I watched Sunder Bai cutting thin oblong pads of cotton wool, wrapping them meticulously in gauze and neatly stacking them into a cardboard box. She wrote on the cover: *Yeh Baisahab ka* pad *hai; isko koi nahin lena* (These are Baisahab's pads; no one should take them).

I knew by instinct that the pads had something to do with chi-chi and blood.

When no one was looking I took out one, felt it between my palms, and rubbed it on my cheeks. I never dared to ask Sunder Bai what they were!

During her periods my mother could not go near my father. She had to sit on a mat made of silk. She wore a silk sari and slept on a special silk sheet. She could not touch anyone. She could not enter the mandir or the kitchen till the fourth day when she washed her hair and became clean again.

I purposely touched her.

'*Kya karte ho babyji* (What are you doing, Babyji)?' Sunder Bai rebuked.

'*Baisahab ko mat chhuna. Unpar chipkali giri hai* (Do not touch Baisahab. A lizard has fallen on her).'

I was scared of lizards and wondered how they kept falling with alarming regularity on my mother's head. I did not want to sit on that silk mat alone in a dark room like a leper.

I sneaked past the walls of my room carefully avoiding the corners, stealthily looking up for falling lizards, clutching Sunder Bai's arm hard. Lizards made me shudder!

There were three airtight compartments in the three homes of my father. All three were sprawling mansions befitting his status. Saraswati lived at *Nau Number* Mansingh Road, a home that had belonged to the Maharaja of Kapurthala. Asha lived on *Pandrah Number* York Road. which was renamed Motilal Nehru Marg three decades later.

Ours was *Teen Number* Sikandra Road.

We were never allowed to mix with our stepbrothers or stepsisters. My father feared that his wives would poison the children of their *saut*. Alka, Asha's youngest child, was stricken by polio soon after her birth, which left her lame. My father believed it was because of a tantric spell cast on Asha by one of the wives. Later I learnt that they had blamed my mother!

I longed to go to *Nau Number* to meet Ila, Sheela and the rest of them, or even *Pandrah Number* to talk to Dhruv, or to admire his twin sister Meera. Meera was as beautiful as Ila. She had sex appeal. Men fell around her like ninepins.

I feet sharp pangs of jealousy. I was neither beautiful nor sexy. Just plain.

Ila had the sweetest voice anyone had ever heard. She could charm the leaves off a tree. Men followed her like puppies. She had spurned many lovers. When someone told me I looked like Sheela, I was pleased but never as much as when I was compared with Ila. Ila was my father's favourite and although looking like her made me feel proud, the comparison made me jealous.

Then my *dadi* died. I had never known her and had hardly seen her. My mother went to Benaras for the funeral with my father. The thirteenth day puja was at Saraswati's home. It was one of the few times that my mother entered her domain. My brother Babu accompanied her. He was the chosen one. I seethed with anger and jealousy and cursed him.

'*Motu,* have they made you *ganja?*' I asked him on the phone later, secretly wishing that his head had been tonsured with the sharpest of razors. I wanted to laugh at him when he got home.

The dormitory that we slept in overlooked a wide garden at the rear of the main home. There was a tall carved marble fountain in the centre that had not been used for many years. Mould had collected along its pillars and floor making a palette of shades of green, brown and gray. One of Cupid's wings had fallen off and the bow and arrow were missing.

The gigantic peepul tree stood taller than the home, bending over it like a nurse tending a baby. Its branches spread in all directions, some touching the windows of the dormitory.

The ground at the foot of the peepul tree had been paved and a platform about one-foot high was created around it. The roots of the tree had torn open the concrete after years of suppression and jutted out from the cracks. The overhanging branches looked like the gray matted beard of a man, hundreds of years old—worn and weary.

This tree had seen four generations of births and deaths of the inhabitants of my home. Listening to fairy tales, sucking my thumb, I would stare out from the window hoping to spot Peter Pan sailing on a cloud, spilling magic dust from his wand on all those who had not slept. The dark branches tapped the glass when the wind blew through them.

'A *churail* that wears a white robe lives on the peepul tree Babyji. Drink up your milk and say your prayers quickly or she'll come down and eat you up. I have seen her many times; she roams the garden at night; she is very tall and has red eyes. *So jao* Babyji. *So jao nahin to churail aa jayegi* (Go to sleep Babyji. Go to sleep, else the witch will come).' Sunder Bai said.

To get to the front entrance of the home you had to walk on a red sandstone path along a wide grass lawn. The tall imposing wrought-iron gates could not be opened unless they were pushed by two men.

The boundary wall had a ten-foot high iron fence that was covered with a dense creeper that blossomed with millions of yellow flowers in spring. Tucked behind the pillar near the main gate was a little wooden shed where the chowkidar lived.

'One chowkidar was found dead here, Babyji,' Sunder Bai told me.

'It was the year *majli* Babyji was born. He slept outside his shed on the *kabar* of the Mussalman Nawab whose con sold this home to Sethji. For three nights he was woken up by a hard slap from someone who said: *"Meri jagah se hat nahin to maar daaloonga* (Move from my place or I will kill you)".'

Her voice dropped to a whisper: 'Don't tell anyone Babyji; these *gorkhas* are very foolish. After three nights his stiff body was found with his neck broken, his head hanging—lying dead. No chowkidar wants to go near that spot. Everyone feels that Sethji should not have broken those kabars... and those pujas that he had done never helped, Babyji... but don't tell anyone I told you. The churail and the Mussalman both roam around the home at night. Don't go near the peepul... They can even read your thoughts.'

I put my arms tightly around Sunder Bai hoping that the Mussalman and the churail had not seen me pour out the milk from the glass that Sunder Bai had brought me, into the garden that afternoon. I hated milk and when no one was looking, emptied it into the fountain pit or at the base of the peepul tree.

I held my breath, scared to think. I did not want to remember the big blob of double-bubble gum that I had taken from my sister's mouth, chewed for a while and then stuck under the *takht* in my mother's room; or the *imli* that I had stolen from the kitchen; or the Macleans toothpaste that I had eaten from the tube on her sink; or the homework I had not completed....

I pulled my blanket over my head and quickly pushed the unopened packet of double-bubble gum from under my pillow onto the ground!

There is a very fine line between complexity and perversity. Sexuality is the strongest motivating force in human behaviour. My father's sex-life was ridden with its own measure of perversity and obsessiveness. His attitude that reflected strongly in his overt behaviour created serious problems in the lives of all his offspring, the most damaging of them being emotional. To him the only relationship that could exist between a man and a woman was sexual.

My mother with her inadequacies in bringing us up as a single parent in a manner of speaking had to day-in and day-out put up with preposterous accusations regarding herself and most of us excepting Padma, and Raja, and also Bunny and Dolly by default because they were the youngest.

The first time she bore the brunt of such accusations, she crumbled and gradually as time healed her she learnt to listen but not react. Even the tears she wanted to shed had to wait till he was gone.

I met my stepbrother Dhruv as a young college-going girl. Dhruv always fascinated me. He was brilliant—something of an enigma. He had shown spark and spunk early in life. His personal turmoil had pushed him into doing drugs. It was the decade that flower-power and the Beatles Mania had hit the streets of Delhi where hordes of hippies roamed around and LSD was the new age mantra to 'instant nirvana'. Dhruv had embarked on a dangerous and unforgiving journey that gave no second chances. Prolonged drug abuse took its toll. But before that he had eloped in the most sensational manner with a gorgeous sixteen-year-old Muslim model from Bombay who fell in love with him because he was both rich and famous. She was Ayesha Sayani—the niece of Amin Sayani whose velvet voice on Radio Ceylon had immortalised the programme of hit cinema songs—Binaca Geet Mala.

Ayesha bore him a female 'flower child'. Dhruv had filmed the entire process of childbirth in the labour room at a private nursing home in Delhi. The act had sent shock waves through the primitive minds of the city and the family. But that was Dhruv, the fearless rebel!

Not surprisingly both his wife and daughter deserted him after some years.

Dhruv was ruthless and fierce. He had scratched Ayesha's name onto his palms with a Swiss army knife. His stare was penetrating and icy. He had made a deep gash in his hand with a blade to mix his blood with that of Babu his stepbrother, who had also returned the gesture. 'We are blood brothers now! Never betray this bond or I shall kill you,' Dhruv had said, sparks flashing from his eyes!

He had knifed my father's bodyguards who had dared to trail him on one of his night jaunts. He had rammed his fist hard into the face of his headmaster at school and broken his nose. He had been expelled five times and no school in Delhi wanted him.

On a cold and dreary morning in the month of January in the year 1971, Dhruv wandered into our life and home. He was stoned and incoherent. I felt naturally drawn to him.

The first time I saw Dhruv was when had come to Padma's wedding uninvited, with his beautiful wife carrying her little baby in her arms—causing quite a stir.

Padma had been married for just over twelve months.

She had gone with her husband to Meerut where she lived unhappily, unable to adjust to the demands of a large joint family. Babu was in his first year of post-graduation studying History. My father had completed his prison term more than seven years ago. My mother in a sense was still serving hers! My *nana* and *nani* had both died. Sunder Bai too was dead. Laxmana was studying Philosophy and was in the final year of her post-graduation. She was seeing a Muslim boy, Aziz Quraishi, who was a national-level football player and her classmate. I had enrolled for my first year of post-graduation in Psychology. Raja, Bunny and Dolly were still in High School.

My father had stopped living with us since he had returned from prison and was back with Saraswati. He visited us for a few hours in the evenings once in every two or three days, which was just as well because those hours were tortuous. My mother was scared to be with him alone and forced us to suspend all activity to sit with him. Most times he sat in silence on his gol gadda. He never touched a morsel of food nor a drop of water in our home for fear of being poisoned. In an effort to please him, my mother also gave up eating during his visits. She fasted every alternate day—in vain. She sat across the room—always in silence. Sitting there was a punishment and each one of us tried to pass on the duty to the other. It was miserable and fearful—because no one knew what he would say or when—for he only said hurtful and mean things to us or to my mother. I prayed to God to deliver me from that hell!

That cold and foggy morning, I sat close to Dhruv, touching him, listening to his crazy ramblings, commiserating with a stepbrother who had been wronged by his father—and who was as persecuted by Saraswati and her children as I. He invited me to *Pandrah Number* where he was living with his mother ever since Ayesha had left him.

Dhruv's room was on the first floor of the home. It was at the end of a beautiful, carved, wooden staircase reminiscent of colonial times. His room was stark. A sickly sweet smell hung heavy in the air like an invisible fog. It went straight to my head. I coughed and cleared my throat nervously. I knew my mother and father would both be mad at me.

There was a thick mattress on the floor and a large picture of Lord Shiva on a low table under a window. Smoke from an incense holder curled upwards forming irregular patterns. There was a pile of unwashed clothes on a reclining leather chair. Books laden with dust were strewn in careless piles in the corner of the room.

A bathtub could be seen through a half-open door that needed polishing. An annoying drip could be heard from a leaking tap.

In contrast a brand new music system with huge hi-fi speakers occupied a prominent place on a wall cabinet. Stubs of stale cigarettes overflowed from a metal ash tray that seemed like it had not been emptied for days.

I sat down on the mattress. Dhruv sat beside me with an old album. He showed me pictures of Alka's wedding and beautiful portrait shots of his daughter and ravishing wife. He read out letters that my father had written to him at boarding school. He recited lines from an unfinished poem that he had written the night before. I felt like I was in a forbidden world with my father—Dhruv looked so much like him! The hours slipped by and I was in a trance.

When I reached home that day my mother and father were sitting grim-faced and in a huddle on the *takht*.

'I know where you have been, Naliya! You have been to Dhruv's home. My spies have seen you go to his bedroom. I know you have been sleeping with him. Go away, you dirty girl. Don't show me your face ever again,' he screamed.

The story spread like wildfire!

My step-siblings still chose to believe that I was caught red-handed in bed with Dhruv!

That incestuous liasons exist in Marwari homes was never more evident to me. It was bizarre but it was real!

My eyes brimmed with hot tears that rolled down my cheeks. I wanted to die. My father's face contorted with rage and his fists clenched into a tight ball that made his knuckles go white. My mother stared at me silently cringing with fear. Two deep frown lines etched her forehead!

'No Papa I didn't…I swear I didn't…You can ask him…'

'Don't lie,' he shouted, 'don't you ever lie to me, you wicked girl!'

My voice was drowned in the deafening din of my frenzied thoughts. I was shouting abuses at him that he could not hear. I loathed him that day and cursed myself for being his child. I loathed my mother for not being able to protect me from his assault!

That night I went to bed hungry. My eyes were red and swollen. I dreamt of Dhruv. He was wearing a dark leather jacket and a black phantom mask. A pair of wide spiked black bands encircled his wrists and there were knuckle dusters on his fingers. He came to my bed, put his hand over my mouth, pushed my thighs apart roughly and entered me squirting his semen into me deep and hard.

I retched in an uncontrollable spasm over and over again!

There was a vast expanse of water all around me… Water was all that there was as far as my eyes could see… I was all alone sinking… down… down. I could not breathe… I tried to come up gasping for breath… I screamed for help… No one could hear me or see me.

Thick, black stormy waves flung me far away and then brought me near again… Two people… One man and one woman swam around peacefully under water like scuba divers… I could see their silhouettes from a distance… They were naked… So was I… Then I saw their faces… They were my mother and father… They glided past me as if they could not see me… I screamed out to them… There was water everywhere… I was drowning… Water in my throat and lungs… I sank to the ocean floor… This is it… I am dying… Save me Mother! Help me Papa… Please!

As my thoughts snuffed out I found myself on my bed anxious and sweating! I've always believed that I had died of drowning in my previous life and that in a strange way my parents were responsible!

Part II

My Father
Ramkrishna Dalmia
(7 April 1893–26 September 1978)

Tall and supple boy of thirteen years stood on top of the highest ship that was anchored in the Calcutta Harbour, the ship that almost caressed the underside of the Howrah Bridge. The sky was painted a glowing pink of early dawn. A few birds could be heard chirping—the glorious melody of sunrise. The sun was struggling to break out of its night cover to drench the earth and its creatures in its warm light.

This was the Calcutta of the early 1900s; the colonial port that housed the Imperial emissaries of the British; the Calcutta that was to be immortalised in Thomas Daniel's lithographs; that was the nerve centre of trade and commerce; the Calcutta that was silently breeding the seeds of revolution!

He saw a group of emaciated fishermen getting ready to cast their nets into the water in the distance. Struggling and dying fish disturbed him. When they gasped for breath he felt asphyxiated. Fish were an extension of his being. It pained him to see them flailing about till they were dead. He spread his arms wide, tilted his head up to the sky, took a long deep breath and closed his eyes. His bare torso arched upwards defining his flat stomach and the muscles on his long legs tensed with pulsating energy. He looked like Icarus with his wings spread wide, ready to fly. He did a mental salutation to the Lord and then to his ancestors, then slowly opened his eyes and looked down at the muddy waters of the Hooghly, his mind soaring miles above him. With the swiftness and agility of a falcon, he dived into the river below making the perfect angular entry on the surface—a natural feat of aerodynamics. He made no loud splash, just glided into the water like a sharp knife cuts through soft butter.

The sensuous feel of the water on his feverish body soothed him. It felt like the soft velvet of his child-bride's flesh on his skin. Water entered the deep sockets of his eyes and rinsed them as he peered underneath. The stinging thrilled him. It entered his large ears and tickled the fine hair that sprouted from his lobes. It made a loud, roaring sound that heightened the mild throbbing pain he felt in his eardrums. It muffled the sound of his Bapu's voice,

'One day you will drown if you don't listen, you will drown ... you will drown ... you will drown ...'

Water licked his broad forehead and protruding brow. It entered his wide mouth as he slackened his full lips into a smile. This was indeed his heaven!

He pushed himself deeper, holding his breath till his lungs felt like they would burst. All of a sudden he could breathe with ease through the water. He had turned into a fish. His nostrils were gills and his arms became fins. His back was covered with shiny scales and his legs changed into a tail. He could keep his eyes open and glide his body at will up and down forward and backward with ease. Water was his own element!

He could not remember when he had learnt to swim but this was his daily morning ritual. He stole out of his house each day before sunrise and sprinted across the sand to the banks of the river before the city awakened from its slumber. It was a race against time and he was competing with Surya the Sun God. He had to be there before the first rays of light touched the surface. That was his greatest challenge and he had never failed.

He ached to be in the water. The free fall from the tallest ship thrilled him to the bone. Each time he jumped he renewed his pledge to himself that he would stand taller than the Sun God and ride the waves of time to the greatest of heights and depths, and he would conquer the kings of the netherworld and the gods of heaven and outshine them in their might and glory.

Each day he remained in there for seven or eight hours and went home only in time for his midday meal—his body erect, stretched like that of an archer, his skin shrivelled, his eyes shining bright and a sweet, mild, throbbing pain in his ears.

Ma and Narbada, his newly-wed bride, would be waiting for him. They would place a thali *laden with boiled rice or thick chapattis made of hand-ground wheat flour, soaked in cow's ghee that he would eat voraciously, his appetite worked up after the rigorous exercise.*

Bapu would be waiting too. He feared Bapu would scold him, but Bapu never did. All he said was, 'Don't swim in the deep waters for so many hours, Ramakisan; someday you will drown, Son … and the water should not go into your ears it will impair your hearing … '

But my father would not be listening. It was as if his hearing was already impaired. He was too busy noisily gulping down the hot chapattis, relishing the taste of the hand-ground flour and pure ghee as he sat cross-legged on a low wooden stool on the floor, wearing only a dhoti and his sacred janeu, dreaming of his next tryst with the Sun God and the waters of the Hooghly. The happy tinkle of Narbada's sweet laughter transported him into his land of ecstasy where he was frolicking in the deep, dark river, taking the free fall before the crack of dawn, feeling the soft sweet tender flesh of his shy bride under the cover of darkness and renewing his undying pledge to himself to be worthy of the genes he had been awarded by the privilege of his birth!

In the sandy village of Chirawa not far from the copper mines of Khetri in Rajasthan, Seth Kashi Ram Dalmia, a man of eighty-five years, lay dying. All his life he had been known to be a man of honour. A pious and religious observer of Hindu traditions, he had been revered and adored for his benevolence and kindness. Never did a poor man come to him for help and go away empty-handed. Nor did he pass a day without distributing food to the needy. Everyone knew him as one who gave away corn, sugar, ghee, cooking vessels, hand-grinding machines, needle and thread, articles of clothing or whatever else anyone needed. He was the oldest living patriarch of the Dalmia tree that had now over two hundred direct branches. Having foreseen his end almost two weeks before he died, he had summoned his two brothers and their descendants, his three sons, their wives, their children and grandchildren from Calcutta, Bombay or wherever else they were, to be with him before he finally departed.

The grand old man lay frail and dying on his bed surrounded by his next of kin, all of whom had been forbidden to cry. His dark complexion had become even darker as death hovered around him and he slipped into a trance—the deep trance that is the comfort zone between the living and the dead. He held on to the last hours of his life with a string of coral beads fixed between his thumb and index finger—the name of the Lord on his tongue, silent but visible from the muscles twitching under his chin. It was a habit that he had followed in all his eighty-five years for he was god-fearing and holy, and had spent as much time as he could taking the name of the Lord.

Seth Kashi Ram had spent the early part of his life in the village of Bhiwani—a part of present-day Haryana. A temple that he had built and which was known as Kashi Ramji Ka Mandir still exists, bearing testimony to his illustriousness, for he had attained in his lifetime the highest *punya* that can be accorded to a Vaishnav Hindu.

An orthodox and pious man, he would rise at two hours past midnight and go to the village well for a bath accompanied by his clean and pure Vaishnav cook. The cook would ceremoniously clean the bucket before drawing water from the well and bathe himself, and only then would his master Seth Kashi Ram take a bath. Cleansed of the night's impurities in body and soul he would return home to begin his *Gayatri jaapa,* the incantation of the paramount mantra of the Hindus, followed by one hundred thousand incantations of the name of Lord Rama—the symbol of the divine male, the incarnation of Lord Vishnu, the epitome of the virtues of duty and sacrifice—a ritual that could only be completed by midday. After that he would distribute food and money to anyone who came to him and only then break his fast by taking his first meal. His wife Amri Devi followed the same routine and also chanted the powerful *Ram Naam Mantra* one hundred and twenty-five thousand times. Only after her husband had finished eating, would she put the first morsel of the day into her mouth, after which the two would walk to their temple to take part in the religious sermons that were held every day for them.

The dusty village reverberated with the powerful sounds of the beating drums and the chimes of the temple bells. The men, women and children would leave whatever they were doing to congregate at the courtyard to participate in the group prayers in the presence of their greatest benefactor, Seth Kashi Ram and his pious wife, who had turned their village into heaven. Everyone craned their necks with half-shut eyes to get a glimpse of their beloved Sethji and his beautiful wife—each one experiencing his own ecstasy. Then, Seth Kashi Ram and his wife would get up and walk regally down the people-lined courtyard distributing temple prasad to all, and food and clothes to the needy.

This was the precursor to the ultimate act of sacrifice that he would commit a few years later, whereby he donated his wealth, his property, his belongings and all his earthly possessions to charitable causes, an act that turned him into a living saint. After renouncing his worldly effects he moved to Chirawa to live with his sons each of whom contributed fifteen rupees every month towards his expenses for the rest of his life.

Seth Kashi Ram was a happy and contented man for he had performed his mortal duties on earth to perfection and had indeed practised what he had preached.

As he lay dying on his wooden cot in his native and ancient haveli surrounded by his descendants, he spoke in a feeble, barely audible voice, '*Ae munna*, where is that *goli-raand?* Tell her to bring me some water. My throat burns and my mouth is parched.'

Someone from the group of women huddled together near him hurriedly rushed to bring water.

The sound of the crude invective did not bother them. They were used to it. It was a term of endearment he used for his daughters-in-law. It was also a warning to them that if they became slaves of their passions and anger, they were like 'slave-widows', who are cursed and doomed. No one had ever dared to disobey or question him. They felt privileged to have the good fortune of serving him!

Shri Ram, his youngest son, who sat close to him, holding his ankles, broke down and as if on cue everyone wept. The wailing crescendo was drowned by the sounds of the tolling bells and the beating drums of the temple in the distance as his soul left his body and his coral beads fell to the floor in what was a glaring reminder of what you take with you and what is left behind when you die. The male descendants were made to strip to the waist and adorn new white cotton dhotis. They brought the bier to the place where he was to be cremated, running a few yards ahead, then turning back, prostrating, getting up and starting all over again till they reached Kashi Ramji Ki Bagichi—the special place reserved to cremate him.

The sounds of the drums and the mourners' chants—*Ram naam satya hai* (The name of Rama is Truth), *satya bolo gat hai* (Truth will bring salvation)—rent the air as the whole village had turned up to pay a final tribute to their beloved patriarch.

Shri Ram stood staring at the pyre. Harjimal, his little boy of five, stood close to him holding his hand, clinging to his knees.

The little boy could not comprehend why death had so cruelly snatched away his Bade Dadaji. He loved his Bade Dadaji for having given him the honour every night of letting him press his legs till he fell asleep. He loved to listen to Bade Dadaji's stories that were told to all the privileged ones who lulled him to sleep by rubbing the soles of his feet. It was his Bade Dadaji who had taken him to heaven for a darshan of Lord Vishnu.

Every night Harjimal had eagerly awaited that jaunt. As soon as he sat beside him with his brothers and cousins, Bade Dadaji's hypnotic voice sent them into a trance.

'Shut your eyes munna...' he said. 'Shut them tight and look at the light in the centre of your forehead...look hard...Now you can see a beautifully decorated *udan khatola* of gold in the sky...Can you see it descending to earth?' Harjimal would nod vigorously, eyes tightly shut, astounded by the imagery and his space odyssey.

'Tell me munna…Can you see it floating down to earth?'

'Yes, yes, Dadaji,' the children would chorus in impatient unison, almost afraid that their voices would make the udan khatola disappear.

'Get up munna…The udan khatola has been sent down from heaven for you…See the doors are opening for you…Step in munna…'

Hypnotised as it were Harjimal would step into the aircraft of the gods that would rise to the heavens amidst a shower of falling stars and magic dust. Bade Dadaji would continue, 'You are flying high, hold tight now…Look, you are crossing *Chandra Lok*…and now *Surya Lok*…and now you are reaching your destination…Look, you are in *Vishnu Lok* now…Get off, you are going to have a divine darshan of the Lord Vishnu and Mata Laxmi…Stand before them…and breathe their fragrance…You can taste the nectar of the heavens…Now prostrate before them…Look, Ma is smiling and Bhagwan is blessing you…'

The children had the most vivid and powerful experience. They had been to heaven. And then the deep, soft voice from above would say, 'It's time to return to earth; we cannot stay here for long or we will be thrown out.' Gradually they would descend to earth full of devotion and ecstatic that they had seen the divine couple.

Harjimal could not rekindle that joy in himself as he stood watching his Bade Dadaji turn to ashes during the cremation. His beloved Bade Dadaji was gone and there would be no more celestial trips. He wept clinging tightly to his father's knees. It did not worry him that his Bade Dadaji's benevolence had left them penniless. He did not know that he himself would father two extraordinary sons—Ramkrishna and Jaidayal just two decades later, who would in their adult years become the most celebrated and dynamic luminaries of the industrial world—a position he would neither enjoy nor be able to take pride in because he would long be dead. Neither he nor his father Shri Ram had been blessed with the longevity with which his grandfather Seth Kashi Ram had been blessed and neither would cross their forty-fifth year.

On his father's death, Shri Ram Dalmia, moved to Amravati, a small town in Berar, to work as a *munim* for his sister's husband, leaving behind his wife and children in the village while he worked to provide for the family—a decision that he was to regret and a position from which he was to resign, not too long afterwards.

Shri Ram's wife, Naraini Devi, was a very fair and, therefore, very beautiful, short-statured pure-blooded Marwari woman who had lived a life of great luxury as a maiden with her father, Mirija Mal Poddar at Churu in Bikaner. Along with her two sisters-in-law, she bore the brunt of their poverty and misfortune ungrudgingly. In the true spirit of the *Bharatiya Hindu Naari* whose prime dharma is *pati seva*, they took to the hardships of a commoner's life in their *sasural* with ease, never looking to their parents for help.

Naraini rose early in the morning, washed, cleaned and cooked, and ground enough wheat grains for the day's meal in the stone grinder with her small princess-like, fair hands. She did all the menial jobs of the house and tended to the children, living within her husband's meagre salary.

Her husband Shri Ram was going through his own travails. As if being a munim with his brother-in-law was not degrading enough, in an unfortunate turn of events, a huge sum of several thousand rupees was stolen from his employer's home. The suspicion for the theft fell squarely on a poor and dejected Shri Ram. Assuming that his own sister and brother-in-law did not believe he was innocent, he silently sent a messenger to Naraini to send all her jewellery to him so that he could make good the deficit, which she did readily. The only one who knew the truth was Dalu Ram, the village priest, whose advice Shri Ram did not heed. Without a murmur of protest he accepted the blame, compensated for the loss and resigned from his job, an act that he could ill afford.

Dalu Ram, however, did not rest in peace and deputed his own spy to track down the thief. The spy chanced upon the real culprit who turned out to be none other than the village potter who also doubled as Shri Ram's employer's cook. In a swift and timely swoop the money was recovered and so was Shri Ram's honour restored. He was relieved of the nightmare but stubbornly refused to go back to his job. He returned sadly to his village and lived there in penury till he died at the age of forty-two, with his devoted wife by his side and his mother's words in his ears: 'Never work for or conduct business with relatives, for money turns men into monsters!'

Naraini Devi outlived her husband and son Harjimal. She died at the age of sixty-six in Calcutta where her last rites were performed in grandeur and reverence by her grandson Ramkrishna, who was a young man of twenty-two by then and had already been noticed as a rabble-rouser in the Calcutta stock market. As if by divine intervention Ramkrishna had just made a great deal of money and used it lavishly to give his grandmother the funeral of a high-caste Hindu queen. Naraini Devi died a fulfilled woman, having experienced the ultimate joy of living to see the birth of her great-granddaughter Rama, Ramkrishna's first-born who was a little over two when Naraini Devi died. Her grandson accorded to her in death what life had stolen from her in her youth.

It was Friday, 7 April 1893. Jadia Devi, the wife of Harjimal Dalmia—the daughter-in-law of Shri Ram and Naraini Devi, and the granddaughter-in-law of the great philanthropist Seth Kashi Ram Dalmia—was in labour for the third time. As she lay writhing in pain with the village midwife beside her, in the east wing of their ancestral haveli in Chirawa, she chanted the name of the Lord—praying for a son. This was the brutal side of procreation—the natural corollary to marriage and the prerequisite to the attainments of womanhood.

Her husband Harjimal was an honourable and strong-willed man who was three years younger than her. She fervently prayed that this time it would be a boy and she could do him proud.

The child born was a male. He was bonny and fair. He had the golden complexion of the sand dunes and his thick dark hair shone like polished ebony. He had long limbs, a very wide nose and small deep-set eyes. He began to suckle his mother furiously as soon as the *dai* put him to her breast—an act that he would continue till he was five, long after his natural weaning years. Jadia Devi, tired and spent, held the baby to her swollen breasts and with each sucking movement of his tiny mouth the pain she felt below her waist eased away. She closed her eyes after planting a tender kiss on the baby's wide forehead and put her head back on the pillow that was a rolled-up cotton sheet. She heard the bells chime from the mandir in the distance and felt at peace. They augured well. They were saluting the birth of her new-born. She lay in the haveli that had housed the grand ancestors of her husband and child, and said a prayer of thanks to the Lord. She prided herself for carrying forth the seed of the Dalmias, the seed of the great patriarch Seth Kashi Ram who had passed it on to his son Shri Ram, and then to her husband Harjimal, and which now lay dormant within her newborn boy. The seed would make him blossom into a grand and lofty tree that would reach high into the clouds of fame and fortune and give her the distinction of having borne the most illustrious and dynamic male descendant in many generations that had preceded her or were to follow. The seed would impregnate half a dozen women and create a family of eighteen offspring from six wives before traversing to the next generation.

Indeed Ramkrishna, as the baby was named, would prove to be the greatest of them all. He would within his own life span of eighty-six years, indelibly and incredibly imprint his personality on the minds of all those who came in touch with him and become a subject of intrigue for all those who did not!

For his was to be a saga that defied the boundaries of the orthodox and the conventional, making him the most controversial link in the chain of the Dalmias. Jadia Devi could never have imagined that within her womb so powerful a life had been nurtured, and from her flesh and blood this exceptional and unique soul had taken its earthly form.

Long-limbed, olive-complexioned, wiry and agile Ramkrishna was an exceptional child. He had a fire in his eyes that was disturbing. Unlike other children he was neither given too much to playing or reading storybooks. At four he commenced his studies under Guru Jhabarmal Pande at the village school, completing them within an unprecedented span of four years because he had a head for numbers, and arithmetic came to him with ease. He learned to write from one to one hundred, and then memorised a set of multiplication tables from two to forty. Tables of one-and-a-half, two-and-a-half, three-and-a-half and four-and-a-half—he mastered them all with the speed of a computer, before graduating to the use of the units of weights and measures to hone his grounding skills that would train him to be a clever trader of goods and commodities. Devoid of pen and ink, notebooks or paper, the little students competed against each other, learning on stone slates on which they wrote with chalk sticks.

As a student, Ramkrishna was gifted. He excelled in his class because of his phenomenal mathematical ability and his mastery over the Marwari dialect that had a script without vowels, so it served as a shorthand. This made him the brightest student in his school and also the most eligible for a future job. Delighted with the experience of having such a prodigy under his tutelage, Guru Jhabarmal, appointed him head boy—a position that he remained in till he moved to Calcutta with his family when he turned nine.

Calcutta was a sharp contrast to Chirawa. It was crowded and vibrant and pulsated with a live energy.

The family rented a small part of a house that had been taken on lease by one Prahlad Rai Dalmia, a wealthy cousin of Harjimal with two sons, Madan Lal and Mahadev, for a monthly sum of eight rupees. Jadia Devi and her four children moved in and quickly settled down in their new home comfortably.

Manmeri and Basanti—her two elder daughters, Ramkrishna—her son, and Godaveri—her fourth child, along with their father Harjimal, took to city life without any trouble or fuss.

Ramkrishna however was restless. The pulse of the metropolis stirred him and stoked the fire in his eyes. He was compellingly drawn to the Hooghly Ganga that beckoned him even when he slept. He only felt placated when he was in the water—at first intrepidly and then with a speed and skill that amazed even himself. The hours got longer and longer and the depths he scoured deeper and deeper! There was something about the water that energised him.

At nine he enrolled in the Vishudhanand Saraswati Vidyalaya run by the Marwari Society of Calcutta. The school system was different. The primary class was called Class Eleven and the students got promoted backward. Brilliant as he was in mathematics, he secured admission into Class Nine and within a few months was given a double promotion to Class Seven. The smattering of English that he had picked up from his master Devkinandan in Chirawa enhanced his academic performance.

Many a time, while his cousins Madanlal and Mahadev took private tuitions, he sat outside the door and picked up spoken and written English, eventually proving to be far superior to them in his grasping and learning abilities.

Soon enough Ramkrishna made his presence felt in the Vidyalaya and his chest filled with pride when he overheard his teacher saying, 'This boy is the brightest child I have ever taught and he shall go places!'

The fire in his eyes shone brighter with the thoughts of the wondrous future that awaited him!

Sometimes, on the pretext of going to school, he sneaked off to the nearby market to enjoy the forbidden pleasure of playing truant, pottering around with little money in his pocket but lots of time on hands. Once in a while as a special treat to his four-year-old baby sister Godaveri, he would carry her to the market propping her astride his waist to buy her an ice-cream. It was a secret they shared. Sometimes he had the money to buy them one each but most times they shared a single one. Ramkrishna gave her the bigger half and kept the smaller one for himself because he loved his baby sister and it delighted him to see her happy. Godaveri licked the ice-cream greedily, and with her soiled hands clutching his shoulders, would ride back home in her Bhaiji's arms, wiping the remnants of the ice-cream from her mouth onto his sleeves—feeling the deep bond between them grow even deeper. At bedtime she would snuggle close to him as he read aloud stories from the *Sukh Sagar Bhagwat,* thumbing the much-used pages with his nimble fingers till she drifted off to sleep.

Ramkrishna stared at the three deep, round vaccination marks on his arm. They had been there since he was six. He remembered the day vividly. Ma had taken him to Malsisar, his *nana's* home where he was jabbed three times by the village municipality doctor.

Three ugly boils had erupted the following day and then disappeared after some time, leaving behind deep scars that had stamped him with a lifetime's immunity. He touched them and looked at them often. They were the only flaws that marred his beautiful golden skin. Something about them disturbed him!

In his tenth year Ramkrishna left school. Jadia Devi's brother Motilal Jhunjunwala, a rich and success-ful merchant who had been named 'Silver King', spotting his potential gave him a job as his cashier for a salary of ten rupees a month, offering to take him to Bombay. Ramkrishna was euphoric and waited anxiously for the day of his departure. He tied his savings of two rupees and ten annas that he had collected in one-pice-coins over six months into a handkerchief and carefully tucked it into the folds of his dhoti at his waist. He felt a sharp stinging pain on his arm as it brushed against his sleeve. He had forgotten the acid burn, that had eaten away the stubborn ringworm infection that had persisted there for so long. No local potion or application could made it go away. He was afraid that it would hamper his trip to Bombay with Mamaji. He thought of consulting his family *vaidya* or ayurvedic doctor, Mungelal. Vaidyaji was their physi-cian and *purohit*. He had administered the sacred thread ceremony to all the males in their family, thereby elevat-ing them to the rightful status of vaishyas. Recognising the urgency, Vaidyaji offered a sure-shot but very painful remedy.

'If you can bear the pain, I can cure you in just three days,' he said.

The little boy was steadfast in his resolve, for nothing could have been more painful than the prospect of getting left behind. So he readily agreed to Vaidyaji's suggestion.

A concentrated lotion of *tezaab* was poured over the infected place, burning away the ringworm, and also corroding a part of the flesh it had infected. Ramkrishna neither flinched nor cried out. He only shut his eyes tight and held his breath. Not a whimper escaped his lips. Vaidyaji was dumbfounded. He had never seen such steely resolve and such power to tolerate pain in anyone before!

Excited about his trip to Bombay, Ramkrishna trotted alongside his mama to the railway station. He patted the bundle of his life's savings tied at his waist and felt secure. Soon they were inside a moving train.

The train gathered speed and after a few hours stopped at a junction where they alighted to take another connection. They were waiting at a platform for the next train that would take them to their destination when an old man, bent over double, approached them. Ramkrishna saw a sad, crumpled face that moved him.

'Please Babuji,' the man mumbled as he stood before them, 'Help me. I have lost my ticket and have no money to buy another one,' he said, tears streaming down his face. 'Please help me.'

Motilal ignored his pleas and waved his hand angrily, gesturing him to move on. The old man hobbled away. But Ramkrishna's eyes followed him. He waited till the old man was out of sight and then, on the pretext of going to the bathroom, ran to catch him before he disappeared.

'Wait, Baba, wait,' he shouted when he spotted him, 'don't be sad. I have something for you.'

The man looked up with hope in his eyes—tears still staining his face.

Ramkrishna pulled out his precious little bag of coins and without a moment of hesitation, emptied all of them into the open palms of the startled old man.

He saw the old man's eyes mist over with gratitude but did not wait to hear his words of thanks. With a deep sense of satisfaction in his heart and a lightness in his step, he ran back to the platform where mama was waiting impatiently.

In the winter of 1904 Harjimal sent his pregnant wife and children to Chirawa where his mother Naraini Devi lived in their haveli. Ramkrishna was eleven. It was the year that India saw the outbreak of the dreaded plague during which thousands lost their lives and fear gripped the hearts of all. Naraini Devi decided to move with the family from Chirawa to Malsisar where she thought she would be far away and safe from the threat of the epidemic. The villagers evacuated their homes and made an exodus to safer havens. The wealthy travelled on majestic chariots drawn by oxen, loading their belongings on camels that followed their entourage.

Naraini Devi was not that privileged. Along with her family, she left on camelback uncomfortably but ungrudgingly, for neither she nor her daughter-in-law Jadia Devi would ever ask any of their wealthy relatives for help and incur any injury to their pride. For two long days they rode to their destination—Malsisar. On the eleventh of December in the Jhunjhunwala haveli, Jadia Devi gave birth to her fifth and last child. A handsome boy with princely features and a very fair skin. Ramkrishna fell in love instantly with his baby brother. The paternal bond between them would grow long into their adult years till the tide of fortune changed—but to Ramkrishna the little boy would always remain closest to his heart—his own child whom he would love and nurture like none other.

Back in Calcutta Harjimal Dalmia had just finished his early morning bath in the Ganges. Standing in waist-deep water, he performed his first *sandhya*, which he completed after sunrise. The ritual commenced after a reverent *pranam* to the Lord and to his ancestors. He chanted the powerful *Gayatri Mantra* with practised perfection to end his *tarpan*. Harjimal was a kind, modest and god-fearing man who loved his wife dearly. He firmly believed in monogamy and had strict and orthodox views on marriage. Never in his thirty years had he looked at any woman other than his wife. To him a matrimonial alliance was only acceptable if the family was pure and untarnished and had a high moral standard. So strict were his criteria for selection that if in several generations of a family, any person had committed suicide or had been suspected of taking alcohol or meat, the family would not be considered worthy of marrying into. In keeping with these high standards he had agreed to the alliance of Mani, his eldest daughter, with Gangadhar Chokhani of Laxmangarh, and Basanti, his second daughter, with Durga Dutt Modi of Jhun Jhunu.

As he waded out of the water on that December morning, Harjimal thought of his pregnant wife and his son. He knew she was safe in Malsisar at her father's home, far away from the treacherous plague. He felt comforted that his mother was with her. He had fulfilled his duties as a son, husband and father. He had instilled in his children a deep sense of devotion to the Lord and to their parents. All of them could recite slokas from the *Bhagwad Gita,* the holy scripture that had moulded his mind and conduct. They doggedly followed the rituals laid down by him in their daily prayers, for he set an example that they admired.

It was only Ramkrishna who unnerved him. Although he was obedient and god-fearing, the fire in his eyes was unsettling. Harjimal could not fault him for his devotion towards his parents, but he was very strong and self-willed and his restless energy was worrisome.

Ramkrishna was eleven and of marriageable age. Harjimal made a mental note to examine the marriage proposal sent by Mani's father-in-law for the niece of his friend Gangadhar Goenka of Nawalgarh. It seemed a good match for Ramkrishna. He had heard the girl was tall and slim and the family was clean.

He said a silent prayer to the Lord to protect his son from harm.

When Harjimal returned home there was a telegram awaiting him with a joyous message from Malsisar. The news of the birth of a boy elevated his mood and the anxiety he had felt, dissipated. The new-born baby, the youngest Dalmia of his lineage, would do him proud. He could not wait to set eyes on him and ached to be with his wife. He voiced a special thanks to the Lord asking for protection for the mother and child.

But fate had ordained for him only a short association with his little boy. Harjimal would not live to see him through his tenth year.

Ramkrishna, the eleven-year-old adolescent, was feeling the stirrings of his manhood. Pottering around in the market place, travelling in trams, walking back from school he felt a pleasant rush at the sight of young and nubile women, particularly fair-skinned ones. Although he had been bred on a fare of spiritualism, a sharp dichotomy within him divided the surreal from the earthly. His absorption in religious books was deep rooted and he tried to live his life and train his thoughts towards simple living. However, a strong innate pleasure-principle dominantly but unconsciously controlled him. Having weaned off his mother at five, distinct oedipal traits that Freud would have recognised, showed up in his persona.

Each day as he romanced with the Hooghly he felt his hormones metamorphose him from boyhood to manhood. He dreamt of living the life of a great king or a great saint, for he held the banner of the Dalmia family tree and took it upon himself to prove worthy of it.

The year of the plague epidemic, but more significantly the year his baby brother was born, unknown to him, talks for his betrothal to Narbada, the daughter of Girdharilal Goenka of Nawalgarh had begun. After brief and appropriate negotiations it was decided that Narbada was fit in every respect to be wedded to him even though she was eleven months older. It was agreed that their marriage would be held in Chirawa where the bride's family would also be invited to stay, unlike the convention where the boy's family goes to the girl's with a *baaraat*.

It was like the wedding of two dolls. Narbada, the innocent and beautiful doe-eyed virgin of twelve dressed in her traditional clothes and jewels, twittered happily as she walked around the fire with her child-groom in the courtyard of their ancestral haveli. The fragrance of the sand dunes filled the air as did the excitement of her beating heart under her prepubescent breast.

Ramkrishna, the groom, agile and athletic, felt his eyes mist more from the smoke of the fire than with the anticipation of conjugal bliss. His face glowed making his complexion shine an even brighter gold.

It was the auspicious time of *godhuli* when the ceremony began—the mystic and sacred moments of the cattle raising a cloud of dust as they return home after grazing lazily in the pastures all day, the moments that have been revered down the ages as the most favourable for uniting in wedlock.

That day, on the dusty horizons of the village, a rosy cloud of suspended particles hung low in the air veiling the two little dolls in an ethereal and romantic mist, and the sun faltered for just a wee second behind a pink cloud to capture the visual joy before it went down.

Hidden behind a veil that came down to her navel, Narbada followed her husband after the ceremony was over and bent down in reverence before his Ma and then his Bapu, touching her forehead to their feet. Then as tradition dictated she went back with her parents, to her native home to wait for over six months before she would be finally united with her husband for the rest of her short life.

In the tiny south-facing room in Calcutta partitioned by a curtain, on a muggy and rainy night, their marriage was consummated. Narbada lay beside her husband, with fear and abandonment, her heart beating wildly. He pulled her to him and smothered her with a deep and urgent kiss crushing her lips savagely as he bit into them. He moved hungrily down her slender throat to her tiny breasts and sucked them hard. She felt a tingling sensation of pleasure and pain, and tears rolled down her face from her tightly shut eyes. He moved his hands down her tender body tracing their path with his mouth. She felt his thumb between the folds of flesh between her thighs. She put both her arms around him in a tight embrace holding back her sobs for fear of waking up Ma and Bapu who slept behind the curtain. She felt him push her thighs apart and guide himself into her passionately. Then he lay still. She did not open her eyes or loosen her hold for a long time till he slept—like a baby, sound and secure in its mother's arms. She felt drowsy and the pain dulled as she slowly drifted off to sleep. Her virginity taken, she had been cast into a different mould irrevocably.

For Ramkrishna, Narbada was a toy, a plaything on which he could rightfully vent his anger and lust, over which he would exercise total control! He was her Lord and Master and she dared not displease him. She was too innocent and too much in love. She did his bidding to the best of her ability without a whimper or complaint, for she had pledged to serve him and his family as long as she lived.

Women of those times had to live in strict purdah and were not supposed to have questioning minds. Marriage was sacrosanct and they had no choice but to be happy with whatever they got. Narbada submitted to her new and difficult role without resistance and even though her husband's demands to remain completely covered from head to toe at all times were unreal and impossible, she never stopped trying. Both Harjimal and Jadia Devi doted on her and she served them dutifully. Ramkrishna maintained his routine of an early morning swim and work throughout the day. At night when he came to his bed, he took on the role of dictator, sadist and lover, for he loved his possession Narbada, but would not discover how much till after she died.

When Ramkrishna turned fifteen he was bringing home about fifty to a hundred rupees every month, a sum that he earned from commissions of brokering the sale of imported sugar to prospective dealers. Harjimal too was earning a salary of sixty rupees every month which made them comfortable. Employed with a firm called Brij Rai Harsukh Rai as its cashier, Harjimal had earned the confidence of his employers and they trusted him implicitly. His daughter Godaveri was happily married to Bashesherlal Vora, who belonged to a traditional Marwari family that was originally from Chirawa but had settled in Gaya at Navada in Bihar. He felt satisfied about fulfilling his paternal duties towards his children. Jaidayal, his youngest child, was four and growing up with the right values in the manner that he wanted. The adulation that he saw in the child for his elder brother and the deep affection that they shared, made him proud.

Ramkrishna indulged Jaidayal constantly. He gave him a few one-pice coins everyday and once in a while a two-anna coin that Jaida, as he had been nicknamed, collected and treasured. But Ramkrishna was restless. Deep conflicting emotions played up within him. He was conscious of his duties towards his family and wife but the teachings from the *Devi Bhagwat* spelt out something else. They pointed to a higher goal that he thought about often, but practical life and his work pushed away these nagging feelings into temporary amnesia. However, he never missed his morning reading of the *Samudra Manthan* before going to work. It energised him and he believed that it always brought him luck.

One night after everyone had retired to bed after a tiring day, Ramkrishna tiptoed into the room where Harjimal kept a strongbox with cash that belonged to his employees, but was given to him for safekeeping. Blocking the voices from his mind he stealthily removed the keys that lay in the pocket of his father's kurta that was hanging near the door. He opened the box with trembling hands and removed five one-hundred rupee notes from it. No one suspected anything when he came home the next day wearing a set of four shining gold buttons on his person, riding a brand new bicycle, for it was believed to be a self-indulgence from his own savings.

Harjimal's employers dismissed the matter assuming that he had been unknowingly tricked by someone in his dealings, for his honesty was never in doubt! No action was taken and the matter was forgotten. But Ramkrishna's conscience did not let him rest. Even after his father left the job and took up another one sometime later, he remained uneasy. He promised himself that he would not carry the burden with him for the rest of his life. A few years later an unexpected windfall in speculation brought him the enormous amount of one and a half lakh rupees. The next day Brij Rai Harsukh Rai received a cash delivery of one thousand rupees, squaring up a debt that had long been forgotten! His conscience finally appeased, Ramkrishna was at rest—but his emotional conflict was rekindled once again. The nagging quest for a better and higher spiritual life just would not leave him!

On his way to work one normal day, impulsively he turned towards the railway station and boarded a train that would take him to Puri, the temple town of Orissa. He carried nothing on his person except the clothes he wore and a blanket. Puri was the place where he believed he would attain the ultimate *gyaana* and thereby all the answers to his questions!

Leaving behind his earthly belongings and his family, he entered the temple city charged with a different energy. As he took in the panoramic view of the twelfth-century structure built by the Kalinga kings, he felt like a speck of dust in the enormous universe. The main towers that rose over fifty metres into the sky, stood on an elevated platform—their swirling pinnacles commanding the landscape for miles around. The sea of people—the pushing crowds—were all charged with the same energy that he felt. He entered the *sanctum sanctorum* of the temple where the three deities Lord Jagannath, Subhadra and Balbhadra stood, wearing the finest attire and grandest of jewels. He was struck by the omnipotence and omnipresence of their aura. He folded his hands and stood rooted to the spot, unmindful of the tears streaming down his face or the crowds jostling around him. It was only when he was pushed aside by an impatient darshan seeker that he moved away to join the line of people waiting to get their share of the free food being distributed at the *bhoga* outside.

For several days and nights he moved about in the vicinity of the shrine like he had never known a life outside of it. Bathing in the *Chandan Talab*, sleeping in different spots, he mingled with the pilgrims who had converged on the mystic beach that was the sacred ground of Lord Jagannath. Sometimes he spread his blanket on the sand and slept under the open sky asking himself, 'Who am I? Where have I come from? Where do I have to go?' Questions that he had posed to himself over and over in his meditation and prayers. At other times he would stare at the moon and stars and wonder, 'Who is it that holds them in mid-air? Why don't they fall? How do they hang in the sky?' And looking far away deep into the darkness, he would fall off to sleep to begin the next day of his quest all over again.

It was the gold buttons that he wore and his clothes that gave him away. Distinct in his appearance and force-ful in his stride, with the fire burning stronger in his deep-set eyes, he stood out. Just when he was beginning to believe that he was eternally submerged in the hubbub of the temple at the feet of the Lord and that all ties with his family had been broken, his Bapu found him.

As he climbed down the gradient steps of the *Chandan Talab* to begin his day with a morning bath, he stood looking straight at his Bapu standing just a few feet away. Ramkrishna began to cry. He wept like a child—tears of fear and repentance—as he fell at his Bapu's feet expect-ing the worst dressing down he had ever received.

Harjimal bent down and held out his arms. He lifted Ramkrishna's head gently and pulled him to his chest. He hugged him hard till his sobs stopped. Then he sat down on the steps of the sacred water tank and in a soft and consoling voice said, 'Do not be afraid Ramkrishna,

I will not scold you. I have come to take you back. Your ma is sick with worry and has not eaten a morsel since you left and *bechaari* Narbada she does nothing but cry. Your brother keeps asking for you and cries too. He needs you like all of us do. Come with me, my son. You are two young to leave home and become a sanyasi.'

Ramkrishna looked into his father's eyes. The softness and forgiveness in them made him sadder. In between stifled sobs he managed a few sentences.

'You only have taught me to become detached Bapu,' he said, 'I do not want these worldly pleasures. I will stay here and serve the Lord as a sadhu.'

Harjimal's patience did not wane. 'Listen my child,' he said, 'A man has three debts to repay in his life—*yagya* for the *devtas,* puja for the saints and *shraddh* for the forefathers. You have to finish paying yours. If any of these remains outstanding you cannot attain peace. Come back with me, my son, your *vairagya* is only temporary and you will repent your actions if you don't listen to me.'

Ramkrishna was pained by the love and compassion being showered on him. He clung to his Bapu and wept bitterly. He returned to Calcutta to his family feeling reverence and love for his Bapu like he had never felt before and hoping that he would be able to atone for the pain he had caused!

Narbada, the raw thirteen-year-old pubescent rustic, who spoke a village dialect of Marwari native to primitive

Rajasthan, could neither read nor write. She was fair and had large limpid eyes. Her laughter sounded like the tinkling of bells. She lived with her husband, who was eleven months younger than her, and his family in a rented room in Calcutta that cost thirteen rupees a month—an amount they could ill afford. The room was so small that it could just about accommodate four narrow cots placed closely side by side. It had a small verandah facing south that was used by Grandmother Naraini Devi.

Every night, she sat up, pressing her husband's tired body and legs, waving the *pankha* over his head to make him comfortable. Narbada was deeply in love. He was her dear and beloved husband—her *pati parmeshwar.* He did funny things to her; he also scratched her and bit her, but she did not mind. It was her fault—try as she would, she could not manage to keep her arms covered and those stubborn bangles, they always crept out of her sleeves and made jingling sounds. She had to be more careful. Months of physical abuse had made her weak and tired. She became gaunt and frail but no one had noticed. The urgency and rush that she had felt when he first touched her was waning. She could no longer cook and clean like she did earlier. She could feel a hot flush in her cheeks at all times. Her hands remained cold and clammy. Soon she developed a persistent and irritating cough but she was too afraid to tell. She didn't want to die so soon. She loved her young husband dearly. And then there was an unfinished task…that woman whom he craved for…the one who occasionally visited him with some relatives…So what if they were related. He was deeply infatuated by her—he told her so. She had to make it happen, some-how, anyhow. It was her sacred duty to please him. It hurt when he pinched her and sucked her breasts but there was a strange and heady pleasure even in that pain. She knew that his mother had suckled him till he was five years old. She often imagined him pulling and tugging at his mother's breast for milk that had long dried. She found it arousing. The touch and feel of his body, agile and athletic like that of the champion swimmer that he was, never failed to thrill her!

Gradually her cough worsened. Once she even coughed up some blood but was too scared to tell him. She deteriorated rapidly, and by the time she crossed her sixteenth birthday she had full-blown tuberculosis.

Narbada died soon after at her father's home where she had been sent for a change of place.

She never saw the copious tears that streamed down Ramkrishna's face as he put her pale, listless corpse on the ground. She did not hear the loud sobs that rent the air as he grieved for her. She could not feel the great remorse that poured out with his cries; they fell on her dead ears. He mumbled broken sentences: 'Forgive me beloved. I have really tortured you. You were my truly devoted wife…a real saint…a divine blessing! O God! Punish me for what I have done to her! I will avenge you my beloved…I will never rest till I can wipe every tear that fell from your eyes and kiss away the throbs of pain that I inflicted on every part of your body.'

Narbada's frail and diseased body was consigned to the flames bringing to an end her tortuous life with

Ramkrishna that had spanned two years—but the remorse and guilt stayed alive in his mind. It transformed into a passionate, restless, unending search for his beloved Narbada whom he so desperately wanted back—this time to love her like he had never loved before—with a tenderness and fervour that she had never known. Narbada would be back—but in the body of Dineshnandini almost fifty years later!

The first setback in Ramkrishna's life and ostensibly the most emotionally damaging one came when he was sixteen years old, after Narbada died. Carrying the burden of a guilt-ridden conscience for not having treated her well, he was overcome by acute depression that did not abate even after he moved to Uttarpara with his father. In Uttarpara he tried to drown himself in his work that entailed assisting Harjimal in selling cotton cloth from a small shop that he had bought. He would load several bales of fabric onto his bicycle and peddle his wares from door to door trying to make a living. As he wandered around doing his tedious job, he would pass the banks of the river where the gloomy sight of millions of fish snared in nets, struggling for their lives, and being hauled out of the water hit him. He stood staring at them, feeling their agony, praying for their release, and then with helplessness and sadness would get back to his business of selling cloth. Dying fish reminded him of his Narbada and that made him even sadder. Even a good sales day did not lift his spirit, for melancholy had become his sole and constant companion.

The cloth business never took off and they sold the shop and returned to Calcutta. Ramkrishna lived a hard and frugal life. He took up a job with Motilal Jhunjhunwala for a meagre salary and privately dabbled in speculation in jute, cotton, and silver. Harjimal also found employment as a cashier with a wealthy merchant, having had no luck in his own work.

Having discovered the lucrative market of shares and stocks and the quick and easy prospects of returns in *satta,* Ramkrishna plunged headlong into it. With Motilal he began handling cash and keeping accounts—a job that he had perfected. Figures and transactions that went into crores remained in his head and he never needed to write books to remember them, for he had the uncanny ability of instant recall. His boundless energy was compounded by his numerical genius and that made him ideal for the work he so enjoyed.

After Narbada's death many proposals for marriage came for Ramkrishna that were judiciously and scrupulously examined by Harjimal. A very slim and fair girl of pure Marwari descent was rejected because her brother was physically handicapped. Several others were turned down for equally inane and flippant reasons. A wealthy Patodia girl whose eligibility and antecedents were satisfactory was agreed upon and finally the two were engaged, till someone informed Harjimal that the girl had some flaw in her eyes. Without even checking the authenticity of the rumour, the engagement was called off for only an immaculate entity could be allowed accession into the Dalmia lineage because Harjimal wanted pure and healthy descendants to carry forth their name.

It was Durga who was destined for the role!

Brought to his notice by the local pandit, he could find no fault with her or her family. So she was accorded the honour of becoming his son's second wife—a position she held for forty-five years. Durga was neither literate nor beautiful, and barring his scandalous pursuit of other women during her lifetime, Ramkrishna remained dutiful to her—always giving her the status of *Griha Laxmi*. So much so that all his subsequent wives were made to pledge that they would love and respect her like an elder sister. Her own life was never free of ailments, and she spent a major part of it in a wheelchair. She gave birth to one girl who was named Rama, and a few other infants, who died—either prenatal deaths or soon after they were born—so she never achieved the distinction of becoming the mother of his son!

Barely three years after Durga was married, death struck again, this time to snatch away Harjimal. He had been keeping poor health that resulted from physical hardships and mental stress. Ramkrishna had accompanied Motilal to Malsisar the fortnight before for a family wedding despite his uncle's reluctance and father's ill health. From Malsisar he rode on camelback to Lathmangarh where his sister Mani Bai lived. He spent a few joyous days with her, being pampered and enjoying her hospitaliy before he returned. At Malsisar he received a telegram with disturbing news from Calcutta. Bapu had taken a turn for the worse. He cut short his trip and went back to find him in the worst agony that he could have imagined. He had been diagnosed with dropsy for which there was no cure those days. His stomach had distended to gruesome proportions and his excretory system was blocked.

'You will be cured Bapu,' he said unconvincingly and then recited slokas from the *Devi Bhagwat* to lull him to sleep. But Harjimal knew his death was near. Rest and sleep both eluded him and his mind and body were only one single sensation of excruciating pain.

On 14 September, the day of an ill-omened eclipse, he breathed his last an hour before midnight. His end finally relieved him of his unbearable torture. It was exactly sixty-five years later in the same month that Ramkrishna was to die!

It was during those trying days that Ramkrishna met Seth Baldeodas Dudhwawala. One of the wealthiest merchants of Calcutta, Dudhwawala had started life as an ordinary munim and by sheer dint of his hard work and good fortune had risen to eminence. A highly principled man, he was respected and revered and the entire community bowed down to his sterling personality. He had the unique quality of forgiveness that overshadowed any other trait in his character, and tales of his kindness, returning good for evil, never ever having lost his temper under the gravest provocation, and his utmost faith in the Lord, were legendary.

Ramkrishna was at a dip in his life. The sporadic and temporary gains from speculation were enough to keep him hooked but not enough to sustain his family. After the death of Harjimal his responsibilities had increased and the duty to look after the family fell singly on his shoulders. Jaida was eleven and totally dependent on him. And there was no one else who could take care of Ma and Durga.

But his inner voice never let him feel dejected. It gave him the power to carry on. Dudhwawala smiled benevolently at Ramkrishna. Taking an instant liking to him, well aware of his firebrand market methods and recognising his ability for hard work, he made him an offer.

'Ramkrishna, you have been a defaulter many a time in the market,' he said. 'Today you are neither creditworthy nor trustworthy. No one will loan you even five rupees, but I shall take you as my partner. You can use my name for the business but I will take a share of fifty per cent in the profit. If there is a loss I shall make the payments and debit your account. You will never have to worry about generating cash against losses.'

Ramkrishna could not believe his ears. Dudhwawala was like a messenger from heaven. His inner voice echoed, 'I told you so ... told you so ...'

Dudhwawala continued, 'Never deceive me Ramkrishna, never, and take my advice, stop indulging in satta, you will be ruined by it. Satta is like termite. It preys on your being and leaves you powerless. We can do good business together and you will never look back. Promise me that you will not do satta ever again.'

But Ramkrishna, the compulsive gambler that he was, did not heed his benefactor's words!

The world of gambling is unforgiving and harsh. Money is the demon and the deity and there can be violent bloodshed if losses are not immediately squared up. The speculative market which is a larger variant of a gambling den can also be merciless with a loser, but the lure of easy money is too compelling and once trapped in it, it is impossible for anyone to get out. It was the turbulence in the market tides that taught Ramkrishna the most vital lessons in fortitude, forgiveness and patience. It was here that he discovered the impermanence of wealth and the mercurial changes it brought towards those who had it or those who did not. Chanting the magic mantra of *Ram Naam* whenever he was on the downswing, he pressed on. Gambling was in his blood and despite his promises to Dudhwawala, he obsessively continued his indulgence. Each time Dudhwawala forgave his waywardness, he renewed his promises to him only to break them the next day!

One such dreary morning he entered the bazaar contemplating on life and his ill fortune, when he was rudely jolted. A man swiftly stepped up behind him and threw his muffler around his neck tightening it into a death-like noose. His heart pounded and his pulse went racing as he felt a wave of terror rise in his constricted throat.

'Let me go ... Who are you? You are strangling me ...'

A sinister-looking, puny man loomed in front of him, tightening the noose even more. 'Pay up you *chor*... Pay me my fifty rupees or I shall only let you go after you are dead!' he screamed.

Ramkrishna remembered the fifty rupees of an unconfirmed debt he owed this insane broker whom he recognised. His eyes filled with tears of humiliation and anger. A huge crowd of amused onlookers had collected around them and were watching in glee.

Ramkrishna folded both his hands and gasping and coughing he said, 'I'll give you the money. I promise I'll pay you as soon as I can.'

After what seemed like an eternity the angered and abusive broker let go of him. He towered above him menacingly. Ramkrishna ached with the wound to his pride. He bent down to touch the extortionist's feet in gratitude and shamefacedly walked out of the vicinity of the barbaric fiend.

He swore to himself—one day he would avenge the insult. All he needed was big bucks! He remembered the banks of the river, the fish being hauled out of the water, writhing in pain and choking to death. It made him feel wretched.

World War I broke out barely two years after Harjimal died. Every being on the planet reeled under the effects of the gargantuan combat in some way or another. Ramkrishna, however, was being consumed by the raging flames of his own private battle. A serious defaulter in the satta bazaar, he had been condemned as a criminal and was despised in the cruel world of business. Ostracised as a debtor he was not even considered worthy of a paltry five rupees by anyone, including his own relatives. The burden of supporting the family was breaking his back. In all his twenty-two years he had never felt such a sense of injustice. He could not understand why he was being sinned against, or why life was being so hard on him. He could not see the larger plan of omnipotent time that was at work in a strange and immutable manner.

Driven by his dire need, feeling utterly forlorn and dejected he went to an astrologer to seek solace, thinking that he would be relieved of some of his troubles. The astrologer, a personal friend and of a saintly disposition, was very kind and sympathetic towards him.

'My dear friend, the end of your misfortunes is in sight,' he said, 'After six weeks you enter the sub-period of Mercury in your horoscope; it will be very lucky for you and you shall come into big money. I see you getting more than a lakh and a half!'

There was a ring of excitement and sincerity in the astrologer's voice.

Ramkrishna felt stupid. Not believing a word of what he had heard he said, 'Don't joke with me Panditji. My time is bad. I have no friends and no credit in the market. I am being hunted like an animal and I don't sleep even a wink. My life is worth less than even five rupees today. Who is going to give me that kind of money?' Panditji interrupted his words and pulled out a piece of paper from his desk. In big bold letters he wrote down what he had forecast, handing him the folded slip when he finished.

Ramkrishna looked at the slip bewildered but not becalmed. 'Empty words,' he thought. He put the note in his pocket and hesitantly and sadly returned to his world of misery uttering the name of Ram as he stepped out. He blocked out the sounds of his inner voice irked by its persistence. Feeling the days drag on heavily he woke up one morning not knowing that his life was going to change permanently thereafter.

One of his agents in London whom he had been acquainted with while working for Motilal and who had also been privately dealing with, sent him a cable informing him about an expected rise in silver prices in the near future. In those days there were only four authorised brokers in London who informed overseas buyers about market trends by cablegram and Ramkrishna had developed his independent contact with them all. The one who was the first to receive the information could usually avail of it to his own advantage, by buying or selling accordingly.

With that vital tip in his pocket and a ray of hope in his head, he entreated some of the regulars in the market to transact some business in his name, but the *persona non grata* that he was, no one came forward to buy his idea. Distressed but not disheartened he approached Panditji, the wealthy astrologer who had so confidently predicted his future windfall. He entreated Panditji not to let go of this god-sent opportunity and managed to convince him to purchase silver worth seven thousand, five hundred pounds for which Ramkrishna would receive a commission of only one hundred rupees—an amount that he said would more than satisfy him. Since he did not even have ten rupees on him to send the cable to London for the relevant purchase, the benevolent Panditji gave him the money to send it. Hopeful of a rich return for his astrologer, Ramkrishna boarded a tram to the General Post Office in Calcutta, but in effect began a journey that was going to change the course of his life in a mysterious and stupefying turn of events!

That night he slept soundly, comforted and secure with his new-found patron's support. He woke up the next morning feeling bright and cheerful, and headed for his bath to the river when a messenger from the astrologer stopped him in his tracks. He was horrified to hear that Panditji had changed his mind about the silver purchase and was no longer to be held liable for the transaction, nor did he want any share in the expected profit. Ramkrishna was devastated. He was saddled with the risky purchase of the metal worth seven thousand five hundred pounds. Even a small drop in the market would be disastrous. Where was he to get the money from? Crazy and random thoughts raced through his head. Panic-stricken, he ran to Panditji to beg him to reconsider his decision. Copious tears fell from his eyes as he pleaded with him but Panditji remained unmoved!

'Main barbaad ho jaunga Panditji; daya kijiye mujhpar. Aap nahin kehte to main chaandi nahin khareedta (I will be ruined, Panditji; have pity on me. If you hadn't agreed, I would not have bought the silver).'

But Panditji had turned to stone. Unknown to Ramkrishna other forces had been at work. Someone had poisoned Panditji's mind against him and he was convinced that Ramkrishna was trying to cheat him. They had warned Panditji that Ramkrishna was a resourceless and defamed defaulter, and would neither give him any share in the profit nor actually buy the silver. He would only be made to underwrite a loss.

Crestfallen and defeated Ramkrishna gave up. He assured Panditji that no liability would fall on him for the transaction and he was not bound to his commitment. Quite evidently Panditji's predictions had been empty words that he himself did not believe.

With a heavy heart and no direction is sight he went straight to the Ganga to balm his burning head. He waded into the river till the water came upto his knees. Forgetting his physical body and blocking all thoughts from his mind, he folded his hands and closed his eyes and began intoning the powerful *Gayatri Mantra*. The sounds of the words *Om Bhur Bhuvaha Swaha*…suffused him with an ethereal energy. His faith unshaken, he stood like a statuesque heron half immersed in the cool water till his mind, body and soul all aligned with the chants and the music of the waves of his *Ganga Ma*. He stood there untiringly for hours after which he returned to the bustle of the city.

After two long and anxious days of waiting, silver prices shot up. A worried Ramkrishna heaved a sigh of relief. His profit totalled a sum of four thousand rupees. His confidence booming, greed and ambition got the better of him. He did not sell his holding, hooked onto the board where the dice had just rolled him his fortune. He became intoxicated with the prospect of a big haul. Unmindful of the immorality of his actions, he stole Durga's gold ornaments and mortgaged them for two hundred rupees. With the money in his pocket, richer and more confident, he cabled the second agent in London to purchase ten thousand pounds worth of silver. His profit in the next few days grew five times and he found himself sitting on a tidy sum of twenty thousand rupees. Now there was no stopping him. He knew he was in the winning seat. Fuelled by the strength of his growing kitty, the gambler in him was raring to go. The spurt in the silver prices was not going to die down for a while and he was riding the crest of the wave. Soon his profit swelled to an astounding seventy-five thousand rupees—a sum that he could not have even dreamed of barely three weeks ago! He mused again and again about his own good fortune and Panditji's folly, and thanked the Lord for his kind benevolence! He was the single owner of so much cash— the thought thrilled him and the desire to touch, feel, hold all that money with his own hands grew stronger. Ramkrishna decided to sell his total holdings, just when fortune was beginning to smile. However it had not finished doling out to him his share.

Ramkrishna cabled one of his agents to sell all the silver he had bought for him and the second one to buy the same amount on his behalf. He calculated that, in that way he would only have to pay a commission for the transaction and not diminish the huge profit he held.

Strange are the ways of destiny! The first cable with instructions to sell got mutilated in transmission, so his agent never sold his stock, asking instead for a clarification of instructions. The second agent with the orders received the cable 'To Buy' on time, and followed the directions with the desired purchase.

The volatile market shot up once again and Ramkrishna hit the jackpot. His profit doubled to a lakh and a half. He instructed both agents to square up the business and sell all holdings. Being inexperienced he never realised that such a huge sale would create a downward slide in the market trend and reduce his profit considerably—but the demand for silver in London during the war was high and all of it got absorbed in the market, leaving him richer by a staggering profit of one lakh, fifty-six thousand rupees! Indeed Mercury had showered wealth into his palms and the astrologer's predictions had come true!

With the money remitted to him in three different banks, he first paid five thousand rupees each to the astrologer and the bank's munim in gratitude and then squared up his debts of over thirty thousand rupees in the satta bazaar. He also cleared his father's outstanding debt to Mama Motilal.

Suddenly he acquired a new respectability in the eyes of those very persons who had loathed him. There was a monsoon crop of new-found friends and relatives that flocked to his door.

Hundreds of fictitious stories spread like wildfire throughout Calcutta. Some called it a 'derby-sweep', others thought it was a lucky streak at gambling, still others said he had stumbled on a hidden treasure, but no one questioned the source. Wealth was wealth—ill-gotten or otherwise! He was respected and coveted—no longer a liar or a cheat. Such is the metamorphosis that wealth brings.

It made him both cynical and bitter but he was enjoying his status immensely—till the real nature of wealth—illusory and ephemeral struck him again. He lost all his earnings in just a few months but his respectability and creditworthiness remained high.

Now, Ramkrishna commanded a respect whereby people trusted his judgment. Reputed to have an uncanny feel of the market pulse, he set the trends on buying and selling. If he bought, people bought; if he sold, they sold too. Taking advantage of this, he formed a syndicate with Motilal Jhunjhunwala and a few other wealthy businessmen of Calcutta with a small share of two-and-a-half-annas in the rupee as profits for himself. Trusting his acumen and sixth sense on forward trading they decided to corner all the silver that was available in the country. Subsequently, silver worth over a crore was purchased in cash by the syndicate and hoarded both in Calcutta and Bombay. To complete their transaction, however, they were short of an amount of fifteen lakh rupees which they could not muster up even after they mortgaged their entire holdings, an act which they had done in complete contravention of an ordinance that made hoarding a penal offence at that time.

The success of the syndicate was in serious jeopardy. Just then, Ramkrishna received a call from the manager of the Bank of Bengal asking him to come and see him. Thinking there to be a solution in sight, Ramkrishna, accompanied by one of his senior associates from the syndicate, went to call on the manager. What they encountered was not what they had expected. Forthright and stern-faced, the man of British descent asked them to disclose to him how much silver they were holding. For fear of being prosecuted, Ramkrishna's associate panicked and left the room.

Ramkrishna followed him out. 'Let's not lose courage,' he said, his words belying his maturity of twenty-three years. 'Lets go back and tell him the truth. You need not be afraid. You tell him that all the silver belongs to me. That way no harm will come to you if we are prosecuted.' His courage and confidence in place they went back into the manager's cabin.

However, they were given another jolt by him. The bank manager only wanted to know how much they were holding because the government wanted to buy silver.

The next day they were informed that the government had agreed to purchase the whole lot. As a result they were delivered from facing the prospect of abject failure of the syndicate and the astronomical losses that would have accrued. It was the first time in the history of the British rule that the government purchased silver from India to be used for coinage.

Ramkrishna made several lakhs in the deal and earned for himself the title of Silver King, that was once accredited to his Mama Motilal. He cornered silver many more times later and like a rubber ball, he was tossed up and down time and again, his failures only pushing him to greater heights of success. His was a name to reckon with in the world of business, and he commanded a control over the markets in both Calcutta and Bombay.

By the middle of the second decade of the century, while World War I raged savagely in all corners of the globe, political and economic changes were churning the belly of the Indian subcontinent. Gandhi had returned from South Africa and had settled on the banks of Sabarmati near Ahmedabad. Feeling the pulse of simmering resentment against the Imperialist rulers, he had begun to travel throughout India to re-acquaint himself with his people. Dressed like a fakir in only a white khadi dhoti, setting an example of sacrifice and ascetic living, he began to loosely formulate his ideas which would help consolidate the disjointed and fragmented struggle for freedom from the Raj. Wherever he went he was mobbed by responsive and milling crowds to whom he preached his tenets of non-violence and truth. The rumbling, discontented masses gravitated to him for they saw in him the messiah who would deliver them from their bondage. He touched a chord in every Indian's heart and their dormant patriotism assumed a dimension that was both palpable and definite. His call for non-cooperation became a burning fever. Homespun and handwoven khadi became the symbol for nationalism, and swadeshi the magic mantra.

Far away in the secluded world of satta, Ramkrishna was not untouched by Gandhi's wake-up call of patriotism. Workers of the Indian National Congress often came to Dudhwawala for monetary contributions. Gandhi and Madan Mohan Malviya, who were frequent visitors to his home, were given generous donations by most of the wealthy merchants of Calcutta including Dudhwawala. Fifteen-year-old Jaida had reached his matriculation in the Vishudhanand Saraswati Vidyalaya which was a government-recognised institute and, thereby, in a sense anti-national.

As Gandhi's call for civil disobedience and non-cooperation gathered momentum, Ramkrishna withdrew his protege and younger brother from his *alma mater* in keeping with the prevailing nationalistic sentiment. A day later a massive rally organised in the college square was addressed by Gandhi and attended by an overwhelming crowd of thousands of people. Jaida too donned his khadi cap and sat listening to him amongst the milling sea of humanity. Mass arrests followed and hundreds of people including the young student Jaida were arrested and bundled off to the local thana. The following day, they were sentenced by the magistrate to thirty days' imprisonment, but Jaida was let off because he was found to be under eighteen.

His studies disrupted, Jaida was subsequently given charge of a small shop to sell khadi by Ramkrishna and following his brother's orders, he dutifully carried the bales from door to door, contributing to the cause and trying to sell his wares.

This was the beginning of the Dalmia's long-standing association with Gandhi and the Congress which lasted till Gandhi died in 1948, but was completely dissipated when Jawaharlal Nehru demolished Dalmia five years later.

The year Jaida turned sixteen, a suitable match with the eleven-year-old daughter of Laxmi Narayan Jalan of Nawalgarh was found, and he was wedded to her. On 19 May 1920, Ramkrishna discharged his final duty towards his brother, that had fallen on his shoulders after Harjimal's untimely death, by getting him married to the girl who would have passed the most stringent of tests laid down by Harjimal's standards of selection.

Krishna was illiterate but fair and fragile. She committed herself to the *sewa* of her husband and his family with exemplary devotion. She soon became skilled in the knowledge of the scriptures under the guidance of Durga, her sister-in-law, Jadia Devi, her mother-in-law, and her husband. During her long and pious life in which she predeceased her husband, she gave birth to seven sons and two daughters that infinitely glorified her status as a Dalmia *bahu* who sowed the seeds of a parallel generation fathered by Jaidayal—that would ultimately come to be known as the 'real Dalmias'. Krishna's entry into their home was followed by another newcomer the same year. Durga gave birth to her first child, Rama, who would prove to be the luckiest of all of Ramkrishna's children who were to follow much later from his other wives. She remained his only and most-loved child till the birth of Krishna's first son, Vishnu Hari, for in him Ramkrishna saw an embodiment of his own soul and therefore invested more time and emotion in him than in any other child of his generation or later. This association grew into a potently meaningful one and only changed when fortune and repeated marriages stymied what could have turned into a legal adoption.

Torn by the contradictions in his mind, bleeding with the internal strife, clamouring to find the path of supreme bliss, a restlessness resurfaced in Ramkrishna. He travelled every weekend to an ashram not far from Calcutta with Durga and his family in search of peace. There he drowned himself in the atmosphere of devotion. He had mastered written and spoken Bengali by reading signboards. His favourite bedtime story book called *Amiya Niami Charita* was authored by the owner of *Amrit Bazaar Patrika;* it was on the life of Gourang Mahaprabhu Chaitanya believed to be a divine reincarnation of Lord Krishna. Deeply moved by Chaitanya Mahaprabhu's life he became his ardent devotee, spending as much time as he could in the ashram, even fantasising that he had been possessed by his spirit.

In the serene and pure atmosphere of the ashram he mingled with the thousand-odd Bengali women chanting *Hari Bole* in a loud musical tenor, while they stood up in abandon, dancing in divine ecstasy, and then fell to the floor in a trance. Sometimes he transcended space and time to become Lord Krishna, or one of the *gopis,* or Radha singing and dancing, forgetting his earthly form. Even when he returned to his hard material world he carried the sounds of the kirtan from the ashram in his heart, while his soul lingered on amidst the devotees there.

That familiar feeling of distance and detachment overcame him again. The urge to find the answers to his questioning mind haunted him. He wanted to be alone. He sent his family to Chirawa and stayed back in Calcutta to be in mute solitude. He spent all day weeping copiously, pining to be united with Lord Krishna, believing himself to be a sad and separated gopi in Vrindavan or Chaitanya in Mathura. He sublimated all his desires and attachments and began to live like an ascetic—his younger brother Jaida, following his example, also became an ardent devotee of Chaitanya Mahaprabhu.

When Rama turned eight, Ramkrishna wished to inculcate in her deep spiritual *sanskars,* and left her at the Bhagwat Bhakti Ashram founded by Rao Balbir Singh at Rewari. Later he also spent a long time there with Durga and the rest of the family. It was here that many freedom fighters and disciples of Gandhi stayed to learn the finer and higher spiritual goals of life. It was in this ashram that Ramkrishna met Madalsa—the daughter of Jamnalal Bajaj and Madeleine Slade who had become Gandhi's disciple, and had been rechristened Mirabehn by him, and it was here that later he developed closer and deeper ties with Gandhi.

For the time being, his desire to pursue wealth and fame was lost but not extinct.

Ramkrishna beheved his mission on earth was to guide mankind to salvation. Honouring his mother's wishes that were of paramount importance to him, he began to construct a new haveli at Chirawa which was a little further away from their ancestral one and purported to be much bigger and grander. He moved to Chirawa with his family, with his higher spiritual goals driving him to live the life of a sadhu even as he remained in his worldly garb. In this state of mental evolution he imagined that he had become *jeewan mukta*.

The new haveli was constructed with a specific plan to suit his reformed lifestyle. In the centre of the courtyard a twenty-feet deep underground tavern was dug out which was turned into a private cave for his meditation. It was paved with white marble and a tiger skin spread on its stark floor. On the walls of the cave he scripted slokas and Bhajans with his own hands. They were meant to remind him constantly of the Divine Being and the aim of his life.

Donning saffron robes Ramkrishna spent several hours meditating in his cave and the rest of the day, holding religious discourses for villagers who flocked around this new avatar. He recited slokas from the *Bhagwad Gita* and narrated tales from holy scriptures to an awe-struck audience that was held captive by his fluency and knowledge.

When the mango season arrived, Mani Bai sent the family a huge basket of the rarest and most expensive

Alphonso mangoes from Bombay. Without keeping a single one for himself or the family, Ramkrishna took the basket to the construction site where the half-clad and impoverished labourers toiled for their living, laying brick by brick painstakingly to complete their task. He distributed them one by one to the astounded workers who had never seen or tasted this transcendent fruit of the gods. He watched the myriad emotions of joy, gratitude, awe, adoration, worship flit across their faces and felt suffused by an overwhelming surge of pleasure—different from any he had ever experienced and far greater than tasting the mangoes would have procured him. The hail of jubilant shouts did not penetrate his ears for they were filled with a different melody from the heavens. He headed towards his cave to return to his meditation.

The celestial melody from the strings of a musical instrument played by the gods filled the air with a resounding wave of indefinable bliss. The notes of the symphony floated around making a tune that no mortal could have ever heard. Each strain had a different colour and hue—a dimension that could be both seen and touched. The crescendo lifted him into a stratosphere of magical peace—the sounds of the stars playing an orchestra, a seraphic serenade that lulled and mesmerised—that was painful to turn off.

He had tuned into it many times on the floor of his cave. He could control the volume—the sound, the light, the colours, the hues and the ethereal lightness of his being—his spirit flying high out of his body like a kite on a string, far away into the deep blue of the sky. He knew one day the string would snap and the sky would swallow the kite into its limitless expanse. The strains of the melody tugged at the string and the kite floated back into his body that had levitated six inches above the white marble floor!

The sharp rays of the sun pierced his half-closed lids as he alighted the stairs that brought him back to his real world. They hurt and his eyes began to water. He had been in the tavern for over six hours and a crowd of anxious villagers were waiting to hear him speak.

By the end of the '20s, the changes that were sweeping the world were also reverberating strongly in the far corners of the Indian Peninsula. The impact of the Russian Revolution and the disintegration of the monarchy of the Tsars had shaken the Imperial rulers as much as it had laid bare the fragility of their control over the Indian subcontinent. The brewing undercurrents of the demands for freedom were threatening to turn into an orchestrated driving force under the aegis of Gandhi.

Quick to gauge the pulse, with no substantial resources to back his plans, Ramkrishna turned his attention to industry which indeed was the right field to be in. Having gained experience as a commission agent of essential commodities at Danapur in Bihar (after moving from Bombay), he had realised the untapped and enormous profitability in setting up a sugar-manufacturing unit. He went about purchasing the land for the proposed project even after a heavy loss in linseed speculation left him with a huge outstanding debt.

His transition from speculator to industrialist was neither smooth nor easy, but the initial problems did little to dampen his resolve, which led to the establishment of the first in a chain of sugar factories that would soon dot the entire southern belt of Bihar. Better known as Seth Dalmia, he was now regarded as a wealthy and successful industrialist, whose support to the Indian National Congress imparted to him a new and highly respected veneer. He took to wearing khadi and instructed all his family members to adhere to the Gandhian principles of *satya*, *ahimsa* and *swadeshi*. He discarded all British-made goods and mill-made cloth and began to conduct his life like a loyal and dedicated soldier of the cause. His regular cash donations to the Sadaquat Ashram run by Gandhi's followers, and headed by Brij Kishore Babu, the father-in-law of the yet-to-be-famous Jai Prakash Narayan, kept it going. Staunchly supporting *satyagraha* and non-cooperation, he toiled sincerely, even managing to garner the covert backing of some highly-placed Indians who were in government service, thus entrenching himself well into the mainstream struggle against the British.

In Bihar the Sadaquat Ashram, generously supported by Dalmia's donations, became the nucleus of anti-government activities. In a sudden swoop on the premises one day, many Congress leaders who had converged there were arrested and thrown into prison. Subsequently as a suppressive measure, a strict ordinance was passed, imposing a ban on all activities that defied government orders.

Hasan Iman, a barrister of very high standing, was the first Muslim president of the Indian National Congress. A personal and close friend of Dalmia's, he communicated his desire to begin a protest march against the draconian arrests of the Congress workers.

Accompanied by his fifteen-year-old daughter Rama, holding the Congress flag upright in his hands, fire and pride shining in his eyes, Dalmia began a courageous and daring march from Danapur with a few thousand people that swelled to over a lakh as they reached the Patna court shouting slogans against the government. Charged with passionate nationalist sentiment he climbed onto a high rampart outside the court to address the mammoth crowd that had collected there, and who cheered with frenzy as he shouted *Bharat Mata ki Jai* (Long Live Mother India) and Congress *Zindabad* (Victory to Congress) in defiance of the authorities. Whether it was the belligerence of the people or the highly volatile mood of the crowds, no arrests were made; the demonstration ended peacefully—as a grand success and the Congress workers were released the following day!

Dalmia's active participation in the cause crystallised his desire to become one with the people who mattered. During that time, encouraging greater participation of the people, the British government had allowed them a set number of elected representatives to the Provincial Assembly. He expressed his wish to contest elections as a Congress nominee from Danapur for the Legislative Assembly but his candidature was shot down due to strong opposition from within the ranks, and another person of Dr. Rajendra Prasad's choice was given the Congress ticket, compelling him to stand as an independent candidate. Due to damaging propaganda against him, he met with a humiliating defeat that injured his pride but did not deter his loyalty and support to the Congress or the cause. Ironically, even the Congress candidate who defeated him was financed by none other than himself! Angry and bitter with the attitude of the ones he had wholeheartedly financed at a time when fear prevented most industrialists from rallying around the revolutionaries, his differences with Gandhi and Dr. Rajendra Prasad assumed tangible proportions, but later with the intervention of Jamnalal Bajaj, who arranged a meeting between them, a rapprochement was brought about and the Congress had his solid support as before.

Meanwhile Dalmia's industrial expansion continued unabated and his empire, that had spread into all parts of the country, foraying into chemicals, paper, light-railways, and then cement and newspapers with unprecedented speed, threatened to swallow the long-established and orthodox houses of the Birlas and the Tatas.

By the '40s Dalmia's name became a household word synonymous with wealth in every rural and urban home, as India geared up to take the curtain call on the concluding stage of the war for freedom. His contributions in cash, and support in body and soul remained undiminished—and his largesse benefited them all. Scaling the heights of success, the emotional steroid that he had consumed, blocked out rational thought and he began to believe he was invincible. In doing so he attracted a growing cesspool of jealousy and hostility.

When Rama turned sixteen she was considered the most eligible and acclaimed child prodigy amongst the Marwaris. Despite financial constraints she had been brought up like a princess with deep traditional values, and was well versed in English, Hindi, Sanskrit and her own native dialect. Although she was not fair and no classic beauty, she possessed the innate charm and polish of a woman well ahead of her times. That made it all the more difficult for Dalmia to find a suitable match for her. A nationwide matrimonial advertisement placed in the newspapers got a tumultuous response and setting aside the not-so-satisfactory proposals from conventional Marwaris, he chose her private tutor Shanti Prasad Jain of an ordinary family from Najibabad. Although rumour had it that Rama had fallen in love and secretly eloped with her private tutor Shanti Prasad, a respectable veneer was given to it by Dalmia who took on the responsibility of the decision of her marriage, and the credibility of the rumour was never established.

Shanti Prasad, a teacher at a local college, was neither Marwari nor wealthy, but being fair with impressive features, even though he was noticeably shorter than Rama, he scored over a host of other prospective grooms and was wedded to her, inheriting her luck and fortune in a well-defined Karmic plan!

This was the first in a long list of benefits that was to accrue to him and his relatives. The alliance was solemnised in a grand ceremony befitting the demands of the Jains. Rama did not make a coy, bashful, conventional bride. On her wedding night, she delivered a fiery speech that she had learnt from her father on social evils and moral values, appealing to the thousands of guests who were present to pledge to wear only khadi and discard the fuss of ornaments and gold in order to promote the sentiments of Gandhi. How far she carried out that pledge in her own life that was filled with all conceivable earthly luxuries is another question, because she inherited from her father a huge slice of his empire some years later and her taste in jewellery and clothes remained something of an enigma. Dalmia loved Shanti Prasad, his only son-in-law, and brought him into his home, showering him with all his affection—a decision he would regret in the later years of his life—a bitterness that would reflect sharply in his last will and testament.

Shanti Prasad was intelligent and a willing learner. He was obedient and devoted to Dalmia who treated him like his own son, grooming and training him to run his vast business, something that Shanti Prasad assimilated quickly. With expanding frontiers in the whole of Bihar where a parallel township as big as Jamshedpur came up at Rohtasnagar and was renamed Dalmianagar, and his business spreading to the entire nation thereafter, he allocated the day-to-day management to Shanti Prasad and

Jaida, and tuned inwards to the resonance of his political ambitions—his restlessness had been stirred up once again.

Dalmia sat on his east-facing swivel chair behind a carved teak wood table. The skyline in the distance, visible from his picture window was silhouetted by the pink rays of the rising sun. A panoramic view of an industrial township in a wide-span photograph adorned the wall behind him. On the other wall was an oil painting of Ma Jagdamba riding a tiger. The rest of the room was bare.

This office was the nerve centre of the nascent township of Dehri-on-son that has been renamed Dalmianagar after its founder. It pulsated with life and activity. The township had sprung up around industries that provided a source of livelihood to the millions of people who lived there.

It was the land that held deep inside its bowels the most potent natural resources of the country—an untapped treasure of mineral and ore waiting to turn into gold.

He took a deep breath. The fresh and familiar morning air filtered into his room—an air emulsified with the myriad smells of rotting sugar cane, paper pulp, crushed stone, chemical fumes and industrial smoke; an air laden with suspended particles of matter each carrying a peculiar Morse code that spelt power. It traced an acrid path up his wide, flared nostrils and snaked right up into the centre of his head.

He leaned back on his chair and closed his eyes. A faint smile played on his lips. A large replica of a sugar cube moulded in lead crystal held down a colourful, fifty-page brochure as if it were anchored to the vein of untapped ore that ran in a continuous ribbon embedded in stone, hundreds of metres below the surface on which the table stood.

Dalmia toyed with the perfectly proportioned, giant-sized sugar cube. As it shifted in his fingers the brochure flapped open, licked by the breeze from the ceiling fan, a historical overview of the Dalmia Empire, his empire unfolded before his eyes.

Photographs, company profiles, messages of felicitation...a list of all firsts in the industrial world reeled past his eyes like the images on a cinema screen.

The first sugar mill 'Rohtas Sugar Ltd.'.

The first privately owned light railway by the same name.

A private ropeway transporting raw sugar cane to be processed into sugar in the factory.

A history of the acquisition of the first privately owned Bharat Insurance Company that had a declared turnover of twenty-five crores within twelve months of its takeover by the Dalmias in 1936.

The first passenger lorry service in remote Rajasthan.

The first hand-operated bioscopes in the native villages of his home state.

The first private trunk-telephone line that connected Dalmianagar to Calcutta.

Cotton and woollen textile mills.

Ordinary, general and fire insurance companies that set the trend for private ownership in terms of their high profitability.

The first private 'Bharat Bank' established in an incredible twenty-four hours by the financial wizard Dalmia. Also prominently featured were photographs of thirty-two-year old Jaidayal, his wife Krishna and teenaged son Vishnu Hari sailing to Germany en route to Denmark to examine the prospects and facilitate the purchase of dry cement and paper plants that could be set up in India.

Dalmia felt the sensuous sides of the glass cube, as he rolled it over on the table, the smooth texture of the flawless material suffused him with an all-pervading energy. He reflected on his life gone by. He had come a long way.

At forty, he stood at the apex of the industrial world, an unchallenged and gigantic mastodon who could make mountains move at his will, and turn everything he touched into gold. The whole world was at his feet, everyone in awe of his spectacular rise. No Indian was unaware of this displaced Marwari from the desert village of Chirawa who had stunned the industrial and financial world by his uncanny wizardry.

A twinge of pride, not unnatural to a person in his situation, spread within him like a warm glow. He remembered his days in Chirawa a wandering minstrel in saffron robes, a spent gambler, a fakir spouting religious sermons to an impoverished and opium-filled audience. His mother's frustrated words echoed in his cars...

'Kya mera Ramkisania bhi kabhi kuch kamayega... Kya kabhi wo bhi bada aadmi banega (Will Ramkrishna ever

begin to earn ... will he ever become a big man)?' she had lamented.

Living far away on the banks of the Ganga in Kashi, Jadia Devi was untouched by the grandeur of her first-born. She had renounced the world to await her final reunion with the almighty in the lap of her Ganga Ma. She has risen too far above an earthly existence to care about the glory and the wealth that lay at her son's feet, but she had not disconnected enough to block out the chill that she felt around her heart when she remembered his recklessness.

Dalmia did a mental salutation to his mother.

'Look at your son now Maji ... Just look how he stands with his head touching the sky ... Are you proud now?

The impenetrable cloud of euphoria that his success had woven around his senses made him feel virile as he had never felt before. He held a tremendous power in his hands, a power that had humbled all the giants around him and brought them knocking at his door. The Maharaja of Bikaner, the Maharajas of Jaipur, Darbhanga, Jodhpur, Jamnagar, the Nizam of Hyderabad, all the rich and famous had befriended him. Jamnalal Bajaj, Jugal Kishore Birla, Subhash Chandra Bose, Gandhiji and many more ... They felt like puppets in his hands dancing to his will. The will that could move mountains to come to men. 'I am greater than them all,' he thought recklessly, dismissing from his conscious mind the time-tested metaphysical law of gravity that establishes that what has to go up has to come down.

An urgent knock on his door broke his reverie. He saw his daughter Rama enter the room.

'Bapu, what are you doing?' she asked. 'Your guest is waiting to have breakfast with you before he leaves for the station. Come on Bapu, he is getting late, he might miss his train.'

Dalmia's eyes misted over as he saw his beloved daughter before him. He reached out and pulled her close into his arms, planting a tender kiss on her forehead. He felt a lump in his throat.

'I have everything,' he thought as he ruffled her hair gently, 'The wealth of Kuber…the brilliance of Surya… the might of Indra…the entire world at my feet…'

Even as he sat inside the navel of the creation of his sweat and blood, the master of all he surveyed, he turned weak and powerless before his adoring bitiya.

Rama held his hand and pulled him out of his chair. He followed her with mock abandon to the outhouse at the far end of the compound to meet with his guest who had been waiting impatiently for him.

The young slender Bengali youth with an unshaven beard that covered more than three-quarters of his face paced restlessly on the veranda of the guest house. He had a rabid fire burning in his eyes and a manner that was reminiscent of firebrand militancy. He wore a white khadi kurta over a dhoti and a flowing silk *chaadar* that had a narrow, red, woven border draped carelessly around his shoulders. A pair of steel-rimmed round spectacles on the bridge of his nose made his deep-set eyes look even smaller. The skin under his high cheek-bones looked slightly sunken into the sides of his handsome face.

The man was a fugitive. He was wanted by the British police for anti-national activities. His will was strong, but his patience had worn thin and he was on a mission that had been completed in the last seven days that he had spent with his benefactor and friend in Dalmianagar.

Over breakfast he exchanged pleasantries with his hosts as Rama chattered intelligently and sweetly in fluent Bengali.

The pensive and unusually quiet guest ate none of the sumptuous dishes that were passed to him. He only sipped lemon tea.

His week-long stay had come to a fruitful end. He had accepted the generous donation given to him with gratitude and grace. The amount was many times greater than the five hundred rupees he had been receiving every month from his ever-willing benefactor in the last few years.

After a brief emotional farewell, he departed—his mind racing miles ahead of him eastwards beyond the borders of Bengal to carry forth his mission of *Azadi*.

Dalmia was troubled. The palpable agitation that emanated from the departed visitor lingered on even after he had gone...

He did not know that neither he nor India would ever see his friend again. Soon the country and the Raj would come to terms with the reality that Subhash Chandra Bose had escaped to Burma, disappearing from the horizon like a vanishing blip from the radar screen of a crashing aircraft.

A frenzied whirlwind stirred up in Dalmia's mind. Subhash's immortal words: 'Tum *mujhe khoon do; main tumhe Aazadi doonga* (Give me your blood; I will give you freedom).' reverberated throughout the length and breadth of the nation. Although they were at sharp variance with his own moderate beliefs of satya, ahimsa, and swadeshi, the words struck a chord in his heart.

Peace eluded him and it was time to move on.

The multiplicity of Dalmia's persona swung him perpetually like a pendulum from the spiritual to the carnal, from the saintly to the sinful, and from the sublime to the worldly, taking in its sweep a wide gamut of sharply conflicting emotions.

The faint memory of Narbada, his strong but sublimated sexual urges that his ailing wife Durga could barely gratify, and his never-ending quest for the path to bliss was roused again. Not content with his success or his material affluence, his mind wandered and to give himself a break, he took Durga to the Bhagwat Bhakti Ashram at Rewari for a course of treatment in naturopathy, completely unprepared for the emotional ambush that awaited him.

Amidst the placid serenity of the ashram one day he sighted Narbada. His hitherto suppressed passions came tumbling out shattering the control he thought he had gained over his base senses. He was shaken out of his delusory state to come face-to-face with hard reality. At first he thought he was hallucinating when he saw her, sitting with her eyes closed, singing a bhajan on the floor of the ashram during the evening prayers. Staring fixedly at her face, he stood rooted to the spot feeling helplessly drawn to her. His mind and heart locked in a spasm as he was fully convinced that the woman who sat just a few yards ahead of him was none other than his child-bride Narbada. The painful memories from his past flooded his mind, drowning him in a heightened sense of guilt that he had internalised for years.

Anguished and saddened he returned to his room to spend a sleepless night reliving the tragedy of his unfulfilled soul, looking to avenge his long-dead wife.

She was the third and youngest daughter of a sanyasi, Bhakt Nand Kishore who had renounced the world after his wife died, to live in the ashram with his three young girls, Godaveri, Subhadra and Kamla. Kamla was tall, limpid-eyed, and fair, and had the grace and attraction of full-blown girlhood that oozed out of the coarse khadi sari that she wore over a long nun-like blouse. Brought up amidst the austere discipline of the ashram she had devoted herself to seek spiritual realisation pledging to remain a celibate all her life. Unbeknown to her, she was going to be jolted out of the tranquillity that she treasured and believed in, by the uncanny resemblance that she bore to Narbada!

Narbada stood before the mirror. She took out a tiny box of bright red sindoor *and meticulously smeared a thick line into the middle*

of her parted hair. She hummed a familiar folk song in her sweet tinkling voice combing her long black hair in slow and deliberate strokes. Slipping a bunch of red glass bangles over her curled fist onto her soft arms, she buttoned her blouse right up to her throat and pulled the sleeves down to her wrists covering her bangles. She carefully draped the pallu of her sari over her head pulling its border to the rim of the big red bindi between her brows.

The reflection that stared back in the mirror pleased her. She looked calm and beautiful in the faint glow of the light that filtered through the room—like an unobtrusive entity that wanders the grounds of eternal peace. Then all of a sudden she felt his arms around her.

He came up from behind holding her in a tight embrace. She was pinioned to his enveloping body. Her pallu slipped down exposing her face, her closed eyes, her pulsating throat and the front of her closely buttoned-up blouse. She allowed him to turn her around and felt his warm lips on her forehead. She felt his mouth trace an invisible line dotted with kisses down her face, onto her throat, between her breasts, onto her navel and below her flat stomach as he gently pulled her onto the bed, not slackening his hold.

'Where did you go Narbada? I have been looking for you all these days…I love you Narbada…I love you…Show me how much you love me…Let me kiss the pain away from your bruises. I will never hurt you again…Just lie beside me and sing me that song…How does it go Narbada? Sing to me my beloved…'

He held her in a suffocating grip. She melted into his arms, her body taking the shape of his as if they were one single mass of flesh. The tune of the folk song came alive in the air and music filled the sky!

Ramkrishna woke up sweating. His wife Durga slept soundly in a comfortable position on the twin–bed beside him. He could feel the loud beat of a drum, that seemed to emanate from his chest. The front of his kurta was drenched with the tears that were streaming down his face. A faint blue light from the window bathed the room in a silvery mist. The curtains moved slightly with the hint of a breeze. A mild fragrance of sandalwood wafted in the air. There was an eerie silence. He wiped his clammy hands and stood up, and walked slowly to the window. The door of his room was closed and its latch in place. He gazed outside but could not see a soul in sight. A silver blue glow illumined the green expanse that surrounded him. He stood still, breathing deeply, soaking in the serene beauty till the drum beats slowed down and he felt slightly calm. Then all of a sudden he heard it—the faint familiar melody of a song he had forgotten. A sweet tinkling voice, singing the words that were muffled but not unknown! A fresh breeze stirred up the curtains and the scent of sandalwood became stronger. It was Narbada! His Narbada beckoning him…his Narbada calling him…wanting him…as much as he wanted her. She had come back for him and this time he would not let her get away.

He glanced at Durga's pale and sickly face and sat down on a mat on the floor. He folded his legs into a lotus position, closed his eyes and began to meditate.

It is human frailty that the longer a thing is denied the greater is the keenness to attain it!

Acute depression overcame Dalmia. The harsh words of Kamla's rejection echoed in his ears as he boarded the train from Rewari to Delhi. Gripped by his frenzy he could not think and had forgotten how it felt to be hungry. All he did was weep. Durga, his devoted and self-effacing wife, tried everything to alleviate his suffering but she could not turn herself into Narbada!

No amount of persuasion worked with Kamla. Swami Parmanand, the Head of the Rewari Ashram; Bhagatji, her father, her sisters, Madalsa Behn, Jamnalal Bajaj—all of them failed. Determined and bull-headed she stood unmoved. For the first time in his life Dalmia felt dwarfed and impotent. It made him realise that his wealth was not powerful enough to provide the fusillade that could break a single woman's resolve. However, neither the humiliation nor the defeat discouraged him and he hardened his determination to attain what seemed so within his reach and yet so far!

The journey dragged on tediously. The hate and contempt in Kamla's words pierced his heart like shrapnels of glass as he sat brooding by the window.

'I would rather marry a dog … a dog … a dog …'

They hurt like a gunshot wound. He stared out onto a station platform where the train had stopped. A scruffy mongrel with a festering wound on its back yelped in pain as some passerby scrambling to climb on, kicked it carelessly. The whining sound made him squirm as he felt an incessant stinging in his eyes that brimmed over with tears.

He could not wait to reach Delhi where Jamnalal Bajaj had arranged for him to meet Gandhi. He knew

Kamla revered Gandhi like a godfather and would not be able to turn him down!

In Delhi at Birla House, Gandhi lay emaciated and tired after a twenty-one-day-long fast that had left him unable to walk or talk. Dalmia looked at him with sincere devotion as his oft repeated words echoed in his ears '...self denial is good for the soul...' but Dalmia's soul was aching with his need for Kamla and he could deny it no more.

He looked at the thin, skeletal, crumpled man lying on a cot beside whom Vinoba Bhave, one of his closest followers and supporters, sat cross-legged on the floor. Gandhi's association with Dalmia was old and deep enough to allow this intrusion at a time when political upheaval ravaged the nation and Hindu-Muslim riots were rife. Gandhi depended heavily on him for monetary contributions and valued his support to the Congress and the cause. Despite his failing health and the crucial situation the country faced, he readily agreed to talk to Kamla. His heart went out to Durga who also pleaded with him in earnest to assist her in making Kamla change her mind—but Durga was as obdurate in her stand, as Kamla was in hers!

Gandhi, the modest little man who had renounced the world for service to humanity, who had mobilised the Indian masses to an electrifying moral crusade that was to succeed in driving out the Imperial rulers and give his countrymen their freedom failed to move this lone woman. Kamla wept before him with her hands folded saying, 'Ask anything of me Bapu. I shall not hesitate to give my life for you but I cannot agree to become Dalmia's wife.' Hurt and rejected Dalmia went into an emotional fugue that lasted for a period of five, long, painful years, during which he only wept or moped. He could not help thinking that if Narbada was indeed in Kamla's body, she had not forgiven him, which made him even sadder.

Jaida, Krishna, Rama, Shanti Prasad and Durga all became helpless spectators to his psychosomatic infirmity. Mistaking his state for a long-repressed carnal need, his secretary of some years, Mrigank Babu, offered him the choice of some beautiful, willing, nubile women, hoping it would shake him out of his hellish melancholia, but beauty and youth had never lured him. So he remained in a state of suspended animation till he met another woman—Pritam Takhat Singh in Ferozepur at the end of that year.

The dusty city of Ferozepur nestles on the line that has mercilessly sliced the state of Punjab into two segments after the Partition of 1947. The vibrant land of the five rivers, of glowing mustard fields and the robust Sikh populace was once the home of thousands of Hindu and Muslim families that peacefully coexisted there. Among them lived a highly respected sexagenarian by the name of Sant Takhat Singh whose message of peace and brotherhood was essentially epitomised in his Sikh Kanya

Vidyalaya—a school of fifteen hundred girls whom he adopted, educated and groomed till they attained adulthood and then married them to suitable boys of his choosing.

Every year at the Annual Day ceremony of the school, a grand cultural panorama was organised after which a special invitee awarded prizes to the students and addressed them to deliver a message that most often echoed Santji's beliefs. Every year the special invitee was an eminent individual chosen from a different field of service.

In 1942, after Gandhi's call for handing over 'India to the Indians', nationwide arrests had led to the imprisonment of over thirty thousand Congress workers. Dalmia's inevitable involvement in the campaign and his frequent visits to Punjab where he had a cement factory in Dandot, (now in Pakistan), brought him in contact with Sant Takhat Singh who acknowledged and honoured the leading philanthropist in him by inviting him to be the chief guest at his school's Annual Day.

Still snared in the pain of separation from Narbada and the memory of Kamla's rejection, he half-heartedly consented. He arrived in Ferozepur where he was received in grand style by Santji and his young, graceful, graduate daughter Pritam Singh.

Earlier that day, Pritam had donned a lemon-coloured *shalwar-suit* with a fussy silver trim as she rehearsed her welcome speech in front of a full-length mirror. Her fair skin and well-toned body was set off by the nicely-fitted clothes she wore. The unfamiliar apprehension she felt in her mind as she looked at her own reflection irked her.

She had addressed chief guests many a times in the previous years but had never felt nervous and shaky as she did that morning. Steadying herself, she adjusted her *dupatta* close to her throat, pulling down the two ends on either side behind her. She reminded herself that the man she was about to meet was more than twice her age and could in no way threaten her composure.

Dalmia arrived at the scheduled time with his entourage. Dressed in a white khadi dhoti kurta, he was modest and unassuming and had none of the airs that come naturally with people of his ilk. 'He will be easier than all the others,' she thought, not realising how grievously wrong she was, as she strode confidently up to the podium for the last time as a maiden.

Dalmia was lost in a world of his own. The garland of fresh roses put around his neck by the young girl in a cheerful lemon outfit lay carelessly on the arm of his chair. Sitting in the centre of the podium behind a long table covered with a starched, white sheet that shone brighter than the clothes he wore he mused absently about his mission and his life. He felt the dull ache in his chest that he had learnt to ignore become sharper. His eyes travelled over the group of girls dancing—a colourful interpretation of a folk ballad—and then stopped at the face of the young one who had garlanded him earlier. 'Santji's daughter bears a striking resemblance to her father,' he thought. Her lemon and silver shalwar-suit sparkled in the sun and the bright lipstick she wore hurt his eyes.

Kamla's words came rushing back: 'Marry a dog...a dog...a dog...' Gandhi's helpless face, Narbada's tinkling laughter and the drumbeats from his chest echoed rhythmically in his ears till he was startled by the thunderous clapping from the crowds that blocked his thoughts.

The girl in the lemon shalwar-suit loomed before his eyes, and on a sudden impulse he walked up to her, took the microphone and made an astounding proposition. Before a dumbfounded audience of giggling, light-headed, teenaged girls, he said a few words of praise for Santji and then asked for his daughter's hand in marriage, catching them completely unawares. The blushing bride-to-be was left gaping and stupefied as the fifteen hundred strong crowd cheered and Santji warmly embraced the man who was to be his son-in-law. Tears welled up in his eyes and in a voice choked with emotion, he thanked the Lord, reverently intoning a *shabad* from the *Granth Sahib*, asking for His blessings, wishing them both a long and happy life together.

But neither Pritam nor the fifteen hundred girls present were listening to his words of prayer for Pritam. Each one of the other fifteen hundred girls, stunned by the sudden turn of events, had been swept away by a wave of euphoria, envying her fairy-tale romance and her future wedding to the industrial magnate who stood before them.

For Dalmia it was not lust for the desirable virgin Sikh girl blossoming with youth and appeal—it was her father's qualities that he had mistakenly projected onto her. Believing that she could appropriately fill the painful void caused by Narbada's death, to become an ideal companion and make him a complete man once again, he added another one to his long list of errors of judgement. His disastrous marriage to Pritam was to last no longer than four months.

Totally disarmed by Dalmia's modesty and simplicity that he found to be inversely proportional to his fame and riches, Santji arrived with Pritam in New Delhi to complete the formalities of the marriage.

In the sprawling but discordantly stark mansion at 15 Keeling Road, (one of the many that Dalmia was to acquire for the other women he married), Pritam was wedded in a simple Hindu ceremony, bedecked with jasmines and roses to the man of whom she knew nothing other than the fact that his name symbolised splendour and wealth of a kind that one only reads about in storybooks.

The chief conductor of ceremonies in the ultimate act of sacrifice, was Dalmia's fragile and ailing wife, Durga.

On the nuptial night, the older and less-desired wife retired to her room in the far corner of the thirty-room mansion while her husband retired to his, to consummate his third marriage in another part of the house. Raging with fever she tossed and turned on a rickety cot content in the delusion that at last the misery that had dogged them in the last five years had come to an end.

Pritam was the antithesis of everything Dalmia stood for. The tall and able-bodied Sikh woman, with great expectations and small ideals had been thrust into his world for all the wrong reasons. Their marriage was ill-fated right from the start. The idolatry that he had showered on her father was all but misplaced in her. Her sophistication and modernity was too much for the simple and earthy man who even on their wedding night narrated to a bored Pritam his favourite parables of devoted, sacrificing wives from the scriptures. He made her pledge that she would be kind and respectful to Durga as one would be to an elder sister, while Durga's own body burned with fever and her mind played havoc with thoughts of the strange woman's union with her husband.

In the very first hour of his conjugal night, Dalmia realised that he had made a grave mistake. The morning after, when Pritam sat in her sheer nightdress sipping tea from a china cup which showed stains of stale red lipstick, he felt a wave of revulsion and remorse rise in his throat. He left the room hastily to think of ways of controlling the damage he had incurred.

Pritam's own expectations too had fallen flat. There was nothing about her middle-aged husband that attracted her and the prospect of living with the sickly, sparrow-like Durga revolted her. She was not going to be dictated by the silly whims of an eccentric man. He did not want her to eat out of bone-china plates; he hated lipstick; perfume made him queasy; and his food habits were impossible. The list of negatives went on and on. Pritam was quite clear on what she did not want and even clearer on what she did. Dalmia accepted his mistake and readily agreed to her demands, feeling relieved that he had rid himself of an earthly debt of one and a karmic debt of many lifetimes.

The settlement was quick and easy. Pritam, who chose to revert to her maiden name, wanted to live as far away from Dalmia as possible. She was given a sumptuous cash remuneration, a house befitting the status of a Dalmia and a one-way ticket to London. Thereafter, she continued to receive a sizeable amount of money each year as her annual maintenance allowance. The separation was a bitter one, and no one heard of Pritam till several years later, when she visited his sixth wife Dineshnandini.

For Dalmia, although the pangs of guilt towards Narbada and his undying love for her never really vanished, he began to see the possibility of attaining peace and fulfilment by finding an intelligent and educated woman to marry who was like-minded. Temporarily forgetting his melancholia he submerged himself deeper into the fight for freedom—both from his emotional shackles as well as from the oppressive Imperial rulers that the entire nation was up against.

The external and internal battles assumed different shapes in the next five years. The first came to fruition when the British departed from India, but the second transformed his life in a manner that destroyed his peace forever.

It was during those years that he married the three women who remained his wives till he died, giving him the dubious but inexact title of *The Man with Seven Wives*—actually there were six. It was also during those years that another rumour was afloat—it was widely believed that

Dalmia sought a male child from the seventh woman he married for, according to an astrologer's prediction that child would be a *chhatrapati* and would deliver him from the cycle of birth and death to attain salvation and eternal bliss. No credence could be given to that, however, because Dineshnandini was his sixth and last wife and male offspring were never an obsession with him!

'The transit of the planets propels human beings along their pre-ordained orbits with the same measure of certainty with which the earth moves around the sun.'

In the fourth decade of the century in which the revolutionary cry for freedom convulsed the people of India, Dalmia, and his three wives-to-be Saraswati, Asha and Dineshnandini climbed up the spirals of their separate existences, waiting for the unforeseen moment that would bind them together. On a broader and much more visible arena, Jawaharlal Nehru was shining bright as the most luminous star on the political horizon. In and out of prison, his literary skills honed to perfection, he was halfway to completing a historic and famous monologue—of letters to his daughter, and a lesser-known but no less intense dialogue with another fiery young woman, writer-poetess Dineshnandini Chordia. Equally charged with the passionate declamation of 'Do or Die', Dalmia had made his presence felt by contributing wholeheartedly to the cause at the behest of Gandhi. Despite his concurrence with the opposing ideologies of Madan Mohan

Malviya who headed the hard-core right-wing Hindu Maha Sabha, his backing to the Congress party never slackened. Spinning within his own private vortex of ambitions and success, he had already begun formulating a plan for a one-world-government—for universal peace to overcome the holocaust of World War II and pre-empt another similar genocide and devastation in the future.

In Lucknow, one of the students at the graduation ceremony had much to rejoice about. She had secured the first position in first division in her Master's degree in Philosophy and her photograph and success story had been splashed all over the local newspapers. An ex-student of the Isabella Thoburn College, she was jubilant with her success and stardom as she was being felicitated at an ostentatious passing-out ceremony in the University Hall. A scholar of both English and Sanskrit with a keen interest in political science, she stood amidst the crowded auditorium, wearing her ceremonial gown, with pride beaming in her large eyes. She walked down the aisle of cheering fellow-students holding the precious scroll of paper that testified her achievement, that was going to take her onto the next and most tempestuous phase of her life.

It was the love for his motherland and the Sanskrit language that drew him to her. Browsing through her piece in the college magazine,—'India, in spite of thy weakness I love thee,' that Dalmia had chanced upon, he boarded a train to Lucknow irresistibly drawn to the brilliant scholar. He met Saraswati along with her father in the most unusual if not romantic circumstances.

The interview was not that of a groom seeking a bride, nor was it a passionate declaration of his love. It was more like a nervous candidate being examined by an expert for a plum job.

Dalmia subjected her to an intense volley of questions pertaining to the *Vedanta* and the scriptures, which she fielded with perfection. She concluded her session by the extempore recitation of a Sanskrit poem that she had composed during her college days—arousing the latent passions of the man in search of the ideal woman who could fuse her identity with his to become one single and perfect entity.

He had found his soulmate! After a brief courtship, during which he began an exercise of spiritual and emotional cleansing of his past phantoms, they were married. The soft-spoken, sugar-voiced Saraswati became the fourth wife of a man whom she deeply loved and with whom she shared a passion for Hindu philosophy and Sanskrit.

She was to undergo the same ritual of listening to a discourse on their wedding night and then repeat the rhetorical pledge to be the devoted, respectful, loving younger sister to Durga.

When the first rays of the cold December sun cracked open the cover of darkness in their unadorned bridal suite, he asked her to recite the Sanskrit verse that he had first heard on the day they had met. She recited the extraordinary words of her composition in her sweet musical voice with the appropriate pauses, sealing the tender bond of a love that had grown between them.

Her newly wed groom, held her chin in his hands and said.

'Saraswati ... at last I have found my true soulmate!'

Drenched in the power of his words, she knelt down and touched her forehead to his feet—oblivious of the pain that had resurfaced in Durga's wasting body and soul, and the wrath that his mother would vent when she would hear of his fourth marriage.

Jadia Devi, who was living most of the time in Kashi by then, did not speak to her son for a long time afterwards and his devoted unquestioning brother Jaida, swallowed the bitter pill with predictable silence, ungrudgingly.

Saraswati moved into *Nau Number* Mansingh Road, her home acquired from the Maharaja of Kapurthala, with Durga, Jaida and Krishna. That would be her domain from that moment and would witness the birth of the seven children that she would have in quick succession to propagate the family name. Krishna and Jaida remained with her till they moved out to meet with the demands of their expanding family, and Durga remained a nominal head in a wheelchair till death delivered her to her rightful place in heaven!

Whether it was a high boredom factor or Saraswati's inability to have a male child in the first three years that fuelled his wandering mind, is debatable, but as soon as Saraswati's eldest girl was born and she had been impregnated with her second, Dalmia had already wedded a school teacher, Asha Chatterjee, the daughter of a eminent judge in Calcutta who gave birth to fraternal twins—a boy and a girl three months before Saraswati delivered her second child.

By the time Dineshnandini Chordia came into Dalmia's life and its ambit, Asha had produced her third child who was afflicted with polio soon after she was born, and Saraswati's third child, also another girl, was on her way.

That tied up all the loose threads that bound the four women to each other and to their single life source, from whom they were to receive the commands that would control their lives even after he was dead!

History is a record of the deeds of great men—but the unrecorded efforts of all those people who make a nation and have helped to make them great, is real history.

As the sun rose over the Hooghly on 16 August exactly one year before India was to celebrate her Independence, Mohammad Ali Jinnah, the founder of the Muslim League and the future father of Pakistan sat far west across the Peninsula, in Bombay reviewing his 'Direct Action Plan'. That was his answer to Clement Attlee's failed Cabinet Mission sent to India earlier that year to discuss the modalities of how to transfer power back to the Indians. His plan revealed his method to prove to the British and to the Congress that the Muslims of India were willing to go to any lengths to get their own separate state.

On that ill-fated day hordes of Muslim mobs spilled out onto the streets of Calcutta screaming in religious fervour, burning and looting shops, brutally slaughtering or beating to pulp any Hindu who came their way. The unrestrained genocide that lasted twenty hours left six thousand people dead on the streets and in the gutters of the smouldering city.

Even as the leaders of the Congress party conferred in Delhi on the maniacal outburst, the worst ever communal riots broke out in the neighbouring state of Bihar, spreading to its villages like wildfire. Camping in Noakhali, a Muslim-dominated area that now falls in Bangladesh, Gandhi had just made public his scandalous and widely criticised experiments of taking naked girls to bed to practice 'seminal continence', which he believed was the only way to attain freedom from the shackles of bodily desires and thereby achieve self-empowerment which is the prerequisite to salvation. As if by a natural coincidence Hindus and Muslims struck out at each other rabidly right across the nation from Calcutta to Lahore, leaving behind them a horrific trail of carnage. Broken-hearted and bleeding with the pain of failure, Gandhi appealed to all his countrymen to maintain peace and harmony and to come forward to support the victims of the riots. He undertook a penitent march through the muddy swamps and the jungles of Noakhali to quell the raging fire that had set ablaze the entire nation, and to restore peace to an embittered and frightened people.

While the nation reeled with the aftermath of the brutal killings, Jawaharlal Nehru and Sardar Patel were each reviewing their own positions as the potential premiers who would guide India safely to the mantle of freedom in just a few months' time.

From the precincts of her *Nau Number* home, the fourth wife of Dalmia, also stirred by passions of duty towards her countrymen sent Gandhi a letter expressing her desire to help. Gandhi accepted her generous donation of a hundred thousand rupees that came from the purse of his long-time supporter and India's most visible industrialist, with appropriate grace and speed. This was no novel deed for Dalmia. Cash contributions amounting to millions of rupees had rained down on the Congress consistently and incessantly in the past and most of its senior functionaries were beholden to him.

Like all discerning Indians, he knew that the fate of India rested in the hands of four persons—Lord Mountbatten, Gandhi, Jawaharlal Nehru and his old-time friend and ally Mohammad Ali Jinnah.

Dalmia was appalled by the brutality of the massacres. He was equally appalled by the apathy and ruthlessness of their perpetrator, his stone-hearted friend Jinnah, and he took it upon himself at that crucial hour to do everything in his power to set the damage right. He was confident that Jinnah would listen to him—and the rest would fall into place.

Jinnah's home in Delhi was barely five minutes down the road from the Dalmias. In his house at 10 Aurangzeb Road he lived as a bachelor with his sister Fatima as his sole companion. Jinnah and Dalmia shared a close friendship with each other and were often seen in animated conversation seated on the wide verandah that overlooked the garden in Dalmia's house. That Jinnah trusted him and relied upon his judgement was evident. He discussed his innermost secrets, his fears and fantasies with Dalmia whenever he got the chance. 'Jinnah' and 'Dalmia', as they fondly addressed each other, were friends bound incredibly together by their polarities for no two people could have been more dissimilar.

A staunch Hindu, Dalmia wore clothes made of only handwoven and handspun khadi, and was strictly against meat-eating and the consumption of alcohol. Like all good Hindus he believed that the cow was a sacred animal, and he had given up the use of shoes or watch straps made from leather. He had none of the sophistication that comes with an elite British education and was dead against the division of India on religious lines.

Jinnah who harboured a mildly visible scorn for his Hindu rivals, was a completely unorthodox Muslim. He wore only impeccably cut suits made of fine linen and relished his fare of oysters and champagne. He had the refined taste of a connoisseur for good brandy and Bordeaux. He drank alcohol and ate pork in abject defiance of the tenets of Islam and did not believe in mindless worship at a mosque.

While Dalmia made simplicity his religion, Jinnah revelled in pomp and splendour akin to that of the Indian Maharajas on whose treasures and palaces he had modelled his plush home.

The only thing they shared apart from a profound love for their motherland was the liberal sanction that both their religions bestowed on them, allowing men to take more than one wife! Paradoxically it was also one of their most perceptible differences—for Jinnah remained single all his life after his estranged Parsi wife Ratti Bai died in 1929, but Dalmia went on to wed six women like a devout and practising Hindu.

In Jawaharlal Nehru, however, they both perceived the cunning of a self-absorbed 'pseudo-socialist' who had never really discarded his essentially British ways—the other common denominator between the two.

Jinnah had serious differences with Gandhi. The initial drive for independence in which the intellectual elite had set aside their religious differences to fight the British no longer held them together. The narrow-minded leaders of the Congress remained adamant about making no concessions to their Muslim counterparts. The violent outbursts after the failure of Attlee's Cabinet Mission had left Gandhi feeling defeated and miserable. The Muslim League, even more resolute in its demands for a separate state, cited the religious violence as a natural enmity between Hindus and Muslims. Gandhi's dream had fallen flat on its face. Jinnah's disillusionment with Gandhi and the Congress had a long-standing history of disagreements—not least of which was the clash of identities between him and Jawaharlal Nehru. Fuelled by the innate insecurity of a man struggling to break out of the psyche of a religious minority, he loathed the power that Jawaharlal Nehru held over Gandhi and the indulgence Gandhi showered on him. This became one of the prime reasons for their fallout. He thought Gandhi's utopian dream of peaceful coexistence between Hindus and Muslims was impossible and impractical, and only a separate Islamic state could restore peace to the anguished people on both sides.

Contrary to what rumour mongers decreed, Fatima, the withdrawn and unobtrusive sister of Jinnah, was never the binding factor between Dalmia and her brother—the two men in her life. Given Dalmia's own liberality in the choice and number of the women he married or was associated with, along with the frequency of his visits to the home of an eligible and single woman, it is possible that a romantic relationship evolved from there. But one impropriety Dalmia could not be accused of was hypocrisy and if he had felt any amorous inclinations towards the accessible Muslim woman, he would have unabashedly and courageously pursued her till it culminated in marriage.

Even though Dalmia's friendship with Jinnah was much maligned, it was sound and it was solid, his romantic liasons with Fatima notwithstanding. He knew Jinnah was a man of 'towering vanity' and 'unassailable personal honesty'—therefore, completely incorruptible. Wealth held no lure for him and perhaps the only intemperance that he could be charged with was his inflexible demand for the separate state of Pakistan. Ignoring the treacherous 'anti-Hindu' tag that stuck to Dalmia, he never failed to exercise his right as an advisor and friend, always deriding Jinnah for his rigidity and fanaticism.

'You are selfish and ambitious, Jinnah,' he said, 'You want to become like the Caliph of Turkey in independent Pakistan. The Hindus think you are a demon and are retarding the progress of the country...'

Dalmia's strong words never offended Jinnah. His thin lips pursed into a downward sneer, making his gaunt cheeks look ever more hollow. Living under the shadow of death, breathing through lungs ravaged by the dreaded tuberculosis, Jinnah said, 'I do not speak frequently, Dalmia, but I speak at the appropriate time. Perhaps we could have arrived at an amicable settlement because of you. Your selfless love for your motherland and your deep affection for me makes you the most competent men to have negotiated it. But mark my words—your leaders are not worthy of your loyalty.' Indeed prophetic words of a dying man!

'I may be a demon in the eyes of your brethren but the Muslims adore me. At least credit me for having brought together the *Jee-huzoors* and the nawabs who had submitted to the British under a common banner to serve their country now.'

Weakened in flesh, ashen from the residues of internal erosion holding his dark secret deep in his heart, a secret that he did not share even with his dearest friend Dalmia, Jinnah continued undeterred in his mission to get for his people their own homeland.

As a last-ditch effort, Dalmia, who like the rest of India knew nothing of Jinnah's fatal ailment, persuaded him to have one final meeting with the Congress leaders to arrive at a softer compromise.

He spoke to his long-time associates Dr. Rajendra Prasad and Sardar Patel to prevail upon Jawaharlal Nehru and Gandhi to meet Jinnah.

'You hold a power over me, my friend. I shall agree to meet them at your house if you so desire, but remember, those are the very people who wash their homes after I have walked inside them and rinse their plates with *Ganga jal* after I have eaten from them. How can there ever be a reconciliation? There is no other solution in sight. You know that Gandhi declined to see me after he returned from England from the last Round Table Conference. His words hurt me even today—"I pray for light but see not light," he said—even then to honour my friendship with you I shall meet with them.' Jinnah said.

Dalmia was pained but hopeful. Jinnah could be prevailed upon to accept a mutually agreeable solution, but providence or personal ambitions had already cast the die, and India was perched on the mouth of a rumbling volcano just waiting to erupt!

That evening a sense of foreboding descended upon the decision-makers of India's destiny, who saw the sceptre of a partition looming menacingly before their eyes. A broadcast on London Radio did not go unheeded. It was heard across the globe in the homes of all those people who had tuned in to observe every move of the British in their transfer of power.

'A wealthy Indian merchant is mediating to arrive at an amicable settlement between the sharply conflicting leaders of the Congress and the Muslims League,' it said.

In the heart of Lutyen's Delhi a lone man had just finished his supper. His forehead was furrowed with a deep frown.

There was an obdurate annoyance visible on his face. He switched off the radio without waiting to hear the rest of the overseas broadcast. Then he made two phone calls. The first was to a colleague in the Congress party and the second to the local office of *The Times*. He had already formulated the words of a statement that he was going to issue.

As Delhi woke up to a balmy monsoon day the following morning, the first phone call that rang through to Dalmia was Jinnah's. They each held a newspaper in their hands. The statement of a senior functionary of the Congress who had not been named loomed large before their eyes. Dalmia felt a lump rise in his throat as Jinnah spoke.

' "No significance need be attached to Dalmia's negotiations," they say. Have you read the morning papers, Dalmia? Your own people have a beastly mentality. I told you your sincerity for them is misplaced and shall go unrecognised.'

Dalmia's enthusiasm and hopes came crashing down. His efforts lay captive in a forgotten time capsule, a secret that only he, Jinnah and Fatima shared. India's fate was sealed!

It may be imprudent to suggest that Dalmia would have succeeded where Gandhi and Mountbatten failed, but it is not unreasonable to claim that he was no featherweight and most certainly deserved a chance. The truth of what could have been lies buried in the tombs of those who held in their hands the destiny of four hundred million Indians—those who witnessed the massacre of their brethren who were sacrificed while their country was being dismembered!

Debilitated in body but jubilant in spirit, Jinnah departed from the Indian soil in the second week of August to hail the birth of his homeland. He left with a sadistic satisfaction that his house in Delhi—the last of his claims on Indian soil, now belonged to his friend—Dalmia. Before leaving, Fatima made one last call to a number that she had dialled many times before. Then she wiped a tear from her eyes as she left with her brother from India and her friend!

As the DC 10 circled over Karachi Airport an impassioned cheering sound of 'Pakistan *Zindabad*' rent the air. Fatima touched her brother's feverish brow tenderly. Her mind was still lurking in the corridors of 10 Aurangzeb Road watching the lowering of the green and white flag of the Muslim League, that had flown proudly over the towering flagstaff that adorned its front and another one of similar green painted with the symbol of anti-cow slaughter being hoisted up with a momentum that matched their descending aircraft!

On 14 August at midnight, three people in different parts of the subcontinent were stirred with violent emotions, though not of the same kind.

In Karachi, Jinnah sat in a crowded assembly hall, waiting impatiently to take the twenty-one gun salute that hailed the birth of his beloved homeland.

In Delhi, an agitated Dalmia finding it impossible to rejoice, could hear Jawaharlal Nehru's words resonating on a national broadcast. 'Long years ago we made a tryst with destiny…' He wilfully blocked the words out and sat down before his deity to invoke her blessings for his new mission—to rededicate himself to the unification of his mutilated motherland.

In Bombay a young Parsi girl stepped out onto the balcony of her flat in the suburbs and silently put out two flags—one of India and the other of Pakistan, her eyes stinging with tears of confusion and gloom.

She was the only one of his kin not by his side when her father was being hailed as *Quaid-e-Azam*—the Founder of Pakistan!

It was a circular table at the centre of an oak-panelled room; a room that had witnessed many spectacular events in the three-hundred-year reign of Imperial Britain over its Southeast Asian colony that was home to one-fifth of the world's population, in which the kings and queens of the most powerful kingdom on earth had presided over many decisions that were milestones in the pages of history. An aura suffused the bulbs of the grand Venetian chandelier that adorned the centre of its ceiling. Emotions of various hues flitted across the faces of the people who had gathered there on that evening in the early summer of '47. The heat from the scorching plains of the capital did little to dampen the enthusiasm that pervaded the air. One by one the august men filed

in and took their places on the plush chairs that were covered in hunter-green leather.

Seated at the head of the table was a handsome Englishman in a resplendent naval uniform. He was the great grandson of Queen Victoria—Lord Louis Mountbatten. To his right sat a small half-naked, bespectacled, dark-brown figure—'the gentle prophet of a non-violent revolution'—Gandhi. To his left sat a gaunt and pale-faced man sporting a monocle, a white linen suit and two-tone shoes. He was the leader of the Muslim League—Mohammad Ali Jinnah. Next to Jinnah was a man with a very wide nose and broad forehead wearing a white dhoti and khadi kurta—intense joy radiating from his small and deep-set eyes—Seth Ramkrishna Dalmia. Then in clockwise order were the Commander-in-Chief of the Indian Army, Field Marshall Claude Auchinleck, Sardar Vallabbhai Patel and then, the eighth Maharaja of Patiala, the Chancellor of the Chamber of Indian Princes—His Highness Yadavindra Singh representing the grandeur of his race of 565-odd rajas and maharajas of Hindustan—followed by Liaquat Ali Khan, the second-in-command of the Muslim League. A fair, aristocratic man wearing a stark white achkan sat to his right. A fresh red rose adorned the third button of his coat. He had a well-sculpted face. That was Jawaharlal Nehru, the Kashmiri Brahman whose manner, reminiscent of his lineage, had made him the most distinct and acknowledged face on the Indian firmament.

Each of them had been summoned in their capacities as representatives of a people and a cause, bound together by a singular and burning passion—the demand for freedom! The lights from the glittering chandelier that had illumined hundreds of conventions in the past were a shade brighter than they had ever been.

Lord Mountbatten's deep rich baritone broke the silence. 'It is a glorious moment of my life that I witness today when all my friends present here have finally arrived at a unanimous decision. I bow my head to the services of Gandhiji as I raise a toast to him, the leading spirit of a cause that cements all of us together forever. I also congratulate my friend, the eminent and honourable industrialist Mr. Dalmia, for his laudable efforts that have brought all of us together on this common platform today. The grave apprehensions that had plagued me since I came to India, about a country partitioned on religious grounds, are gone. It gives me great pleasure to acclaim hereby that His Imperial Majesty of England, King George V, has decided to hand over the power of governance to an undivided India, and the dreadful spectre of a partition has passed over. The transfer of power shall be peaceful and has the united consent of all those present here—who represent the feelings of the four hundred million Indians that we propose to set free.'

As Mountbatten completed his oration, a hushed silence fell on the room and then all of a sudden, a rumbling applause reverberated amidst a noisy chatter that broke the silence. A soft strain of instrumental music permeated the air as liveried waiters bearing silver trays on gloved arms came floating in, the tinkling of the ice from their crystal buckets providing the perfect rhythm to the score.

Tears welled up in his eyes as Dalmia's gaze travelled from face to face and then stopped on one man's face that was cold and impassive. A distinct chill emanated from his person. He was the only one of the nine present who had neither smiled nor moved— and the bright red rose in his buttonhole stared back joyously—in sharp contrast to the mood of its wearer!

Dalmia clasped Jinnah's hands and hugged him warmly. 'Bring more light into the room; we have accomplished what we fought for Jinnah,' he said. 'India shall be free and you our first Prime Minister... We have swaraj *... and it is on our terms... Why is it so dark? Bring more light...'*

The click of the switch of his bedside lamp flooded his senses with a bright light that almost blinded him. He opened his eyes and saw his youngest wife Dineshnandini wiping his feverish brow. His nightshirt was drenched in sweat. His body was covered with red welts of a nasty rash and he was mumbling deliriously. As his eyes focused on the red bindi on Dineshnandini's forehead, he sensed a soft fragrance of sandalwood around him. Everything else had faded away. They were all gone.

His friend Jinnah, Field Marshall Auchinleck, Mountbatten, Gandhiji, the Maharaja of Patiala, Sardar Patel—all of them had vanished. The only thing that remained was the icy stare from the eyes of the man who sported the red rose!

Lying under a fan that whirred mechanically in its vain effort to cool his burning and aching body, reality hit him hard once again. The British had left India—a fragmented and restless nation—totally unprepared to face the aftermath of a partition that was to corrode the essence of its unity.

He thought of his friend Jinnah sitting hundreds of miles away in Karachi, ruling his own crumbling *jagir* that was the plum that had fallen into his basket by his tenacious design. He wondered if peace eluded Jinnah too.

His own failure in trying to prevent the dismemberment of his motherland was a grim reminder of his powerlessness in the circumstances—but the challenge that lay ahead of him was too enormous and he would not accept defeat. He would begin the monumental task of rehabilitation and relief for the hundreds of thousands of his countrymen who had been rendered homeless at that ill-omened hour of midnight. He would dedicate himself to assist the refugees that were trickling past the borders in the greatest and bloodiest transmigration that history would ever witness! Stray thoughts hounded him. Mother India has delivered twins by a Caesarean section. They have been separated from each other and her at birth. The post-partum haemorrhage has to be stopped. It is a day cursed by the stars.

As he drifted back to sleep overcome by fever and fatigue, phantom voices from the dome of the hall in the viceregal estate came echoing back. 'Hail Gandhi, the messiah of undivided India...Hail Jinnah...Hail Dalmia...Hail friendship...'

It would be another twelve hours before reality would hit him once again and he would wake up from his unfulfilled dream, wake up to remind himself that it was an illusion—real in every other way except the most vital one—its outcome!

He would shed a silent tear for his dying friend Jinnah and another for his untraceable and presumed-to-be-dead friend Subhash Chandra Bose. He would not be able to hold his thoughts in check: Had Subhash Babu not escaped to Burma, had Jawaharlal Nehru agreed to allow Jinnah to become prime minister, had Patel been made prime minister, it would have been another day for India ... As he tossed and turned deliriously on his bed to spend a sleepless night, the blood from India's severed veins flowed out incessantly and unchecked!

For Dalmia the material and financial losses that the Partition brought did not disturb him. It was the incalculable loss of lives in the unending trail of destruction, the bloodshed that dogged a blinded and panic-stricken horde of human beings in search of safety and relief that haunted him. His empathy had been stirred as much as his anger. A handful of self-seekers had orchestrated this man-made catastrophe. They had to deliver the victims from the present-day calamity. The people in power owed them a responsibility. He was driven by a spirit of service as a patriotic Indian on whom God had bestowed the means to afford help to the needy, and he too felt it was his prime duty as a Hindu to do so.

General Mohan Singh of the Indian National Army, formerly a close associate of Subhash Chandra Bose, was allocated the charge of organising his tours in the refugee camps of the Punjab, and an enormous fund was sanctioned to him for the purchase of requisite relief materials to be distributed. A firebrand Congress critic himself, General Mohan Singh accompanied Dalmia on his extensive tours of the refugee camps, where he spoke provocatively against the Congress.

Everywhere Dalmia went the unbearable horror of the people's plight struck him. Wailing with grief and despair they swarmed around his open jeep much like the flies that hovered above their heads in their desperate need for food, clothing, blankets, bedding or even words of solace, grabbing and snatching whatever came their way like wild animals fighting over a piece of flesh. In the heat and dust of the harsh summer of '47 that was swiftly rolling into a cruel winter, no one knew if he would be alive to see another day. Breeding, eating, defecating, dying under the open sky, they were no different from hapless animals that had been given temporary shelter before they would be led to the slaughterhouse.

Standing atop the bonnet of his jeep, with his wife Dineshnandini and General Mohan Singh by his side, Dalmia addressed the people, his voice tempered with pain and sincerity. He moved from camp to camp, village to village, city to city, round the clock, fired by an untiring energy that propelled him forward. After a long and tedious day, riding silently in the back of his jeep, even though he would fall asleep, his mind would still be with the festering and miserable lot of human beings to whom he had afforded temporary succour. Each day he would be planning his tours and speeches for the following day.

But another seed had silently taken root within and was threatening to assume overwhelming proportions. Dalmia had discovered the ideal platform to air his own grievances against Nehru—the man whom he believed was singly responsible for the present-day crisis and on whose governance lay the absolute responsibility of rehabilitating the milling masses on the cleaved borders of Punjab and Bengal.

Each day his diatribe became stronger and his speeches increasingly incendiary. Egged on by the wily and slick astrologer Haveli Ram who had opportunely latched on to him, Dalmia lashed out at the policies of Nehru—'the incompetent Prime Minister', squarely blaming him for what he maintained could have been a completely avoidable disaster. Reinforced by the accuracy of Haveli Ram's earlier predictions, believing his prophesy that Dalmia would become the finance minister of India one day not far away in the future, Dalmia went ahead like a fiery tornado with his double agenda—to help the refugees and demolish Nehru.

The battle lines were drawn. His open denouncement of Nehru with the obvious intent to discredit and topple him became the breeding ground for a long-lasting and bitter animosity that would fester between them. But Dalmia in his fearless frenzy, did not heed the sounding of a death knell that heralded a diabolic end, neither did he heed the rumblings from within his own backyard.

His two lieutenants Jaidayal and Shanti Prasad who did not share his kamikaze passions, did not possess the intrepidity to challenge the most powerful man in the country. Just like the Congress party of independent India had no use for the esoteric ideals of its founding father Mahatma Gandhi, Dalmia's ideals too were grievously unacceptable to both. Inhibited by prudence and natural fears they wanted no part of the backlash that was certain to fall upon the perpetrator of an insane and suicidal mission.

Even as the front pages of *The Times of India* splashed pictures of its owner addressing mammoth crowds of uprooted Indians across the borders, quoting in bold headlines his vituperative diatribe against Nehru—the two of his most trusted allies—his brother and his son-in-law were working out crucial schemes for self-preservation, knowing better than to wait for the worst to happen. They were fraught with the mortal fears of ordinary men and Dalmia's defiant behaviour and the doom it portended terrified them! While Dalmia continued to inhabit in his surreal world, perceiving himself as the incarnation of Samrat Ashok or even Alexander of Macedonia— dreaming about his grandiose future as finance minister, trampling over his enemies, his brother and son-in-law were holding urgent and secret parleys on how to escape the dragnet of the prime minister's ire. Mistakenly they presumed that Dineshnandini, his youngest and most beloved wife, was in control of his mind and that he was being egged on by her on this path of self-destruction. Perceiving her to be the spectre of their doom the latent hostility that they had harboured against her was fanned with each passing day. After repeated and failed attempts to prevail upon his brother, Jaidayal made a fervent appeal to her by means of a letter to either prevent his verbal assault on Nehru or to initiate a family partition whereby they could segregate themselves from his view and functioning. They also demanded that he should, in a public declaration, clearly establish that his anti-Nehru stand was entirely his own and not shared by the other two, and also discouraged his plans of bringing a newspaper edition of *The Times* to Delhi which they believed would be unwise and ill-timed.

Meanwhile, encouraged and charged by the extensive publicity and media-coverage, a demonic energy fuelled Dalmia's egoistic mission and he felt vindicated to some extent in his angst against Nehru. In an effort to expand his outreach even further, he began working on bringing the publication that was hitherto confined to Maharashtra, to the capital. Soon after, *The Times* was published in New Delhi along with a Hindi daily and weekly edition that were given the poetic names *Nav Bharat Times* and *Dharmyug* by Dineshnandini.

Jubilant and heady with a feeling of power, travelling extensively between Delhi, Punjab and Bengal, each day presented a new photograph, a new speech, a new challenge but the same bold antipathy towards Nehru!

To be able to challenge the power of the prime minister and hurl vitriolic abuses at him was perceived by the rest of his dumbfounded family as the ultimate act of ineptitude. That it was an unparalleled act of daring that no one could have ventured to do at that time was all but lost on them. However, much like the battle fought thousands of years ago at Kurukshetra by the Pandavas and Kauravas as documented by Rishi Vyas in the ancient Hindu epic, the *Mahabharata,* Dalmia too believed that his was a fight of good versus evil and that he would emerge the supreme victor. Unfortunately all his strategists deserted him at the crucial hour, and he was left alone to fend for himself with his wife Dineshnandini, whose pen for once could not match the power of the sword. Encapsulated in her own ethereal world of romance and poetry, struggling to fight the private insecurities of her expendable conjugal status, nurturing the growing embryo of her first child within her womb, and the shadow of Narbada in her psyche, she was busy dreaming of presenting her husband with a son. She was neither equipped with the shrewdness to steer his conduct nor the craftiness to avert the recrimination that was to fall upon her frail shoulders!

The game of dice was yet to take another turn. Secretly flattered by the recognition bestowed upon her by the two most powerful associates of her husband who had never acknowledged her presence in his life with any seriousness, she innocently forwarded Jaidayal's proposal to Dalmia.

Her naivety mistaken for machiavellianism, she would be disgraced as the evil and calculating perpetrator of an ill-fated family partition that would ultimately bring Dalmia to his ruin. The brunt of the arraignment would fall by crafty design upon the scapegoat who would await her final execution thereafter, never quite knowing what she had done wrong!

Meanwhile, burning with a rabid fever that rivalled the fiery state of Dalmia's mind, sleep had eluded two other men since the night of 14 August. They had boarded a train from the Victoria Station in Bombay. The two were on a chilling mission. A mission so meticulous, so secret and so violent that it would rock the world in just a few months' time.

The only thought uppermost on their minds was—
India is divided but Gandhi lives…As the train chugged out
eastwards to Delhi, a loud slogan resonated in two pairs
of ears…

'Death to Gandhi! Death to Gandhi!'

The prime minister was a troubled man. The governance of a country ridden with ailments, torn apart by
bloody riots, had already stretched him to the end of his
tether. He hardly needed a rabble-rouser who had the
voice and instrument to incite public sentiment against
him. Criticism made him testy and short-tempered, and
Dalmia's verbal assault could neither be trivialised nor
ignored. Jawaharlal Nehru had spent many years of his
life in British jails orchestrating his battle against their
formidable might. Dalmia's was not a threat that was
insurmountable, his widely read newspapers and diatribe
notwithstanding. Ridden with his own failings, anger and
vindictiveness, he felt infuriated by this defiance. With an
egocentricity that few of his ilk could have rivalled, the
adored and admired Nehru, his Janus-face neither beautiful nor saintly, raged against his opponent. His most
vocal antagonist—the messiah of the miserable refugees,
the should-have-been-finance minister Dalmia—was to
become his vilest enemy. The man who found himself
duty-bound to alleviate the suffering of the masses, pro-
claimed loudly that Nehru was incompetent and had been
unfairly favoured by Gandhi and providence. Since his

was a voice that rang with candour and sincerity, and was complemented with practical measures of aid and relief, the masses listened to him.

Their association dated back to 1931. Already established as the mainstay source of funds for the Congress party in Bihar, moved by a call of service for the nation, Dalmia wrote a letter to Nehru after his father Motilal Nehru died:

Dear Panditji,

I understand that after the death of your revered father Motilalji, you are in financial difficulties. You may not know me personally as my activities have been confined mostly to Bihar.

If hundreds or even thousands of persons like me sacrifice their lives for you, it is too little. I am enclosing a cheque of Rs. 5000. On a word from you I can send you some more even though my resources are limited. If you do not want to accept it as help kindly take it as a loan.

On 13 March the cheque came back with a brief and laconic rely:

No doubt my position has been adversely affected by my father's death. However, I can manage to maintain myself. Even if I was not in a position to do so, I would rather choose to work hard than to accept (unearned) help from a friend. If you desire I can spend this money for the *kisans* (farmers).

Even though it was unlikely that Nehru was unaware of Dalmia's unstinting support to the party at that time, the mild rebuff from him had no adverse affect on Dalmia. In fact his respect for Nehru increased tremendously as a result.

Shortly afterwards, Mohanlal Saxena, a prominent Congress worker, came to Dalmianagar. He expressed Jawaharlal Nehru's desire to start a newspaper called *The National Herald* from Lucknow to bolster the movement. He requested Dalmia to purchase a twenty-five per cent shareholding that would generate enough running capital for the venture. Knowing of Dalmia's keen interest in politics and the print media, Saxena was aware that a cheque of five hundred rupees was being sent by him every month to maintain *The Searchlight* published from Patna—the only Congress paper of that time, with Murli Manohar Babu as its editor.

Since monetary help did not come easily those days, Saxena was certain that Dalmia's name heading the list of shareholders would attract others to invest in it—if only as a promising business proposition. He appealed to Dalmia saying that since Nehru had devoted his life to the cause of national freedom, it was only befitting that his call should not be ignored by the people who had the means to help.

Far in excess of Saxena's expectations, Dalmia purchased thirty per cent of the shares, totalling to an amount of ten thousand rupees, for the proposed publication— saying that for the great patriot Panditji, no amount was large enough!

He appointed Shanti Prasad as director and *The National Herald* was born. Later more cash funds were needed to sustain the issue so a further twenty five per cent was paid up to keep it going. By now, Dalmia virtually owned the newspaper. It was in a sense his first stint with media-ownership, and infused him with an infinite feeling of power.

It was also in a sense his first brush with the petty side of Nehru and his inexplicable dislike for him.

The National Herald needed more funds. Already strapped for cash—at a time when business was not at its best, Dalmia expressed his inability to comply with another request for additional funds, after which he received a nasty note from Nehru: 'You people first make promises and then go back on them...'

Dalmia was surprised. Either Nehru was ill-informed which he had no business to be, or he was targeting Dalmia for reasons that the latter could not understand. He had purchased shares that were four times more than what he had agreed upon in the first instance. His anger and hurt found expression in his reply:

'I would rather forfeit all my shares than listen to this...I have done nothing to earn this ire and do not deserve your ingratitude for I have not gone back on my word. In fact I have more than honoured it!'

Shanti Prasad was made to step down from the post of director. The misunderstanding was subsequently cleared and Nehru apologised to Dalmia for his hasty reprisal. It left a bitter taste in many mouths. Feroze Gandhi, Nehru's estranged son-in-law, was Editor of *The National*

Herald at that time. Most perceived this as the beginning of the ill will that would slowly acquire epidemic proportions two decades later. It would also go down in Feroze Gandhi's memory to come up in the form of a question raised by him in parliament in 1951, alleging an unholy nexus between his father-in-law—the prime minister, and the owner of Bharat Insurance Company—Ramkrishna Dalmia.

The attack aimed at his father-in-law whose dislike for him was no secret would also claim another unintended casualty.

It would give Nehru the much-awaited opportunity to checkmate his old and established foe Dalmia—and lead to the setting up of the Vivian Bose Commission of enquiry in 1955 to investigate the irregularities of the privately owned insurance companies with the specific intent of exterminating Dalmia.

This would also be followed by a dirty trial by the press and a prolonged and painful trial by the judiciary—with a predetermined outcome—and scores finally settled.

Dalmia's support to the Congress was indeed invaluable. It came at a time when few would have ventured to fund an overt anti-government cause. Never having attained the recognition and gratitude that he merited, he always remained on the wrong side of the law. So, when freedom came, where most others would be richly rewarded for services rendered, he would remain on the other side to become entangled in a savage clash with Nehru and ultimately be reduced to ground zero by the unforgiving witch-hunt that followed.

Nehru disliked the business class. A 'latter day Fabian Socialist', he was a Brahmin snob. With the exception of the Birlas who came to his rescue during the expensive treatment of Kamla Nehru's tuberculosis at the time of her confinement in Switzerland, his disdain for the community as such was hardly disguised. While the Birlas reaped a rich harvest for services that were both opportune and calculative, Dalmia was singled out ruthlessly and systematically pursued to his end.

Nehru had assiduously laboured to rid himself of his British manner but his aristocratic and Western veneer had never quite dissipated. Labelled by Jinnah, his most vocal critic, as 'a Peter Pan who should have been an English professor, not a politician,' his other side was as pedantic and insular, as self-absorbed and vengeful as any ordinary mortal. With his Harrow, Cambridge education, he inwardly scorned Indianness and had no place on his agenda for Hindu eccentricities.

But post-Independent India saw Nehru personally troubled and politically uncertain. The restive masses that were mainly Hindus and whom he had been instrumental in liberating from the British, were on the brink of other serious dissensions. The polarisation of minority sentiments and the exodus of a major part of their brethren into Pakistan had only served to heighten the residual rancour that they were compelled to deal with. The brutalities of the killings during the days of Partition were fresh and their wounds were raw.

Dalmia was a staunch Hindu. He was also powerful. His voice had an outreach that touched millions of readers of his newspapers. Multitudes moved with his fiery rhetoric—his words struck their souls. The Hindus were an angered lot and his was a cause symbolised by a movement, banning cow-slaughter. His attack forayed into hitherto untapped Hindu sensitivities. It also threatened to disturb the fragile structure of the newly formed republic. Dalmia with his high-blitz publicity had an uncanny ability to connect with his grieving and injured countrymen. The freedom of speech, a right bestowed upon every citizen by the essential structure of the nascent Indian Constitution, reflected his notions, that became the source of profound annoyance and provocation for Nehru.

Strategising from his newly acquired office at 10 Aurangzeb Road in New Delhi, a legacy sold to him by his friend—the head of India's newest Islamic neighbour—Pakistan, his aggressive anti-cow-slaughter campaign, supported by strongly worded speeches against the prime minister, awakened the fanatic instincts that had lain dormant within the psyche of the traumatised Hindus. As he orated louder and stronger, the crowds swelled to gigantic proportions and shouted emotionally charged slogans along with him: '*Gau hatya band karo. Gau hamari mata hai. Gau Mata ki Jai* (Ban cow slaughter. The cow is our mother. Hail Mother Cow)!' Every meeting ended with acts of charity and largesse that rained down from his treasure chest on an expectant and needy crowd. The movement became the flashpoint for greater unrest and hysteria and Jawaharlal Nehru could ill afford to trivialise it any more.

In one of his letters to his sister Vijaylakshmi Pandit he would say: 'Dalmia is proving to be the greatest thorn in my side. He makes crazy and frenzied speeches directed against cow-slaughter and the Congress. The crowds are listening...'

Something needed to be done and needed to be done without any delay. Meanwhile, quite oblivious of the counterattack being carefully formulated against him, Dalmia was unstoppable. Every week at the refugee camps he conducted mass marriages of orphaned girls and widows, distributing sewing machines, cycles and other articles of utility by the thousands. Each week he indulged in his favourite sport of Nehru-bashing with enhanced militancy after which he retired to a sound sleep, having rivalled the lofty ideals set by his ancestors to pave the way for his own nirvana.

And while his eldest ailing wife and three younger pregnant ones were individually vying for his attention and running a race for first place in his heart, Dalmia was living his fantasy life on many levels as an ancient *samrat* of the Vedic Era who was governing, warring, propagating, reigning, administrating, strategising and ridding himself of his mortal karmas—all in one single lifetime so that he would never have to assume an earthly form again. But fate had ordained (as it is wont to) quite another hand to be dealt out to him and shatter his utopian dream!

Nathu Ram Godse was an aberration in a race of Hindus that had rarely displayed murderous and bloody fundamentalism. Indoctrinated very early in his life with hardcore anti-Muslim sentiments, he was a true misogynist with overtly homosexual leanings. Along with his covert group of fanatics, he held Gandhi responsible for the mass genocide that his brethren had suffered at the hands of the Muslims—a genocide that Gandhi would have to pay for with his life! Godse arrived in Delhi with a name and the phone number of a man he urgently needed to see—a wealthy and powerful Hindu whose voice had reached the far corners of the nation. Godse felt he could help to bring his holy mission to its natural end. He knew nothing else about the man other than that he was the unquestionable crusader for the cause of the downtrodden, that he was a devout and practising Hindu, and that he publicly displayed a poignant antipathy to the Congress. Like most other Indians, he knew him as the most visible and vocal media baron of free India.

From the Old Delhi Railway Station he put a call through to the number written on a page of his little black book—a diary that was to fall into the hands of the Bombay C.I.D. a few months later.

Of the many distinguished and ordinary people who visited Dalmia's home for the morning darshan, as he was being anointed with generous doses of mustard oil by two agile masseurs, some intuition made him refuse to meet this man—a rare decision, since he never turned anyone away. The urgent caller from the Old Delhi Railway Station who had a distinct Marathi accent had no known antecedents or references.

Dalmia was too deeply engrossed in his verbal warfare with Nehru and his domestic responsibilities towards his four wives and their offspring, to allow a precious half-hour to the caller who seemed to be on a charity-seeking mission.

Reclining on an oil-soaked sheet that covered a thick mattress placed on the floor, with only a loin cloth on his smooth body, neither he nor Dineshnandini knew that he had just turned down a request to meet an assassin and that he would later be perceived as having abetted this assassin. The name of the caller would mean nothing to them or to most people till four months later when it would hit the headlines of all national and international dailies in connection with the most macabre assassination in modern India.

Two months before Dineshnandini was to give birth to her first child, Nathu Ram Godse would pump three bullets into the chest of the aging Mahatma on his way to an evening prayer meeting on 30 January 1948, ending the glorious life of a man who had lived and died in service of his fellow-human beings. The obscure phone number scribbled in the assassin's diary would lead to a blank salvo being fired in the C.I.D. investigation that would follow, and that would, however, in no way be able to link Dalmia to the assassination much to the chagrin of the Congress party—and Jawaharlal Nehru!

The entry of the charlatan astrologer Haveli Ram into Dalmia's life was not perchance. It came at a time when Dalmia's political ambitions had taken firm root and had turned him into a megalomaniac who was beginning to self-destruct. He had a compelling and chronic addiction to the science that decreed that the governance of all life on earth was due to the positioning of the planets. His own conviction came from a deep study of the prophesies of another astrologer of South Indian origin, known to him by the name of Shri Satyacharya. The latter had achieved great recognition by deciphering the words that were inscribed in a dialect that was a mixture of Telugu and Tamil, on ancient palm leaves. Legend had it that these leaves contained the horoscopes of all living beings on earth and had been handed down the ages from an ancient sage. It was from these leaves that many startling predictions had been made for him, including his multiple marriages, his fathering more daughters than sons, and also the apt comparison of his life to a rubber ball that continuously bounces up and down—depicting the rises and falls that marked his life's graph. It had suffused in him an untiring optimism and energy that propelled him to rise again forcefully each time he struck rock-bottom.

So impressed was he by Shri Satyacharya that he had taken him to the Wardha Ashram to meet Gandhi, who did not share his own enthusiasm. Not surprisingly,

Gandhi said, 'I have no faith in astrology,' to which he retorted, 'You may say that the sun does not exist Bapu, but does that mean that the sun will not be there?'

Undaunted, Dalmia made Shri Satyacharya read the birth charts of Jamnalal Bajaj, a contemporary freedom fighter who also lived in the Wardha Ashram, and of Kaka Kalelkar, along with that of Gandhiji's. Reportedly the predictions made by the astrologer tested favourably to a ninety per cent accuracy—a claim that few of his genre could have matched. Taking timely advantage of Dalmia's fatal attraction to astrology, the wily operator Haveli Ram, who claimed to be in possession of the original *Arun Sanghita* found his way into Dineshnandini's home *Teen Number.* Her own childhood interest in the supernatural and the occult compounded their enthusiasm in welcoming the newcomer. Slowly and steadily their dependence on Haveli Ram grew into a neurotic obsession. So much so that Dalmia put aside all his proven business acumen to buy, sell and speculate according to the whimsical and crazy advice from his new counsel. Dineshnandini meanwhile plunged into a deep study of the science herself. Erroneously she believed that it would keep her closely linked to her husband holding his ever-wavering attention in check, and provide her with the lever to control and direct him. She developed that learning into a fine art. Coupled with her own keenly developed intuition, it would later bring her the adulation and reverence of her own fan-following, but also the condemnation of being an evil, tantric occultist by all those who wanted to grab any opportunity to denigrate her.

Meanwhile the process of the family partition as desired by Jaidayal and Shanti Prasad had commenced. In an unparalleled spirit of magnanimity, Dalmia ordered Shanti Prasad's brother, who was also his employee, to draw up a partition deed in accordance with their wishes.

'Barring *The Times of India* and Sawai Madhavpur Cement Company, let them take what they want,' he said.

Even these two were not to remain in his possession for long due to an ill-timed speculative loss incurred on Haveli Ram's advice!

The family partition of an estate of an incomprehensible vastness was completed within an uprecedented time-span of merely seventy-two hours. The vast empire that was worth billions was divided irrevocably without Dalmia's intervention or, in a sense, consent. When he saw the details of the partition deed, in an aside to Dineshnandini's brother he said, *'Arre Bhaiya! Yeh makaan toh hamne lene ko nahin kaha tha!* (Heavens! I did not tell them to take the houses in Mussoorie)!'

The Mussoorie estate which now belongs to the descendants of Shanti Prasad Jain, is a group of seven beautiful bungalows on a hillock that spans tens of acres in the famous hill city. But the Mussoorie estate takeover was only a tiny one of the many surprises that awaited him!

At this time there was a perceptible lack of a back-up support system for Dalmia, as none of his own children were old enough to assume the responsibility of taking charge of his business. Grabbing the opportunity, Haveli Ram crept into the invisible vacuum created by the two deserters who had also been his most trusted soldiers. Dalmia's dependence on Haveli Ram grew into a frenzied obsession that ultimately led to the painful losing of *The Times* and The Jaipur Udyog Industry, and heralded his financial ruin.

On his daily visits to *Teen Number* he made astounding readings from his documents, most of which had come true. Haveli Ram had also been the adviser to and astrologer for many renowned political leaders at that time. He had predicted that Gulzarilal Nanda would become the Prime Minister of India and that there would be a split in Nehru's cabinet. He had foreseen that there would be an internal revolt in the Congress and the country would be thrown into a state of anarchy. These predictions, some of which came true, also echoed the secret desires of Dalmia's inner mind and helped to further tighten the astrologer's stranglehold on him. Mesmerised by stories from his past life that he was ever eager to know, and vulnerable enough to believe, he was completely in Haveli Ram's clutches.

The astrologer fed his fantasies by telling him that he was a reincarnated yogi who had been in a spell of meditation for thousands of years, and Lord Indra, the King of the Gods, feeling threatened by his powerful *tapasya,* had taken it upon himself to destroy his concentration. As a result Dalmia had been doomed to the cycle of life and death as a mortal on earth. Haveli Ram said that in his previous lives, Dalmia had taken birth successively as Gautam Rishi, Satyawan, Raja Harishchandra and Raja Dashrath—all grand kings and rishis in Hindu mythology, and in each of these lifetimes, his wife had been Dineshnandini in her earlier forms. This addenda was appended on her insistence in her own desperate effort to hold on to the man whose faithfulness was always in doubt.

Anyone with the slightest rational discernment would have seen through this conman, but such were the anachronisms in Dalmia's nature that Haveli Ram had him completely fooled!

Totally taken up by Haveli Ram's predictions during those two ill-fated years, he believed that the Soviet Union would dump currency notes into India and plummet it into the worst ever economic recession faced by independent India. On his advice and in a bid to buffer the impending disaster, Dalmia began to reduce his own industrial holdings and dilute his interests. He sold his extremely lucrative drum-manufacturing factory located in Bombay for a pittance of twelve lac rupees.

At a throwaway price he disposed off two textile mills also located in Bombay that he had bought from His Highness Jiwaji Rao, the Maharaja of Gwalior, and for which he had paid a staggering forty million rupees. The heavy, mindless speculation he indulged in necessitated the desperate sale of a posse of military vehicles and army disposal goods that he had acquired at scrap value from the departing British rulers at the time of India's Independence. Had these been properly managed they could have become a vastly profitable business on their own. He was forced to abandon midway, the construction of a colossal temple that had cost millions of rupees at the Sawai Madhavpur Cement Factory premises near Jaipur.

By the time Haveli Ram was through, Dalmia's losses amounted to an astounding twenty-five million rupees in cash, and incalculable losses in company stocks and other assets.

When things can go wrong, they do so with a vengeance. And so it was with Dalmia. Money that was lost in speculation had been taken out of the securities from the cash reserves of the Bharat Insurance Company that belonged to him. This was in blatant violation of the existent company law. Dalmia was being watched by people in high places and the opportunity thereby fell right into the laps of his patient detractors.

'He's an ugly man with an ugly face and an ugly mind and an ugly heart!' Nehru blurted out in a fit of rage. 'Just because he owns a few newspapers, he claims to be an expert on foreign affairs.'

The angry outburst had been prompted by Dalmia's longstanding and consistent denigration of Nehru's policies. Dalmia had strongly denounced Nehru's socialist tilt towards the communist bloc and the government headed by Moscow, which he believed to be detrimental to the basic policy of non-alignment. He declared that the programmes of the government had created an economic imbalance, and that despite the multiple five-year plans, appalling poverty plagued the country. He called Nehru 'an ideologue with blurred vision and bloated rhetoric', and his party unfit to deal with social and economic issues.

In 1955 Feroze Gandhi's clamourings in Parliament provided Nehru with the chance he had been waiting for, and with the setting up of the Vivian Bose Commission of enquiry, Dalmia was trapped in the worst Catch-22 situation possible.

To put the money back into the Bharat Insurance Company he needed a cash pool of twenty-five million rupees which he did not have, and if he did not put the money back, his actions incurred charges of criminal breach of trust, felony, cheating and fraud. Given the prevailing hostility of the government towards him and his precedent and direct confrontation with the prime minister, there was no one in sight who would come forward to bail him out of his mess, by either loaning him the money or buying any of his companies that he was forced to put up for sale.

Ironically he was compelled to turn to his deserters Shanti Prasad and Jaidayal, both of whom expressed their inability to come up with the cash that he so desperately needed, though not for the same reasons.

As a result Dalmia was driven to offer both his most treasured possessions, *The Times of India* and The Jaipur Udyog Industries to Shanti Prasad Jain, which the latter took over against the requisite payment. So ruthless was to be his amputation from *The Times* that during the ostentatious celebrations that were held in its hundred and fiftieth year, much after his death, the name of its first Indian owner would not merit even a fleeting mention! It was to also lead to a bitter imbroglio spearheaded by Jaidayal's first grandson, Sanjay, between the Dalmias and the Jains three generations later!

Unfortunately, even returning the amount to the company coffers as per all legal and friendly advice, was not enough to absolve Dalmia of the crime. Under the cover of the findings of the commission of enquiry, the government in a cruel backlash initiated criminal proceedings against him that eventually sentenced him to two years of imprisonment, and in a run-up, led to the nationalisation of insurance companies in the country.

Even though Dalmia put up an expensive and spirited fight that lasted seven long tedious years, the stars had turned against him, his change in fortune ironically precipitated by the most wily soothsayer of his own choosing. His counsel, the famous British barrister, Sir Dingle Foot QC, who later became the Attorney General of the Labour Government in the United Kingdom, fought his case with appropriate flair and competence, but in effect he had been sentenced even before the trial began. In a single stroke he lost everything—his honour, his money, his reputation and his freedom. The indictment sent ripples of shock into a stunned India. He went down fighting like a gladiator—alone!

No one knows what happened to Haveli Ram thereafter, but the immeasurable damage caused by him stared Dalmia and Dineshnandini in the face. Expectedly she got her share of the flak.

Life turned one hundred and eighty degrees for her when Dalmia returned from prison exactly two years later!

Around the time that Haveli Ram's influence on Dalmia grew and Dineshnandini gained ground indirectly, another tantric-astrologer Harishwar Prasad gained entry into the impregnable precincts of Saraswati's home. If Haveli Ram was slick, Harishwar Prasad was histrionic! In an effort to counter Haveli Ram and Dineshnandini's consequent elevation, Saraswati accorded Harishwar Prasad the status of a spiritual guru for her family. Rumours of his incredible supernatural powers and his possession of old manuscripts of the *Brighu Samhita* started trickling in. The parallel was absurd if not uncanny.

Claiming to be the reincarnation of Rishi Brighu (also one of Dalmia's revered deities), he was reported to have magically lit up nine oil diyas, made of gold by the mere wave of his hand from a distance of twenty feet! He could materialise holy prasad from thin air in the form of laddoos and rose petals at will. Awestruck by his magical feats the entire family prostrated at his feet. He came to be worshipped as the Lord incarnate and was showered with offerings that comprised gold, silver, jewels, land, cars and generous amounts in cash.

The greatest flaw in Dalmia's character was solely believing and trusting the person who got to his ear first. And by a sheer accident of timing, Haveli Ram wielded greater power than Harishwar Prasad. However, being his own worst enemy, Haveli Ram's inherent ability to self-destruct led him to lose his position and hold, as fortunes nose-dived and financial devastation became a hard-hitting reality.

Meanwhile, in a fit of anger, Saraswati went to Sardar Patel who was a personal friend and the Home Minister at that time, to complain against her erring husband's conduct. No one knows what transpired between them but Dalmia was summoned to the Home Minister's office and clearly Saraswati got a reprieve. Her self-preservation instinct, born of a deep desperation, further heightened the animosity between her and 'the other woman', Dineshnandini. That the fallout would take the shape of a bitter and posthumous lawsuit between Dalmia's progeny over his dwindling estate, was inevitable.

In an uncharacteristic turnaround the man who had taken on the entire nation through his blatant defiance of its Prime Minister, cowed down after getting a strong rebuke from the Home Minister. The cryptic change in him was puzzling.

Dineshnandini, on her part, suspected that it had more to do with a burden of guilt that he carried for some unknown breach of promise to Saraswati whom he loved and feared more than any of his other wives. He spent all his life thereafter trying to appease her.

Her guru Harishwar Prasad, who was later also adopted by Dalmia, exploited the situation ruthlessly and amassed enormous riches from his only-too-willing benefactors. The consequent power bestowed on him corrupted him completely. He indulged in all the vagaries of a sham-godman that were possible, not least of which were gambling, alcohol and womanising.

After the speculation fiasco and Dalmia's incarceration, Haveli Ram was banished from sight but Harishwar Prasad remained entrenched in *Nau Number.* He was to outlive Dalmia, only to be thrown out by Saraswati's eldest son Gun Nidhi in a clean-up job after Dalmia's death.

Dineshnandini was numb. Her life had taken a terrifying turn. Her ideologue, Nehru had turned against her husband—the one man for whom she had sublimated her entire existence. This was not the Nehru whom she had passionately worshipped like every maiden in the pre-Independence era had.

As her husband read out an emotive farewell message to his grieving family before being carted off to prison like a low-grade criminal, she drifted into a painful re-enactment of the years that had preceded this dismal calamity.

Part III

My Mother
Dineshnandini Chordia Dalmia
(16 February 1925 - 7 October 2006)

On the banks of the Ganga in the ancient city of Benaras—home to the pantheon of the greatest of Hindu gods, the seat of the Kashi Vishvanath temple that boasts a history dating back to the sixth century, on 11 October 1946, Dineshnandini Chordia commenced her stormy life with my father, as his sixth and last bride. The eldest child of Shyam Sundarlal and Harak Kumari, her union with Ramkrishna Dalmia, after two years of feverish pursuit by him, proved to be more convoluted than anyone could have ever perceived.

It was the last quarter of a year that preceded the birth of independent India. The palpable energy in the air matched the passion and fervour of the newly-weds. The bridegroom, a highly volatile, very controversial man who was as renowned for his industrial genius as he was maligned for his multiple marriages, wore a stark white kurta that contrasted with the green emerald buttons on his chest. He wore no watch on his wrist and no adornments on his person. On his face was an expression that bore testimony to a sense of *déjà vu*. He was enacting a pantomime that he already had with the same fervour five times before!

In a mansion that stood on the shoulders of tall carved pillars that rose majestically out of a swirling river, flanking a gradient flight of flat marble steps, they walked slowly around a *havan-kund* amidst loud Vedic chants from a shaven *panda* in a saffron robe—a janeu prominently visible on his shoulder. A row of life-size statues of *Yaksha* and *Yakshi* in different poses stood mute witnesses to the ceremony. The petite, five-foot tall bride wore a red sari embellished with intricate silver and gold thread through which the ground fabric was barely visible. The sari had been woven by the weavers of the same city. The pallu covered her from top to toe in an effort to shield her from something unknown and unseen. On her arms were red and white ivory *churas* that gradually widened upwards into her choli sleeves. On her forehead was a small gold *tika* with a row of delicate pearls that caressed the vermilion bindi marking the centre. A thin circular *nath* made of gold pierced her nose. Its arch swept across her cheek ending in a crescent of fine pearls that flirted with her lips which quivered in unison as they moved. The faint pockmarks on her half-veiled face looked like the play of light on her honey-coloured skin. A soft fragrance of rose attar permeated the air around. There were no *baaraatis* with the *dulha,* no *shehnais,* no bedecked horses and no band playing. The only people present were her three younger sisters, four brothers, her mother, her father, and her nurse-turned-companion, who with unabashed joy scattered rose petals on the bride and groom.

It was the union of two human beings that portended the fragmentation of an individual to a magnitude that would make the heavens shudder. It threatened to destroy three generations of a complex family-fabric that spanned almost a hundred years, and would precipitate a personality disorder so serious and damaging in its brutality that it would shatter the lives of seven innocent people who were yet to be born and the ten who had partaken in the ceremony. Dineshnandini had turned the tide of events onto the course that destiny had paved for her by accepting the persistent proposal of her suitor despite his disturbing status of a man who had married five times earlier and had lost count of the numerous women he had not!

Her union with Ramkrishna Dalmia was a union with a man who would be obliterated by another, also known to her, who was to become the first prime minister of the new republic, ten months later. Jawaharlal Nehru boasted an aristocratic, Kashmiri lineage. Impressed with her writing skills, he had invited her during an intense exchange of letters to join the freedom movement.

Regrettably she had turned it down, to unite in wedlock with another who was to become his single arch foe!

Like the countless lambs that were sacrificed at the altar in the historic Kashi Vishvanath Temple to appease the gods in the holy city of Benaras, another unsuspecting one was being led for sacrifice at the altar of a 'human deity' who would never be appeased. There were no butchers, or knives. No blood or hymns of sacrifice. Only a strange, eerie and deafening silence of a closed and secret ceremony.

Predictably, the marriage was consummated and almost immediately though not predictably, the couple parted. The groom left for his destination, Calcutta— alone, to guard the secret he had so carefully kept from his mother in particular and kin in general. The bride, with her brothers, sister and companion-nurse, was packed off without any fanfare or fuss, in solemn secrecy, on a train to Delhi, the place that was to become her home thereafter.

She entered the gates of her new home with faltering steps, uncertain and unsure. There were no lights, flowers, lilting shehnais or relatives to welcome her. She had moved from the humble home of her father to the grandiose but desolate home of her husband, alone!

In steps small in linear terms, but gigantic in figurative terms, she walked into her home in New Delhi which she had chosen over another equally grand one at 10 Aurangzeb Road, because she thought it was bigger and would be better to bring up the numerous children that she intended to produce. That home too, had a history of its own, closely and intricately woven with hers. It had been sold to her newly betrothed husband by his close friend and associate Mohammad Ali Jinnah, who was to become the founder of Pakistan in the following year. But more significantly he was the brother of an attractive woman called Fatima, who it was rumoured, had had a brief but intense romantic involvement with the man who was now her husband!

Silent tears streamed down her face as is natural for a newly-wed when crossing over the threshold of a new life. Mixed feelings of fear and confusion descended on her as she lay alone on the *nivar*-bed—quite a comedown from the bridal suite that most girls dream of and that a man of her husband's stature should have had! She placed her clammy palms on her swollen eyes as she slept, blocking out the phantom sounds that flooded her senses in the silence!

'Poverty is the destruction of the poor itself…'

'Don't marry him … It is a trail of self-destruction…'

'There will be no comeback…'

'You will have the life of an empress … Riches and comforts will be at your feet…'

'Your eyes haunted me all night…'

'How dare he? This middle-aged man with so many wives!…'

'So what if he owns half the country … He cannot own me …'

'Why do you want me in your harem?'

'I want to marry your daughter…'

'I don't need to see you. I know what you are… Don't say no … Ojha will meet you at the station…'

'Who do you think you are… making a mockery of womanhood?'

'You will make so many women unhappy…'

'I could never live with it on my conscience…'

'Your mother has cancer… Who will look after all of you when she is gone?'

'We shall keep the marriage a secret…'

'Marriage can never be a *secret… It is a sacred union…'*

'I'll send you to America… You can take your family with you… I'll keep visiting you…'

'Never… never… You'll have to declare it right away…'

'Why is she marrying him? Is it his money or her pride…'

'Your eyes haunted me all night…'

'No one will marry her… Her pockmarks are too big… No one will marry her…'

'She'll have a hard time finding a groom…'

'Poverty is the destruction of the poor itself…'

'Poverty is the destruction of the poor itself…'

'Your eyes haunted me all night…'

She tried to block the sounds out of her mind. She felt a faint throbbing around her temples… The words of a lyric began forming in her mind:

Why did you bring me to your nest, Oh! Restless One, when your heart was not free!'

She buried her face into the damp pillow to muffle the phantom sounds.

1944 was a particularly significant year. The independence struggle was nearing fruition. Jawaharlal Nehru, imprisoned in the Ahmednagar Fort had begun writing his last and most famous book *Discovery of India*. His son-in-law Feroze Gandhi had fathered a male child, born to his daughter in an expensive nursing home in Bombay.

Not far from there in the city of Nagpur, Dineshnandini Chordia, a young woman in her twenties had already established her name as writer. She was highly acclaimed as a literary genius. Three of her works had already been published and she had been awarded the coveted Sakseria prize for the best Hindi literary creation in 1937. She wielded the pen with the deftness and ease of a skilled swordsman. Her prose and lyrics had a freshness and quality that stirred the deadest of souls. Her pieces *'Aurat Gulam Kyon Ho* (Woman, Why Are You a Slave)?' and *'Are We Born to Live in Shackles?'* were already questioning gender inequality.

A true liberal and a feminist her writings showcased unmatched brilliance and a deep knowledge of Philosophy and the scriptures. The pain and pathos felt by separated lovers, particularly Radha-Krishna, found an echo in her lyrics and invited a comparison with a reincarnate gopi who was living the tragedy of not being united with her beloved Krishna.

Fearless and free, empowered by her pen, flying high above the pedestrian existence of the women of her times, she was surely in an enviable position. Her writings had attracted the praise and adulation that she deserved from literary stalwarts like Munshi Prem Chand, whom she had read as a child, and Mahadevi Varma who observed traces of her own flavour in her works. They had flooded the senses of all those men and women, sensitised and galvanised by the frenzied atmosphere in a country that was bursting with energy—on the brink of its freedom!

This was to set off two separate chain of events that were to become indelible cenotaphs in the karmic tapestry that Dineshnandini had woven around her.

Meanwhile in New Delhi, Saraswati, the fourth wife of Ramkrishna Dalmia, had also become aware of the existence of this young and dynamic poetic-genius. She shot off a letter to her, in admiration of her work, inviting her to come to Delhi and stay with her, not knowing that she would be sharing her life and her husband with her not too long afterwards!

It was at this time, in an unrestrained spirit of adventure, to fulfil a daring challenge that Dineshnandini began writing letters to Nehru, beautiful and prolific compositions under the assumed name of Nero. Why she began this chapter of her life under this name is not very clear but it clearly illuminated an anomaly in her behaviour where she lived in compartments within her psyche, and each new chapter of her life began under a new name, as a new person with an entirely new identity: a split that had first manifested itself when she was a young girl of fourteen and was to manifest itself with much graver ramifications as the sixth wife of her husband-to-be, Ramkrishna Dalmia.

Why did she assume the identity of Nero, the cruel emperor of Rome who played the fiddle as the city burned; whose name symbolises callousness and indifference; who went down in the annals of history as the most debauched and scandalous ruler of his time? Was it a cavalier mask of someone she wanted to become, or was she hiding behind an underlying insensitivity rooted in sado-masochism festering within the complex folds of her mind?

Whatever the reason, there is indeed no greater aphrodisiac than success and nothing attracts more than the aura of a powerful man. Jawaharlal Nehru, extraordinarily handsome and charming, was known as the 'uncrowned prince' of India and must have kindled the ardour of many a young woman.

As the days went by this ardent exchange continued. In one of his letters he wrote: 'Come and meet me mysterious one. I don't know who you are or what your name is, what you look like, or why you write to me.'

In the throes of this fervid passion that had elicited an even more startling response after a period of two long years she was invited to meet him at the Gandhi Ashram in Wardha at a predetermined time.

This was to be the event that would bring her to the crossroads of her life. It would landmark the beginning of a second phase in an existence that would become like a highspeed-roller coaster with all its giant loops, corkscrews and terrifying drops.

Those days the Gandhi Ashram in Wardha had become the nerve centre of the national struggle for freedom.

It was Spartan and austere in keeping with the ideals of the leader. Nehru too, had long discarded his aristocratic and Western attire for the coarse, hand-woven khadi in the spirit of swadeshi. The only activities inside the premises were spinning the charkha and singing bhajans.

Accompanied by her brother, Dineshnandini arrived punctually at the ashram in nervous anticipation to meet the man she had so passionately admired; the man with whom she had boldly initiated a dialogue and who had sustained a long romanticised relationship with her.

He was standing in front of her, welcoming and warm. His presence made her heart flutter and she could hardly contain her joy and triumph! This challenge, like all the other earlier ones, too had been effortlessly met.

There in front of her eyes stood Jawaharlal Nehru, the man who was accustomed to the tumultuous adulation of the teeming Indian masses and was riding the crest of an unprecedented popularity wave. He held her up as she bent down to touch his feet.

Those warm hands that were to release scores of white doves in a symbolic gesture of peace and freedom on 15 August a few years later did very little for the little white dove, held captive inside her heart, hammering away at her chest to be set free. She sat down beside him on a mattress that covered one half of his room. He summoned his secretary.

'Upadhyaya, get some tea for our guests.'

'Thank you! I don't drink tea.' She could barely speak.

'Come try our tea today. It's made with lemon and honey.'

A neat tray with three glass tumblers the size of coffee cups was placed dutifully on the low table in front of them.

She sipped the steaming, frothy, pale, gold-coloured liquid slowly and deliberately as she heard him say, 'Speak your mind, little one…Do not be afraid…You write beautifully and your letters have moved me deeply…'

The background blurred…she was *wandering in a garden full of roses, Phirdaus from the gardens of paradise… her eyes drifted to the soles of his bare feet… his soft cushioned heels were the texture of a freshly bloomed bud. She wanted to touch them.* She froze that moment of incredulous joy into the folds of her mind, a kind of joy that she would never experience in her life again. The familiar sounds of a bhajan in the distance broke her reverie. She found herself saying— 'What should I do? I am utterly confused. I have done my graduation, and am being pressed by all those around me to get married. I don't want to be married, I want to give my life for the service of the country…' A torrent of words came gushing forth: 'If only I could serve someone like you or else, please keep me here with you. I will also give my sweat and blood for the cause of freedom.'

Nehru smiled. Her innocent though passionate naivety touched him. He melted on hearing the confession of the frail woman, in the full bloom of her youth, offering herself to him with abandon and devotion like a flower at the feet of a deity.

The idol of the adoring Indian masses spoke.

'There cannot be two Nehrus can there? And then where can I keep you? I am a nomad within my own home. I never stay in one place for long, but we need bright girls like you. Come and join the cause. I'll write a letter to Maulana Azad. Go and meet him and I am sure within no time you will rise to be a leader and become part of us.

'Take my letter to Azad. He will tell you what to do. In your spare time spin the charkha. It will help you gather your thoughts and make you feel better. You are young and very intelligent. I have no doubt you will meet with great success.'

Her vision blurred and the images faded into soft focus... There were millions of rose petals raining down on them from heaven... She was drowned in the sight, touch and sounds of the moment.

He put his arms around her shoulder lightly and she closed her eyes in a trance as if she had been truly baptised.

The interview lasted for ninety minutes after which he saw them off to the door. She walked out slowly, with a feeling of lightness, a joyous anticipation, leaving behind reluctantly the man whom she would never see in this vista again; but who would perpetrate the most vicious act of vendetta on her husband a decade later!

And Nero got buried deep into her subconscious forever, reiterating the famous words on his suicide note: 'Alas! What an artist is dying in me!'

She felt a faint throbbing around her temples and the scent of those raining rose petals lingered on.

Dual personalities constitute a dramatic hysterical reaction in individuals to escape from an intolerable situation. They lead fairly autonomous existences each having a memory of its own. There is usually some vague awareness of the co-personality; the transition from one to the other follows sleep or sometimes the waking state. One personality recedes and is immediately replaced by the other whose actions, speech and behaviour are radically different from that of the previous personality. The person in charge may or may not deny all knowledge of the other.

James D. Page

Narbada, the child-bride of fourteen years was sitting at the foot of a worn-down takht wearing a coarse sari that covered her head. She kept tugging at her pallu in an effort to hide her bare arms as she pressed the legs of her husband with one hand. Her husband too was a child of thirteen, just eleven months younger than her. In her other hand she held a pankha *that she fanned rhythmically and silently in a sweeping circular motion over his head; she had been doing this for long ... Her arms ached ... She was afraid ... If her pallu slipped, she would be scolded and beaten by him ... The nail marks on her forearms were deep and the scars had not healed. The stinging pain had diminished but it had not gone ... She had to be careful ... If any part of her body showed it would be disastrous ... She had been taking these beatings for sometime now ... She never complained ... She did not know better ... All she knew was that her adorable husband loved her dearly ... He excited her and made her tremble all over ... She found no reason to complain to Maji ... Maji loved her dearly too ... So did Bapu ... But she should never go in front of them without her face fully covered in her* ghunghat *... No part of her skin should show ... She was not troubled. That was the way girls had to be. Whatever their husbands said or did was to be taken* *as a blessing from heaven. She had been taught not to think, feel, see or hear.*

There had to be a complete sublimation of her female identity as soon as she had been given away in Kanyadaan *after she had walked around the fire to take the sacred vows of marriage. Once she had bent to touch Bapu's feet, and the pallu of her sari had slipped down. Her pubescent bosom half-covered with a coarse* kurti *untidily held together by a safety-pin, was visible for a fleeting moment. She sprang up as she retrieved her pallu and swiftly wrapped it tightly around her shoulders. ... That night he bit her hard ... She thought he would never let go ... The crescent shaped purple mark on her breast did not go away for months ... It hurt but it gave her a deep sensual pleasure ... She felt a warm glow climb up her back and fuse upwards into her chest. He scratched her with his nails savagely again and again, scraping long, angry, red marks on her thighs. ... He put a hand on her mouth to stifle the sobs that escaped her lips. She shut her eyes tightly to stop the tears of pain ... Then like a beast he entered her mercilessly in a brutal and carnal release ...*

Dineshnandini felt a throbbing around her temples as she woke up in his arms. He was gently caressing her forehead beaded with drops of perspiration ... carefully kneading her brow!

'Wake up Dineshnandini,' he said, 'Wake up. I am here with you, do not be afraid ... you are with me.'

The throbbing in her temples grew less as she focused. She was in her own plush bedroom, the familiar ivory and gold pattern on the walls, her double-spring mattress, dishevelled and crumpled. The duvet was sprinkled with fragments of her broken red bangles.

That day, from within the complex folds of her mind had emerged the person whose search had driven her husband over and over again to the many women in his life—a quest that would not be over till very long after.

When Dineshnandini conceived Padma, she was going through the most trying period of her life. An earlier pregnancy had been accidentally terminated in its first trimester. She grieved the loss for she thought it had surely been a boy. Saraswati who had two daughters, three and two years old, was pregnant again. Asha's twins, Dhruv Hari and Meera, were toddlers of two years. She too was pregnant with her third child.

Dineshnandini was not at peace. Within the walls of her vast and lonely home she spent sleepless nights, agitated and anxious. It was always a long wait. The city was rife with bloodshed and slaughter. The glorious midnight that had preceded the dawn of freedom only a few months ago, was drenched in the blood of thousands of massacred Hindus and Muslims. Outbursts of violence gripped the city. At the Old Delhi Railway Station dozens of Muslims had been slaughtered. Hindu mobs were looting shops and butchering the owners. The Old Delhi vegetable market had been set ablaze. Loud cries of *Allahu Akbar* and *Har Har Mahadev* struck terror in the hearts of all those around.

As if in fine tune, the inside of her high-walled fortress was also fraught with the paranoia, compounded with a panic and hysteria that was bursting from within. She had sensed a slackening in her hold over her husband. He seemed to be slipping again. She rabidly feared his wanderings and the shifts in his attention. He had promised her in their unwritten, pre-nuptial arrangement that he would never marry again. In what was to be the ultimate testimony of her self-worth she had accepted the challenge but that unmistakable restlessness breeding in him made her nervous. It was the same restlessness that had driven him to heights of insanity again and again. It was the compulsion that made him seek partial relief through a conscious recourse, only to start all over again. It was a repeated psychological detour that had given him a protective subterfuge in the arms of any woman in whom he found the wronged wife of his prepubescent years—the reincarnated Narbada from whom he sought just one more chance. It terrified her.

For Dineshnandini there was no greater challenge than this. If he got married again she would be scoffed at. Ravaged for her infamous liaison with an equally infamous man. Braving the storm of controversy she had wedded him, defying all reason and logic. She began to realise that if she did nothing to break out of the mediocrity of the normal, she could never regain total control. A life energy with no perceptible form was propelling her. It tore at her insides fiercely. The fear of rejection and personal failure gave birth to an urge so insistent and pervasive that it overtook her as an individual. The sensation was not a new one. She had felt it before. She was losing the love of the man whom she could not share with anyone anymore—surely the strongest death wish had sprung out of her psyche to destroy her.

Unobtrusively but stealthily alongside the growing foetus in her womb, grew another equally important entity deep within the folds of her mind. Narbada became a distinct life-form that would spring up again and again with greater insistence in the next two years.

Narbada sat on the bed propped up on the sumptuous pillows against the bedhead. She wore a coarse, pale-coloured sari and a choli with sleeves that came down to her wrists. A bright red untidy line of sindoor stretched from the tip of her widow's peak right upto the back of her head, dividing her long uncombed hair into two equal halves. It spread unevenly into the hair roots on either side of her parting making a broad and irregular pattern. Her husband's head was in her lap and she slowly pressed his temples in rhythmic movements. She softly hummed the tune of an old folk song she had sung as a child. As if in a trance he spoke in a hushed voice, 'My own Narbadi … my dearest … my beloved … Don't leave me again … I have been looking for you for as many years … I will never let you go … I am worthless without you … Please forgive me … I have been an animal … I don't want that woman I had told you about … I am related to her by blood … This is a sin … a vile act … You have saved me from eternal damnation in the fires of hell …'

He wept bitterly as he went on. Uncontrollable sobs racked his body as he drifted into a semi-conscious stupor. He pulled her to his chest and circling his arms around her, held her in a tight embrace. She lowered her face onto his shoulder. Her large vermilion bindi left a visible mark on his sleeve. He kissed her gently again and again, gentle kisses on every inch of her body right from the soles of her feet to the arch of her brow as if he wanted to draw an unseen ache away. Then he turned her over as if one would a little child. 'Narbadi, I will love you so much and will never let you go...' and then in the gentlest manner he held her close and slept soundly like a baby in his mother's arm, clutching her bosom.

Narbada gradually tiptoed away leaving Dineshnandini sleeping beside him. Inside her womb the growing foetus of four months was carrying on a battle of her own.

'Why do you let Narbada go to him, Mother?' she asked.

'Hush child! Let her be. I can call her back whenever I wish... but just look at the ecstasy in your father's eyes. He has never loved me so 'passionately and tenderly as he does her. He does not know... Narbada is none... she is me... my alter ego... I can make her disappear at will...

'Go back to sleep child... it is too soon for you to start thinking and questioning...'

The growing foetus swung around, feeling the pain searing away at her rapidly beating heart, and Narbada was loved more and more, with greater and greater passion controlled and conducted by her creator Dineshnandini.

Narbada did not have to worry about the child growing inside her womb. It was not her child. The unmindful damage that was being inflicted on the unborn foetus was not her sin... She was only sharing space with that undefined life-form. For many days she had not even known that the foetus lived there—till one day it kicked her, but she did not mind its presence as long as it would not take over her beloved husband.

To Narbada's husband it had never been better. He could grieve and avenge his dead wife. He could demonstrate his undying love to her in flesh and blood and cleanse his soul. The therapy became addictive to the middle-aged man whose power to think had been completely eclipsed by his feelings of guilt, and the albatross that hung heavily around his neck for so many years was finally shrugged off. Also, whenever the need arose, he could be with his highly educated, urbane wife who had shown him the path to his final exorcism.

This constant tussle between the two individuals wreaked havoc on the poor, helpless unsuspecting foetus, who suspended all thought and feeling and would be born to merely exist.

One day just as Narbada had crawled back into her retreat and Dineshnandini was in overt control, Padma the foetus gathered up the courage to speak to her: 'Who are you Narbada? Why do you come to my mother's womb?'

Narbada looked at her and answered, 'This is my home, my body … You are the alien and you are not wanted here … Move away or leave … This is my space …'

'Give up this charade Narbada … please … You suffocate me …'

'No never … This is my shell … He is my husband … You are not his child … He doesn't even know you … I am his lover and his child … Get away from me …'

Padma pleaded, 'Please don't push me out … I have nowhere to go … I am not an intruder …'

'*Quiet, you foolish creature ... He only loves me ... He wants me ... He needs me ... He knows no one but me ... Kick away you fool ... Your tantrums won't help ...*'

'*This is my mother's womb and I am his seed ... Don't you see I look just like her ...*'

Padma was screaming but her agonising cries were not heard by anyone! Her mother felt a throbbing pain around her temples as the seven-month-old foetus kicked violently inside her womb, and Narbada slept triumphantly, safe inside her haven!

It was the first quarter of 1948. Padma who was born a normal child, was barely a few days old when Dineshnandini conceived again. Saraswati, almost as if in competition, was also pregnant. Her two girls Ila and Sheela were plodding along merrily, landmarking the normal milestones of their existence. The twins Dhruv Hari (who had been nicknamed Mickey) and Meera, in their formative stages, were each bearing the onslaught of their personal turmoils. Very early in childhood Dhruv had seen his mother, Asha, attempt an abortive bid at suicide. It was a wound that was to fester within the fragile folds of his mind for a long time. Unable to cope with the pressures of her life and the repeated marriages of her husband, his mother expectedly crumbled. She had no desire to live.

Although she knew that Saraswati was not in total control, she still had influence on him. Long before, he had got rid of Pritam Takhat Singh, that beautiful Sikh girl whose vulgar use of lipstick had pushed her the farthest away from him. Pritam Singh was sent far away to live peacefully in the United Kingdom. But that was all over before she arrived on the scene. She envied her. Her own position was in graver jeopardy ever since he had married Dineshnandini, and she never knew when he would start roving again. Even the arrival of Mickey had done little to alleviate her misery, proving all the soothsayers wrong. Evidently it was not the quest of a male child that was driving him to these women over and over again.

The lean and dark little boy had stood behind the half-opened door, watching his father by the side of his listless mother, while she cried piteously as the nurse and doctor who had just washed her stomach, left the room.

'*Aami Mickey ke chaaee naa; aami tomake chaaee* (I don't want Mickey; I want you)...' she kept rambling deliriously in her native Bengali that had so endeared her to him.

Dhruv clenched his jaws together tightly. It was a twitch that was to become characteristic of him. It made his cheeks taut and his teeth hurt. His nails dug savagely into his palms as he saw his mother lying crumpled on the bed, her face pale and swollen. There were beads of perspiration on her forehead. Her chest heaved up and down as she breathed heavily. She tossed and turned restlessly from side to side, rambling on and on: '*Aami tomake chaaee, Mickey ke naa! Aami tomake chaaee—Mickey ke chaaee naa!*'

The bright red glass bangles on her forearms stood out in sharp focus but the red bindi that she always wore on her forehead was gone.

Somehow Dhruv thought it was his fault. It became clear to him that his mother did not want him but then he had no doubts about his father not wanting him either.

He hid behind the curtain as his father left the room.

Asha survived the suicide bid but her marriage sunk to such abysmal depths that it became impossible for her to lead a normal life ever again, the natural casualties of the fallout being her children. Her husband's cruelty and impatience had made something inside her harden.

Even though she would attempt to kill herself once more, she was destined to outlive him. But before that she would give birth to one more girl.

No one noticed the little boy, standing behind the door, wipe the tears that fell from his eyes as his ayah hurriedly led him away, his jaw still tightly clenched!

The same year, as the newborn republic of India was yawning in her cradle, Jawaharlal Nehru had begun his tenure as the nation's first Prime Minister, a position that remained unchallenged for a period of seventeen years till he died. In a parallel, though not entirely secluded world, another giant was towering above the ordinary and the mundane, threatening to overshadow all those around him.

He was the man who after a fifteen-year-long struggle, had risen to become the indisputable Sultan of the Indian Industry. He was to be hailed as the 'Indian Rockefeller' by the American press just a few months later. He was also to launch and propagate an international peace mission that would make him celebrated around the globe. His meteoric rise, not surprisingly, had compelled the already established giants of the Indian industry, the likes of Jamshedji Tata and Ghanshyam Das Birla to sit up and take notice of him. The rolling juggernaut that he was, there was no stopping him!

The list of the companies he owned read like a stock inventory of the industrial world. He also owned a group of cement factories, electric-power companies, chemical works, numerous collieries, and jute and textile mills that spread through the expanse of Pakistan in the west to the state of Bengal in the east. He was in the envious position of being in the right place at the right time, favoured by the stars and the climate of the country. Anything he touched bore fruit. Even his mistakes turned into money!

He had an airline that had an incredible paid-up capital of three hundred and fifty million rupees. When he wanted to acquire *The Times of India* from its Imperialist owners, he had deputed the Chief Editor of *The Statesman* to negotiate the purchase, who in turn took six months in London to persuade the managing director of *The Times* to come to meet Ramkrishna Dalmia in Bombay.

The managing director said, 'You want to snatch away my baby whom I have nursed for forty years?'

He was undaunted: 'Now the baby needs two nurses instead of one, sir!' he said.

Those words became legendary and in the most startling chain of events, *The Times* along with its allied publications, came into the hands of its first Indian owner.

The deal was clinched within twenty-four hours in total secrecy after Ramkrishna Dalmia placed a signed blank cheque on the table. It cost him an astounding sum of twenty million rupees. Surely, the Englishman could never have met an Indian of this genre ever before!

The takeover made Ramkrishna Dalmia the undisputed leader of the Indian industry of the century.

Subsequently he went on an expansion spree wherein he established a chain of eight more newspapers all over undivided India—a position that he believed would make him the most powerful Indian. His business conglomerates spanned the length and breadth of the nation leaving no territory or state untouched.

The energy driving him, comparable to that of Emperor Alexander of Macedonia, was bursting at the seams to make a global impact. This, coupled with the profound faith that he had in *Ma Jagdamba*—his divine Mother Goddess—his *Adi Shakti,* the single most powerful guiding force that would impart to him a different quality of life, led him to the doorstep of the highest powers of the world.

The idea had first originated in 1942 at the height of World War II. He had been greatly inspired by a book, entitled *One World,* written by Wendell Wilkey who was at one time a candidate for the presidentship of the United States of America.

Ramkrishna Dalmia had harboured a deep-rooted desire since then to establish world peace through a universally accepted concept that could put an end to war and destruction forever. Subsequently he theorised the idea of a single-world government that could cut across all barriers of caste, creed, religion or territory. He believed that it would lead to the ultimate evolution of a spiritually empowered global family and to supreme and universal bliss.

In this spirit of peace he embarked on a trip to the United States to spread his message.

What followed was a glorious panorama that aptly illustrated the interaction between the 'Grand Moughal of Indian Industry' and the highest decision-makers of the world.

It is only natural for someone wielding power of such magnitude to attract displeasure and jealousies from other powers outside of his arena, who felt threatened by him, and even though the ruling Congress had benefited from his support financially and otherwise over the years, a sharp conflict was to come to the forefront bringing the two titans, Jawaharlal Nehru and Ramkrishna Dalmia face-to-face on the battlefield and that would ultimately destroy the latter.

On the flip side, in the isolated world of his wife Dineshnandini, a conflict of another nature was also threatening to corrode her secluded sanctum in an equally dramatic saga.

On 4 November a chartered flight took off for its destination—Capstone—in the last lap of a grandiose and flamboyant mission of universal peace. The main occupant of

the ten-seater Lockheed Lodestar was an equally flamboyant man of fifty-five, accompanied by his youngest wife Dineshnandini, her sister and a staff that comprised four persons. The two pilots Lloyd Rondeau and Roy Bach were reputed to be the best in the business. The aircraft belonged to the *New York Tribune* and was readily available for news coverage.

It was under the direct supervision of the city desk and could also be leased for private transportation at the behest of the man in charge. Known for the accuracy of its coverings, it was equipped with the best foul-weather instruments known in aviation history. It had undertaken nation-wide surveys in the most adventurous and hazardous of missions that had rightfully earned for it the title of Flying Newsroom. Everything about it was indeed in keeping with the profile of the high-powered media baron from India travelling in it. The only aircraft of its kind in those days it equalled in distinction the grandeur of the man whose peace mission had hit the United States.

On the flight, as it cruised at a speed of two hundred miles per hour, his wife Dineshnandini sat uncomfortably, strapped in her seat, in an advanced stage of pregnancy. She wore a dark-coloured silk sari with a Kashmiri shawl draped loosely around her shoulders. Her feet were swollen due to the long hours of flying and she was restless and tired. Her sister, sitting in the seat on the other side, was also asleep. They had been on a whirlwind tour, travelling on and off for over three weeks. Ramkrishna Dalmia sat in a seat near the window, staring out pensively. The crackling sound of the radio interrupted the hum of the engine now and again. He wore a dark flannel topi on his head, and an ivory-coloured silk *kurta-pajama* adorned his body. His thoughts were racing faster than the speed of the aircraft that he was flying in. He was happy. He had been well received. The Americans had hailed him and his message. The tabloids had covered his mission prominently. He had announced a peace prize of twenty thousand dollars to be given every year to the most outstanding individual who worked for world peace. He had also declared another annual award of four thousand dollars for the person who authored the best book on the subject.

His speeches at the universities of Louisiana, Alabama and Indiana, and his lectures on television both in the United States and Europe, had received a tumultuous response. He had placed a wreath on the grave of Wendel Wilkey, with a reverence that touched his heart even as he thought about it.

The packed hall of the law students of the Allen courtroom had been a memorable experience. The Americans had lapped up every word that he had uttered in his accented and imperfect English. Yes, they had fallen in love with him! His mission had been a roaring success. The reception that had been organised in his honour in London had been attended by important dignitaries including V.K. Krishna Menon, the Indian misogynist who was visiting at that time. The global impact that he had envisaged was imminent.

He glanced sideways at his sleeping wife. She sat in an untidy bundle. Her overgrown stomach was protruding defiantly from under her crumpled sari. Her face was puffy and pale. 'If you look pale during a pregnancy it will be a boy,' he had heard someone say but that did not interest him. The initial rush that he had felt towards her had long evaporated.

She looked unattractive and try as he did, he could not see his Narbada in her. He felt restless. His mind wandered to the fair-skinned, light-eyed American woman who had sat beside him at the banquet the night before. He had watched her eat gracefully with a knife and fork and sip wine slowly from a crystal glass.

Her toned body was silhouetted against the fabric of her dress. He had not eaten anything. His food had to be cooked by his wife, for he would never eat anything that was made in a kitchen where meat ever entered. But it was not food that his mind dwelt upon. It was Juliana. She had stretched her hand forward but he had folded his hands together in a polite namaste. It was not within the permissible limits of his culture to shake hands with a woman, but her enticing smile and the heady scent of her body ... He was happy that Juliana had befriended his wife and had spent two hours with them in their suite that evening. She intrigued him. The fair alien woman with large light eyes had a deep knowledge of Sanskrit and spouted slokas from the *Bhagwad Gita* with the same ease as a child would a nursery rhyme. Somewhere she touched a chord in his heart. Fair women attracted him but the power this woman exuded was deeper than the layers of her skin. It stirred in him a familiar passion that he had not felt in a long time! He encouraged his wife to spend more time with her and sent them off shopping together. The impact she made on him was subtle but definite. He wanted to see more of her, to listen to the slokas from the *Bhagwad Gita* in her sweet melodious voice.

It stimulated him. He was happy when she promised to meet them in New York after two days. She knew where they would be staying. She would check into the same hotel. He felt aroused. He quickly turned his gaze away from his sleeping wife but could not push Juliana out of his mind. He felt her scent permeate the air once again as the aircraft droned on, rocking him gently to sleep.

At the Chatham Hotel in New York the schedule was hectic. The press and other visitors swamped the hotel in a scramble to interview or catch a glimpse of the departing Indian delegate—the Ambassador of World Peace.

Juliana too had arrived in New York and was staying in a room three floors above. No one suspected anything when Dalmia informed Dineshnandini and her sister that he would be busy at a press conference, followed by another meeting all afternoon. To keep them away would pose no problems. Dineshnandini had not even known that they were being trailed by Saraswati's sister right through the trip, and that she too was staying at the same hotel!

All arrangements were made to send them to see a film. He made certain that neither of them would be anywhere in the vicinity of the hotel when he met Juliana.

Everything was working all right except for Dineshnandini's well-honed sixth sense. It was working overtime. She sat restlessly through the first half-hour of the film shifting in her seat. Something kept nagging her. She kept feeling that all was not right. She whispered to her sister, 'Let's go back, I don't feel well. My right eye is twitching and it makes me nervous. Please. Let's go back to the hotel. All is not right there!'

Her sister who was completely absorbed in the film and irritated at the interruption led her out of the hall reluctantly.

When they reached their room at the hotel it was empty. Instinctively Dineshnandini knew that Dalmia had been lying about the lunch-meeting and she would surely find him in Juliana's room.

She rushed into the elevator followed by her sister and pushed the fifth floor button impatiently. She saw a 'Do Not Disturb' sign hanging defiantly outside. Ignoring it she knocked urgently and without waiting for an answer pushed the door open!

Earlier that afternoon Juliana was waiting in her room on the fifth floor of the Chatham Hotel. She was wearing a pale blue dress that stopped just short of her knees. In all the twenty-five years of her life, she had never met a person with such a powerful aura as the newspaper baron from India who spoke a quaint, broken, accented English, who as a rule never shook hands with a woman, who was a vegetarian, and had never tasted alcohol in all his fifty-five years. She felt an immense pull towards him. She had not expected to see him again after the banquet where they had first met. She had struck up a friendship quite easily with his wife, feeling so superior to her.

Juliana had learnt Sanskrit for her own pleasure from a swami she had met in Rishikesh on her first trip to India many years ago. India had fascinated her. Chanting slokas always made her feel at peace. Then this enchanting Indian was evidently attracted to her fluent recitation of the *Bhagwad Gita* in Sanskrit. He was the owner of an industrial empire worth billions. The stories of his harem and six wives had gripped her imagination. She wondered how it would feel to be the seventh wife of this very famous and virile man.

As he entered her room, she rose to greet him. He folded his hands in a characteristic namaste that had so charmed her. They sat across a coffee table laden with a bowl of red grapes as he talked. She listened to him attentively, straining to catch each word. The undercurrent in the air was intense and palpable.

He wore a white kurta-pajama made of the finest pashmina. His dark hair peeped out shyly from the sides of his topi, belying his age. Juliana noticed an unusual tuft of hair growing on his ear lobes. His nose was the widest one she had ever seen. His small penetrating eyes pierced right through her. His protruding brow reminded her of the bust of Socrates that she had seen somewhere. The gold-skinned Indian in his charming quaint attire intrigued her. She wanted to touch him. His oriental and mystic aura transcended her into some other space and time. She wanted to get into his mind and body to unravel the enigma and hold him captive inside her. She knew that the orientals were renowned masters in the art of love-making—this alluring package was impossible to resist. She felt compellingly drawn to him. She drifted into a reverie as he spoke, holding his hands between her palms.

She was wearing his white silk kurta on her body with nothing underneath … The feel of the soft fabric aroused her … Her skin tingled with the sensuous caress of his garment as she glided in a slow rhythmic movement … She was in a holy trance. She saw a golden glow of light around his head. He rocked her gently back and forth as he held her in his strong embrace. The hair on his ears tickled her cheeks teasingly … She was experiencing an exalted and ethereal act of communion with an extraordinary man! She felt inebriated with a new joy that would remain inside her forever …

Her reverie was broken by an urgent knock on the door. A harried and impatient looking pregnant woman followed by another stormed into the room. Juliana noticed an expression of guilt and embarrassment in those small, round, penetrating eyes that she would never see again, as she left the room. She muttered audibly, 'I never called him to my room. He came on his own.'

She never saw the pregnant woman lurch forward dramatically and fall to the floor. The incongruity of the climax puzzled her!

As Dineshnandini stormed into Juliana's room, she saw the white woman sitting on a two-seater near the window. The heady smell of a Parisian perfume hung heavy in the air. She suddenly felt her body freeze, as if the *rigor mortis* of a corpse had come over her. She saw a blur of blue on a person hurrying out. She heard a faint voice from the distance calling out, 'I never called your husband to my room…He came on his own…' As darkness swirled around her, she did not hear her husband call out her name and she fell to the floor.

When she came round, she was in her own suite. She felt a cold towel being pressed on her head and splashes of water on her face. She could faintly hear her husband's voice—'Get up Dineshnandini…get up…It is not what you think…' She saw a man in a white doctor's coat standing near her. He dipped her hands into a basin of steaming water but she felt no sensation below her elbows. Even the profuse apologies that poured out from her husband after the man in the white coat left did nothing to break her out of her fugue. She was motionless and numb and it scared Dalmia to see her like that. She neither cried nor uttered a sound. She felt no sensation in her limbs. Only a deep ache and a sense of betrayal. An ache so intense that it forced her to suspend all motor responses to insulate her from the outside world—an anaesthesia typical of a patient suffering from conversion hysteria. She felt a pain searing the insides of her chest.

Her husband rubbed her lifeless arms in a vigorous motion. She could not assimilate his broken sentences as she watched him with glazed eyes. She did not want to believe his lies. Try as she did, she could not bring Narbada out to make him feel greater remorse for his breach of fidelity. Her own failure stared her hard in the face. She felt tired and alone. It would be twelve hours before she would be well enough to fly home.

It all began in her birthplace Udaipur. Dineshnandini was two years old when she was struck with a virulent attack of smallpox that should have left her dead in its fury. It was by far the most dreaded virus of that time that scarred brutally if it did not kill. As a result, the fair, pretty, bright-eyed, two-year-old, the eldest and adored child of her parents, lay for days in her dim and ancient ancestral haveli on a sheet full of rose petals that would soothe the cruel and raging pus-filled blisters that had not spared any part of her body. From her soft and tender eyelids down to the soles of her little feet, they ravaged her outer frame as if to take revenge for some untold and grievous act of felony. In a cruel paradox, her parents had avoided vaccinating her to protect her from the pain of a needle prick. So, instead of the two permanent round marks she would have had on only one of her upper arms, she got scarred on every millimetre of her body, leaving no part of her skin free from the wrath of its eruptions. They mocked at the pink, soft, fair baby face and tattooed deep irregular patterns on the rest of her. Even more damaging were the invisible ones on her insides, that were to come into focus in strange ways some years later.

The child was named Dineshnandini after Apollo, the rising and radiant Sun God, and deservedly so because she was to outshine all those around her, first through the brilliance of her writing and later by the nature of her marriage. But just like the sun that is merely a fiery mass of gases burning at a temperature that is potentially more destructive than any nuclear weapon produced by mankind, within her raged an inferno of passion that was waiting to explode from its shell to attain a height of unsurpassed glory. A glory so resplendent that people would be compelled to take note of her, extol her virtues, admire her genius and fall in love with her despite her physical disfigurement. The event that actually ignited her craving to be recognised and acclaimed took place early in her life.

One dreary misty cold winter evening when the haveli was engulfed in a strange, dim shadow and the city was settling down to its evening chores, an old relative unexpectedly came visiting. Dineshnandini was five years old. The visitor called out to her mother as she climbed the deep, narrow staircase, trudging heavily.

'*Binnie,* bring the lantern,' she said, 'Let me see your little girl. I have heard her pockmarks are bad. Bring her to me I want to take a look at her.'

She was led unwillingly by her hand to the unwelcome guest who settled down noisily on the cane stool near the small jharoka that faced the main street. She stared at the old woman whom she had never seen before, half hidden behind her mother holding onto her pallu in a tight grasp. The woman was dressed in a densely gathered black *ghagra* that encircled her veined and bony legs. She wore thick rounded *pajebs* around her muddy ankles.

Dineshnandini hated her instinctively as she hissed from her toothless mouth.

'Come here child, close to me, my eyes are bad. I can't see well. Bring the lantern here, binnie. This light is poor. Bring it closer to her face.'

As she snatched the lantern from Dineshnandini's mother's hand she raised it high above her ears with her thin leathery arms that moved about menacingly.

'*Arre binnie,*' she growled, 'What have you done? Her marks are big and so deep. They are bad. Much worse than I had thought. Her whole face is finished. I feel bad for you. *Bechari chhorri.* What are you going to do, you poor thing? You will never be able to get her married.'

As she lowered the lantern, she looked like an evil witch casting a spell on a poor unsuspecting Sleeping Beauty, that would put her into a death-like stupor for a hundred years. The little girl hurried away from the glare of the wicked witch with the jarring cackle resounding in her ears. She moved forward in firm and resolute steps into an unlit courtyard swearing to herself that this was not to be. She would prove them wrong. She would do something that would make her the most attractive woman of her days, pockmarks and the evil curse notwithstanding!

Truly Dineshnandini was to become the most coveted and desired woman of her time, and the same wicked old witch would have to swallow her own words. She would be one of the many women to beg for the hand of the same pockmarked girl for her son and repudiate her own unholy prophesy of doom.

Udaipur in the '20s was a sleepy, old-fashioned, culturally opulent capital city under the rule of His Highness Maharaja Fateh Singh of Mewar. The Rajputs are traditionally robust, tall, strapping and handsome men with sharp features, prominent jaws and a ruddy complexion.

Theirs was a completely male-dominated society where the women lived in strict purdah. Even the houses were constructed with high walls dotted here and there with tiny, narrow jharokas that prevented the invasion of their privacy by even the rays of the sun. The women led cloistered lives from birth to death, tightly swathed in the customs that did not permit them to encounter any male other than their husband and only after they were married.

They dressed in bright-coloured ghagras tied to their waists, that fell down to their ankles in hundreds of gathers. Their upper bodies too were covered from their necks down to their hips, and fitted choli sleeves encased their arms upto the wrist. They wore long flowing *odhnis* that were draped from head to toe, so that not even the slightest silhouettes of their bodies could be seen. They wore thick anklets of silver on their feet and long intricately carved earrings that sometimes touched their shoulders. The married women wore ivory chooras on their wrists that continued upwards to their upper arms enclosing them in a forbidding grasp.

Women could not step outside the walls of their homes unless their faces were covered with long and opaque layers of their veils. With such an impregnable shroud around them, their role was confined to tending and feeding the men in order to keep the race strong and going. They lived like mindless cattle, meant only to be healthy receptacles for procreation.

Going to school for girls was rare and interacting with males considered a transgression. In such a society to be born a woman with a mind that questioned and rebelled was indeed to be cursed!

Dineshnandini's birth too was accompanied by the natural gloom that usually accompanies the arrival of a girl child, but more significantly it was shadowed by the perils of being born a woman with an intelligent and questioning mind. It portended a phase in her life that would unsettle the foundations of her primitive home and plot out a blueprint bound by parameters that would be the antithesis of the ones she ought to have stayed within. Much like Eve in the Garden of Eden, she would commit the original sin of tasting the forbidden fruit of knowledge, and then fall hopelessly and blatantly in love!

Dineshnandini had decided early in life to be different. She did not belong in this citadel of old-fashioned human beings. Her father with his eminent doctorate in English Literature and liberal bent of mind was utterly indulgent with his first-born's whims. On her persistent demands he employed a private tutor to educate her, in outright defiance of all conventions that were the order of the day. This provided her with the initial escape from the stifling existence that she dreaded. The free spirit that she was, she sat up into the late hours of the night with her tutor Shambhu Lal, much to the dismay of the elders and in sheer contempt of the women. Her exasperated mother close to tears often cried out, 'It's only when you have a girl just like yourself that you will understand what you have put me through!' A curse that was to fructify in her own fourth child!

Dismissing all the norms of a primitive society caught in its own time warp, reminiscent of the Dark Ages, this free-spirited young girl grew up wearing clothes that were meant for her brothers, talking and joking only with men, studying with a male tutor and continuously breaking every rule that could be broken.

An old maid who had been assigned the duty to sit in her room as she took her lessons, was heard complaining to her grandmother, *'Baisa* does not listen to me, *Hokum*! She laughs loudly with Shambu Master all night and they speak strange words in English. I cannot understand what they say but I know they are up to no good! She tells me to go out of the room if I stop her. Only you can put a stop to this *Hokum,* only you!'

The maid was ignored as was the grandmother. The more anyone tried to stop her, the more defiant she became. She flirted openly with all those whom it was considered taboo to even be seen near. She cared for nothing because she had her father's support. Undaunted she continued to soar above the stereotyped purdah-clad women of the clan to which she belonged.

In the same city not too far from her haveli, also lived a very handsome six-foot tall, middle-aged *jagirdar* who had a glamourous and enticing personal lifestyle.

Mohan Singh Mehta, although not a Rajput by birth, had all the trappings and features of Udaipur royalty. A man of forty-five, he had a long list of accomplishments, not least of which included a grand, princely life style. He rode his own Arabian horses, lived in a palatial home, wore traditional ornamental attire and was the younger brother of the minister of revenue in the Royal Darbar. He himself held the glamourous and gallant post of Scout Commissioner. His wife who had died sometime earlier was said to have been one of the most beautiful women of her times. An educationist and social worker, he had founded a very renowned school called Vidya Mandir that had brought him great acclaim.

He had one equally dashing young son Jagat who showed great promise and was to become the Secretary of Foreign Affairs in independent India in his adult years.

It was Shambhu Master, a Scout himself, who introduced Mohan Singh Mehta into his young pupil's life. He regaled her with tales of his gallant and handsome commissioner and described his aristrocratic lineage to her in great detail. He told her about his lavish lifestyle, his beautiful horses, his deceased wife and her beauty, his school, his riches, his home...the list was endless. Starry-eyed she would listen to him again and again, fuelled by admiration for the prince who so enthralled her. She goaded Shambhu Master to repeat every little detail that he knew about Mehta's life. A passionate adulation was steadily growing within her. She would often imagine herself being lifted gallantly in his soldier-like arms while he brandished long swords and was adorned with jewels.

She would imagine him putting her gently onto the saddle of his tall black Arabian steed, and with her tightly clinging to him, him riding off across the golden sand dunes, his steed galloping faster than the speed of wind, kicking up clouds of dust into a glowing pink sunset in the deserts of mystic Mewar.

Mehta became the sole purpose of her existence and she eagerly awaited her sessions with Shambhu Master to enact her daily charade of becoming the frail, helpless, little princess waiting for her knight in shining armour to deliver her to the land of rainbows and gold astride his majestic black steed!

As time went by everyone in the haveli became aware of her frenzied obsession for Mehta, the man whom she had never seen, who was ostensibly the most incompatible suitor for her, who was a few years older than her father and more than twice her own age. No amount of admonishments or reprimands deterred her. In fact they only served to strengthen her resolve. Even her grandfather's desperate pleas whereby he placed his turban at her feet, begging her not to play with the honour of the family and retract from her obduracy, fell on deaf ears.

She was madly in love with him and would marry only Mohan Singh Mehta, age, status and other imponderables notwithstanding!

So against all feeble or fierce opposition, with the help of Shambhu Master's writing skills, she wrote a letter laying bare her unabashed passion and feelings to the man of her dreams. It ended in a dramatically poetic line: 'Your compliance encompasses my entire world!' Indeed a poignant and bold disclosure from a fourteen-year-old of those times!

The missive was carried to its addressee by a trusted personal messenger. Dineshnandini had, very much like Meera Bai, already married her *Bhagwan Krishna* whom she adored and worshipped with matching fervour. When the predictable reply came, it plunged her deep into gloom.

'You are young enough to be my grandchild, little girl! I am almost thirty years older than you. How can we be married? Put your mind into your studies and forget about me. This alliance is neither practical nor possible…'

His rejection was cold and detached. All her dreams of a fairy-tale romance followed by a grand wedding came crashing down. His cruel and insensitive response jolted her badly. She pledged in her mind that she would get him at any cost! She also pledged that since she was wedded to him in soul, mind and spirit, she would never agree to marry anyone else. She had wilfully taken him to be her husband and if he did not accept her, she would remain single and celibate all her life.

From there on began a seven-year-long saga of pain, anguish, suffering, tears and self-destruction, not only for her but for all those who lived and breathed with her. Her thin and frail mother tried hard to crack her perverse obsession by presenting her with several other attractive proposals that came knocking at their door but nothing changed. Her father, on the other hand, stood steadfastly behind her fighting all assaults with just one single resolute stand: 'I will never oppose my daughter, no matter what!'

Dineshnandini on her part became a physical and emotional wreck. Buckling under the pressure of rejection and unrequited love, she became acutely depressed. She was withdrawn, would neither bathe or change her clothes and stayed without food and water for long spells of time. Her long, thick, dark curly hair turned into an untidy, unkempt badly knotted matt because she would not let anyone comb it. She wore only tattered and worn-out clothes, roaming around the haveli night after night as if she were sleepwalking, like a phantom, calling out his name again and again. Her face either contorted with pain or remained expressionless, with eyes unfocused and blank. It was a painful sight, but no one could help.

One night under the cover of darkness she quietly stole out of her bed, went to her grandfather's room and snatched up his sword to put an end to her life and the agony that went with it! That was the only way Mehta would be punished. He would carry the burden of her death on his conscience forever, she thought... A timely intervention by a vigilant Shambhu Master saved her, but she fell down unconscious on the cold floor of the haveli, totally broken and emotionally wrecked.

The years that followed turned her into a convulsive-hysteric and transformed her hitherto peaceful haveli into a veritable sanatorium for the mentally ill.

As she lay on the floor writhing in agony, her body convulsed in an impossible spasm. Her jaws clamped tightly together, her eyeballs rolled up in their sockets and all her limbs cramped into grotesque postures as if she were possessed by a demon.

She was diagnosed with the symptoms typical of hysteria—a form of psycho-neurosis that more commonly afflicts women and manifests itself as a result of childhood experiences. It is characterised by a psychogenic loss of sensory or motor functions, temporary amnesia and dissociation states. The person undergoing such a mental breakdown profits in two ways. The primary gain is the reduction of anxiety and the avoidance of an unconscious sexual conflict. The disabling symptoms also permit a retreat from other disagreeable life-situations and have a sympathy-earning value. This is essentially the second but more overt gain.

In a sudden shift life turned around Dineshnandini. As the onset of her hysteric episodes became more frequent, they drove her despairing father to the door of Mohan Singh Mehta—begging him to alleviate her suffering. It was only when Mehta would come to her, talk to her gently and try to ease her cramped limbs with his hands, that she would respond. It was only his magic touch that slackened the *rigor mortis*-like cramps that convulsed her body.

Her helpless mother and father spent hours holding her head in their laps, trying to loosen her locked jaws with a spoon, pouring water into her tightly closed mouth after which she would slacken and lose consciousness. Often she lay staring vacantly at the ceiling, re-enacting her dream with the man she loved more than her life, calling out his name in an effort to make him hear her cries for help. She talked to him in her sleep, saw his face in every object she looked at. In every nook and corner of the haveli she saw only him and all she could do was either convulse or cry.

At the behest of her parents, Mehta tried to do whatever he could to revive her and relieve her, but he did not change his stand.

The pain she felt got embedded deep in her psyche and was to manifest itself in the poetry that she would write some years later. It was to become her signature stamp. Quite in accordance with the Freudian belief that relief from accumulated tension can be obtained through sexual sublimation that directs the libido into socially approved channels like poetry, art and music, she took to writing intense verse that depicted the torment and melancholia of separated lovers. Her rich, sensuous, thought-provoking words stirred the deadest of souls. Indeed the sweetest songs are those that tell the saddest thoughts. Weary and beaten by her prolonged illness and recurrent relapses her father too sought refuge in his own rationale proclaiming that she was a divine soul in a mortal form—an avatar who could see God wherever she looked, and thus deserved to be worshipped and revered.

So strong are the powers of auto-suggestion and so mysterious the ways of the mind, that she converted from the emotionally wrecked, spurned lover, into a reincarnated Devi blessed with supernatural powers of divine healing and holy enlightenment—a role that she was to conduct with practised ease, that would transport her to the doorstep of Her Highness Devendra Kunwar, the ailing Rajmata of Doongarpur, a small *riyasat* in the state of Mewar. In an uncanny connection it would also foreshadow her doom because the *Raj* Mata was a close associate of her husband-to-be, and she would be dragged into a slanderous controversy for perpetrating the vilest con game, and be defamed as the greatest of cheats in connivance with her father two and a half decades later.

For now, she was hailed as a spiritually empowered *bal yogini* by the locals, and as is natural in small towns, the press was rife with her magic powers. The rejected, hysteric, melancholic lover got buried into the deep layers of her id forever. With the prominence and fame that her new role accrued to her, Mohan Singh Mehta became a fading reality continuing his life outside her ambit but within the city as a widower till he died several years later.

The symptoms of her neurosis also faded into a forgotten corner of her mind only to surface in the form of Narbada in her post-marriage life more than ten years later. But for the time being her identity had metamorphosed from that of a suffering tragedy queen into a spiritual child-guru who had the divine power to heal with her touch, who could spout Vedic slokas with the fluency of a high-priestess, who donned saffron robes and a *mala* of *rudraksh*-beads and was hailed as a *paigamber* from heaven!

It was more than an earnest attempt on her part to be extolled, recognised and revered far above the ordinary for self-actualisation and glory!

In the third week of November in 1948 Ramkrishna Dalmia and his wife, accompanied by their personal entourage of officers and staff, took off from La Guardia Airport in New York for their last and final destination, India, after completing the peace mission that had taken them around Europe and the United States. In the aircraft the couple sat separated by an aisle as if it was a grim reminder of the crack that had showed up in their already fragile relationship after the Juliana episode.

Dineshnandini was still in an extended sulk with mixed feelings of sadness and confusion. She was looking distant and numb. She was homesick. She missed her little baby Padma whom she had left behind in the care of Sunder Bai, Sister Mary, and a houseful of servants supervised by her brother. Her impatience intensified at the thought that she would not be able to see her for another eighteen hours. She wondered if Padma had begun to crawl or speak a few words. She felt uneasy. Padma was going to be ten months old and showed no signs of speech. She seemed shy and was only happy when she was with Sunder Bai or Sister Mary, her governess. She shied away from strangers and was most joyous when she saw birds or animals.

Dineshnandini felt a sharp kick inside her stomach and smiled. The thought that very soon she was going to be a mother for the second time comforted her. Her instinct told her that it was going to be a boy and his birth would surely change things for her. It would give her a new standing, and the stability that she wanted in her twenty-four-month-old, shaky marriage. She glanced at her husband who slept soundly like a blissful child. She wondered if he ever ruminated about the sex of the unborn baby she was carrying. He was always distant and aloof. She also wondered if it was with his consent that Saraswati's sister had followed them on this trip, and if she too had left for India the same time as them. She had only discovered this by accident as they were checking out of the Chatham Hotel. Sharma, the secretary, had been evasive with her. He had been trying to hide something. She wished they had brought Nathu along with them. She would get Nathu to dig out all the information when she returned. Nathu was on her side. He always explained to her all the things that puzzled her.

He understood his master's ever-changing mind and was privy to the intricacies and internal intrigues of Saraswati's household. She was sure that Saraswati had somehow orchestrated sending her sister to trail them on this trip to the United States, but she dared not ask. She never wanted her husband to know that she was possessive or jealous. Saraswati's deviousness appalled her. But Nathu would work it all out. She trusted him.

It was Nathu who had told her the minor details of his life with his dead wife Narbada, and Durga, and his four-month-long marriage with Pritam Takhat Singh, the daughter of Sant Takhat Singh of Ferozepur, and Saraswati, and Asha...and everyone else she wanted to know about. Neither Pritam Takhat Singh, nor Durga, nor even Asha ever unnerved her—it was Saraswati. Her husband's tenderness towards Saraswati made Dineshnandini cringe with envy and fury. All the magnanimity and tolerance that she had professed vis-à-vis Saraswati came to naught everytime he mentioned her name. At that time, even Narbada, she felt, took a backseat. She fantasized and visualised her husband making love to Saraswati. She was sure they made great lovers. She personally found sex distasteful and her own inadequacy frightened her. Even though she knew that sex *per se,* was never an end in her husband's life, she was aware that she was unable to provide the raunchy, nautch-girl kind of copulation that he needed. She could never get herself to call out to him those crude, local invectives that she had heard only from street women and *tongawalas* in her home town. It was incomprehensible to her how his carnal pleasure could be enhanced by a reviling act of that nature. Her inhibitions were the greatest impediment in establishing the bond that largely controls compatibility between a man and woman, and if sex is the prime determinant of a harmonious man–woman relationship, she was at a serious disadvantage. She could do nothing about that. She was, however, always thankful when she became pregnant because it forcibly suspended sexual activity till the baby was in the womb, albeit temporarily!

Back at home in her familiar surroundings she took two days to get over the travel fatigue that had overcome her. Much as she tried, she could not get Padma to come to her. She felt upset. She had brought back nothing for anybody. Her luggage was not laden with expensive gifts, curios and perfumes as would have been expected from the holidaying wife of an industrial tycoon. In fact the sole gift she did carry was a small doll which did not even elicit the gratitude and joy that she wanted from her own ten-month-old.

Padma had left it lying carelessly on the sofa. She had not even cared to look at it or take it out of the wrapping. She felt Padma had rejected her more than she had rejected the gift. She felt guilty for having left the child alone for so long, but her guilt vanished as soon as she began dreaming of the impending birth of her next baby. The long hours of waiting in the last trimester, the tedious countdown for the new arrival—it would soon be over. She wondered whether Saraswati's child would also arrive on the same day and wondered what her own state would be if she had another girl and a boy was born to Saraswati. Who would be given the higher status? On whom would her husband heap his tenderness and attention? Before Padma had been born, the anxiety, the anticipation, the fear of a gender betrayal, the hours of impatient suspense had stirred the sensitive poet in her and she had written a beautiful ode to the unborn baby entitled *Parichaaya*—a reflection. It mirrored the complexities of her mind and unlike many of her previous works, this one was flavoured with optimism and joy to augur the birth of her first child! But this time things were different. Her mind was as weary as her body and the inertia she felt was almost terminal.

On 21 January that year she gave birth to an eight-pound, fair, bonny baby boy but her joy was greatly diminished because he was born with club-feet. She could not comprehend why this curse had befallen her. Exactly ten days later, Saraswati too gave birth to a boy who was to acquire the distinction of becoming the most adored and favoured child of his father—a position that would breed jealousies and antipathy in all his other siblings, some of whom were yet to be born.

Even as Dineshnandini sat in her *Surya Pujan* in front of a Vedic *havan-kund,* in the customary yellow *pilia* and *nath* allowed to be worn in the Marwari tradition in a glaring gender-bias only to the mother of a son, the news of Saraswati's newborn male child came like manna from heaven. Her sister-in law with some of her relatives, rushed almost off in a stampede to hail the arrival as it were of the Prince of Wales. The half-finished puja was abandoned by them alongwith the proud father midway. Dineshnandini was left alone with the baby on her lap, and only the pandit, her mother and her sister to comfort her.

Her own momentary joy had been, like so many others in her life, snatched away in an instant.

The pandit resumed his ritual chants after the interruption, and splashed holy water on the mother and child, but what touched the cheeks of the newborn were not the drops from the priest's sprinkler but the tears that fell from his mother's eyes. She held the infant up to her breast, holding him tight as if to block out the pain, but hearing his hungry cries, the nurse came and took him from her. She felt empty and dejected. Even her baby did not afford the comforting that she so desperately needed.

Strangely, the cynical countenance of her predecessor zoomed into her head. Pritam had been on one of her visits to India ostensibly to collect her allowance from Dalmia when she had called on Dineshnandini. Dineshnandini had welcomed her with charming ease. Pritam had settled on the cane chair in the verandah which overlooked the garden drenched in the winter sunshine. She talked about inane and neutral things as she sipped tea and patted Padma casually on her head.

Her clothes were fashionably fitted. Dineshnandini could smell a floral fragrance emanating from her and she noticed a huge round solitaire diamond on Pritam's ring finger. She had beautifully manicured long nails painted a bright red. Dineshnandini had felt confused. She could not decide whether she liked Pritam or disliked her. There was something unsettling and patronizing about her manner.

Dineshnandini stared at the red lipstick stain on the rim of the cup. Nothing's changed she mused, as she said goodbye to the older woman. As she rang the bell for the bearer to clean the table. She kept feeling that Pritam wanted to say something to her. She never saw her again.

She felt a sharp twinge of regret at having taken the wrong turn at the crossroads of her life after she had met Jawaharlal Nehru at the Wardha Ashram.

Surely a different fate would have awaited her had she made the alternate choice. It was a pain that would persistently nag her in life. Even writing did not procure the same kind of joy in her anymore.

That evening when Dalmia returned he appeared cold and aloof. She desperately searched his face for clues that would give her a picture of the other side but dared not ask. She was curious to know what the child looked like: was he fair, how much did he weigh; who was more beautiful...but she sealed her lips. He sent for her baby to look at his feet again. Since his birth just ten days ago, there had been a flurry of doctors and specialists from all over the country who had been consulted to diagnose his condition and oversee his treatment. He took off the infant's blue booties and touched his tiny feet—or whatever was visible of them. They were two pink stumps of flesh with no defined toes or cute nails that babies have.

'Don't worry Dinesh,' he said after a while, 'Don't worry, we shall get the best orthopaedist in the world to set his feet right. Your child will walk, you have no cause for fear.'

He looked up at her as if he could read her thoughts.

'Just look at him, my own little, loveable Babu...He is so beautiful and fair...His eyes and his ears—aren't they just like mine? He is my seed, Dinesh, he can never be anything but perfect. I know he is a great yogi reborn still sitting in the lotus-position in samadhi. Ma Jagdamba has sent him to us and we are truly blessed.'

He held the wailing child to his chest for a few minutes when the nurse appeared to take him away.

Dineshnandini was in acute post-partum depression. There were no more tears left in her dry eyes that burned when she blinked. She could not help wondering why Ma Jagdamba had not sent the yogi to bless Saraswati's home, and why she could not have had a baby with two perfectly formed feet instead. The cold January breeze chilled her right to the bones. A strong draught made the floral curtains of her room flap about wildly. She stood up to shut the window.

'Come here Dineshnandini,' he said, 'I want to say something to you.'

He held her hand as she sat down heavily near him. Her stitches had not healed and hurt as she folded her legs beneath her. He placed his palm on her forehead as she closed her eyes leaning on his shoulder, feeling slightly comforted. His voice sounded like it was coming from faraway…echoing from inside a deep well…She could not tell if she was imagining or he was really talking.

'I know I have hurt you Dinesh. Please don't be angry with me. I will keep my word to you Devi. Juliana was not what you think. I want no more of her or any other woman. You will be the last as I had promised. I have had enough, and even Narbada. I don't want her anymore. I want her to go away. I never want to talk to her again, I only want to talk to you. Narbada is a ghost from my past and I never want to see her again. Its only you I want. Send her away to where she belongs. We have a happy life ahead of us. Why should we need a phantom from the past to hold it together? This newborn yogi, my guru of so many lifetimes has made me see the light of truth. Go away Narbada and don't ever come back…'

Locked in his tender embrace, Dineshnandini couldn't help wondering whether he had held Saraswati in the same manner just a few hours ago. She would never know that Jaidayal had sternly warned his brother for having been taken in by the greatest con job of Dineshnandini impersonating Narbada.

She lay still in his arms feeling the touch of his body all along her…His soft palms were on her eyes…now on her forehead…moving gently…Tears welled up in her eyes again. They flowed in an incessant stream down her cheeks wetting her ears, nose, and throat. He wiped them away gently and then placed his lips on her swollen eyelids…tracing the path of her tears down to her breasts…She felt as if she was standing outside her own body watching two strangers like a voyeur, making love. An unusual serenity engulfed her.

That very instant she saw Narbada, the alien life-form fading out of sight…kicking and screaming wildly in protest…leaving vacant the fertile space inside her ready to receive the seed of another life—that of her next child—which was to germinate within the next few months. What unnerved Dineshnandini was that Saraswati too would be pregnant just a month later.

Asha was to produce no more children, glaringly highlighting the fact that he was visiting her no longer. Her last child, a girl called Ganga and who for some reason, was later called Alka, was born ten months before the birth of Padma. Unfortunately, she was stricken with polio that was to put her through a series of painful surgeries and a lifetime of calipers, leaving her with a permanent disability.

Dineshnandini was aware of the sea change taking place around her but she did not know how she was going to realign herself with the growing polarities.

Meanwhile another leaf had been added to the dossier being prepared on her to establish her role as a sorceress, conwoman, and self-seeker!

After the century crossed over at halfway, the ten years that followed were interspersed with events of varying significance both within and outside the lives of Dalmia and his wives.

All of them trudged along uneasily, bravely bearing their own trials and tribulations. Dineshnandini had given birth to all her seven children and Saraswati had finished producing hers in equal strength. Dalmia's estate and family stood sharply divided. The two breakaway factions headed by Jaidayal and Shanti Prasad flourished as if they had been held back only by the link that joined them to him. Both Dineshnandini and Saraswati were separately involved in rearing their children to the best of their abilities, and with the divided attention of their father. Asha had been reduced to the status of a *persona non grata*.

Her children Dhruv Hari, Meera and Alka, as if to compensate in some way, continued to have a fine rapport with Jaidayal and Shanti Prasad's families, a privilege that was taken for granted by Saraswati's progeny but unfairly denied to Dineshnandini's.

Just before the end of '57 death struck Dalmia's home. His mother, who had been living in Benaras for many years, died at the ripe old age of ninety-four on the banks of the Ganga, and as per the Hindu belief, attained immediate salvation.

Like everyday she had risen at four that morning, woken up the pandas, gone down to the river for her bath, done a *parikrama* of a tulsi tree a hundred and eight times, and then returned to her home after her daily morning puja at the Shiv Mandir. She died peacefully in her home that had tall glass doors from where she could view the holy Ganga flowing all around her. It was two hours past midnight on 6 December. Only her daughter, her younger son Jaidayal and his wife Krishna were by her side when she breathed her last.

The news of her death was communicated to Delhi with appropriate promptness and her body was readied with the ceremonial rituals before the arrival of her older son the following morning.

As she lay in her mortal shell, wrapped in a white khadi dhoti on a bier decked with roses and marigolds, an air of calm descended on all those who sat around her. Incense sticks were lit up and placed all over the stark room and two pandas sat on grass *chatais*, reading hymns from the *Ramayana* loudly. A group of women who were part of her regular *kirtan-mandli* sat in one corner singing bhajans in soft chorus as they had done every morning and nothing seemed to have changed, The colour of the roses and marigolds, heaped around the body, sharply contrasted the deathly pallor of the uncovered face and the white of its shroud.

The entourage from Delhi was to arrive at dawn. A special chartered flight brought all the mourners and their relatives to bid her a final and ceremonial farewell. It included her son and daughters; Shanti Prasad, his wife and children; Saraswati and her daughter Ila; and Dineshnandini with a friend, Sitara, whom she had brought along for moral support. The hustle and bustle continued in the home though there was a distinct pall of gloom all around.

As the aircraft touched down at Benaras Airport, mixed feelings of nostalgia and pain overcame Dalmia. He was coming to the holy city where his mother had lived and died, where only a few years ago he had performed a *Sahasra Chandi Yagya* on the banks of the Ganga. The chanting of the *Maha Chandi Path* by the congregation of Brahman priests still charged him with a powerful energy. It was the city where he had wed his wife Dineshnandini in a secret ceremony eleven years ago. That day, as he landed, he felt a pain deep within.

His mother was dead. She had died as she had wanted to—in the lap of her *Ganga Ma* and attained nirvana. He wondered if she had suffered when her soul had left her body, but he knew that his mother would never suffer the cycles of birth and death again. The thought comforted him. He would give her a grand farewell.

Inside the home Dalmia approached his mother's body with a large wreath of roses, and then sank to the ground. His face was contorted with a pain that he rarely ever showed. He burst into loud uncontrollable sobs as he held his mother's tiny lifeless feet that death had painted with a pale yellow hue. His shoulders heaved up and down heavily as an endless stream of tears flowed from his eyes. Dineshnandini's heart went out to him, as her own gaze misted with the tears. She had an irresistible urge to get up and hold her husband in a tight embrace and comfort him. But such a public show of affection was taboo.

Since her childhood, death had terrified Dineshnandini. Nervously, she entered the hall where the body lay in rest, clutching Sitara's hand in a tight grasp. She knelt down reverently at her mother-in-law's feet, heaping rose petals on them. She held them with her hands as she bent forward to touch her forehead to the ground, after which she sat down, almost crouching into herself, trembling with fear. The cold marble floor felt rough and hard. The women, all in white, sat on one side and the men, also in white, sat on the other. Some stood huddled in a corner whispering inaudibly.

She sat paralysed, rooted to the spot. The grave austerity of the surroundings intimidated her. She had never seen such an emotional outburst from her husband before. His sobs continued for a long time till they were finally drowned in the rising chants of the hymns and the strains of the kirtan that grew louder as they filtered in from the two corners of the room with stereophonic effect.

Dineshnandini's eyes stayed glued to her husband's face. Then she looked at the woman lying on the floor, who had been dead for over eight hours. Her face was pale and swollen. Her forehead was marked conspicuously with a large round tika of sandal paste.

Her mind drifted to the day she had met Maji the first time.

She had been married only a few weeks, and had accompanied her husband to the Old Delhi Railway Station where Maji would halt briefly en route to Benaras.

She had suitably worn a red handloom silk sari from South India that had a wide, dark, intricately woven border. She had pulled her pallu down to the large round bindi on her forehead, that matched the colour of her sari.

As she entered the first class air-conditioned compartment of the train she saw a frail, formidable-looking woman wearing a plain white cotton sari and a full-sleeved blouse made of coarse khadi, sitting comfortably cross-legged on the berth. She wore no jewellery but around her shoulders was draped an oversized natural-coloured shawl of rough wool.

A round white tika of sandal paste marked the centre of her broad forehead. She had protruding brows and a large nose that Dineshnandini felt she had seen before. Her face was framed with two deep lines that stretched from the sides of her nostrils to the upturned corners of the widest mouth that Dineshnandini had ever seen. Her dark eyes had sunk deep into their bony sockets and they flickered like tiny bulbs from behind the round glasses that perched precariously on the bridge of her nose.

She bent down nervously to touch her feet.

'Who is this, Ramakisan?' she spoke in the familiar Marwari dialect that by now Dineshnandini had mastered. Her voice was husky but commanding. Dalmia bent over double, reverently placing his head on his mother's folded feet. She looked at him inquiringly. His sister, who sat quietly on the next berth, rose quickly and whispered something into her mother's ear. The smiling face froze into a grimace. It was as if she had visibly shrunk. Her frown-lines deepened and a furrow etched her smooth brows. Dineshnandini could remember it as if it were a moving sequence in an action-replay. The face of the woman sitting in front of her clouded with antipathy. Her wide smile transformed into a mean downward sneer.

Before anyone could react, her daughter answered crisply, 'This is Bhaiji's new bride, Maji.'

Dineshnandini did not raise her eyes as she felt her face being pushed up roughly by his mother. Her veined and bony fingers dug hard into her chin. The pallu of Dineshnandini's sari slipped back from her head revealing the broad line of sindoor that she had so meticulously smeared into the parting of her hair.

Then after a long and agonising silence she heard his mother speak. Her voice was heavy, more with anger and resignation than with curiosity, 'where are you from?' She stressed on the 'you' and then without even waiting for a reply fired her next salvo.

'How old are you?'

Dineshnandini answered in a barely audible voice without raising her eyes from the floor.

'Twenty-four,' she deliberately took a few years off hoping in vain to appease her.

She could see the fire flicker behind her spectacles as the frail lady stared at her.

'*Tere baap ne tujhe hamaare hi liye itta bada kar ke rakha tha kya* (Did your father bring you up to such an age only to dump you on us)?'

Those acid words seared right through Dineshnandini's heart like a sharp knife.

Fighting back the tears that welled up in her eyes she stood silently still looking at the floor. She had never felt so naked before.

The rhetoric continued...

'I don't like you, do you hear me?'

Sensing the palpable hostility, Dalmia hurriedly touched his mother's feet and led his new bride out of the train compartment. His face was deadpan.

His mother's voice trailed behind them as she shouted, 'Now you keep him happy and be happy yourself!'

Dineshnandini did not hear her as the shrill whistle sounded by the guard signalled the train to depart.

The sound of those words and the high-pitched whistle reverberated loudly in her ears as she was came back to reality in the room where the woman lay dead in front of her. It seemed as if all the mourners had heard those words as clearly as she had.

Dalmia sat at the feet of his mother's body for a long time. His own mind travelled back thirty years in time. He was in Calcutta. Maji had had one of her severe asthma attacks. Her asthma was chronic but had worsened. She could barely breathe. The *vaidya* attending to her had said she was really bad. Anything could happen to her that night. He remembered how he had run to the market and bought six yards of a red cotton fabric to wrap her in were she to die. He had even bought the bamboo and grass *arthi* on which to place her body for the cremation. He had kept it ready in the adjoining room, watching her painful breathing, mindlessly waiting for her last breath...

He never forgot the anguished look on her face when she had seen those things and the tears that had streamed down her cheeks and not stopped for long afterwards... and the pained words in between her gasps for breath... 'Can any mother expect this from her son?' she had rasped. Her tears had never stopped flowing for long afterwards…but eventually she had recovered.

Dineshnandini saw him rise laboriously as if in a hypnotic trance. He cupped his mother's cold lifeless cheeks in both his hands and wiped the tears that he could still feel fresh on her face after thirty years!

'Forgive me, Maji,' he sobbed inconsolably, 'I have caused you so much pain but you always loved me…and my beastly madness…please forgive me Maji. I am your child.'

He cried like a small infant confessing his crime in front of a forgiving mother to unburden his guilt-laden conscience in his concluding apology.

He felt dwarfed in front of her as she slept peacefully for the last time on a sheet full of red and orange flowers. The loud echoes of his mother's voice flooded his ears.

'Ram Ram Beta! Ram Ram! Bahut Baar Ram Ram! Bahut Baar Ram Ram!'

He put his shoulder tenderly to the bier and carried it down to the Manikarnika Ghat with his brother.

Amidst the loud chanting of Vedic mantras, with great reverence and solemnity he walked around the pyre that had been erected with huge sandalwood logs drenched in ghee, before lighting the mortal remains of his mother in his final send-off.

He stood staring pensively till the rising flames engulfed her. A strong draught the cold December air blew around him and pricked the pores of his skin. All he could hear in a rising crescendo was the sound of his mother's voice calling…

'*Ram Ram Beta! Ram Ram! Bahut Baar Ram Ram. Bahut Baar Ram Ram!*'

The acrid smell of burning flesh mixed with sandal fragrance singed his nostrils.

He would be back on the same banks of the holy Ganga with the body of his ailing wife Durga in less than twelve months.

Nothing in life happens by chance. We tend to create the same circumstances for ourselves over and over again till we have learned our lesson by repeated trial and error. The drill continues till we are perfect and thoroughly baptised. No matter how the choices present themselves to us, the outcome is almost always pre-ordained.

Dineshnandini could not bear to see her children cry. The thought of them wailing and screaming while being dragged off to nursery school mortified her. It was a weakness that was to be exploited by all those who desired to, including her own growing seven. To avoid that painful sight she founded a nursery school in her own sprawling backyard. She found an Anglo-Indian woman of thirty named Iris Flory who had teaching experience and who agreed to run the school for her. She also had a neatly worked out model for a primary coeducational institute.

Six roomy, unused garages and storerooms were converted into classrooms. A quaint cobblestone courtyard was fenced off for morning prayers and a playground of decent size was fitted with jungle gyms and slides for

the children to play in. A smart maroon and white uniform accentuated the animation that suddenly sprang up
around the building.

The school turned into a children's delight. It soon
grew to a strength of two hundred boys and girls. This,
for the time being, took care of the problem of sending
her own ones away and also generated for her a private
income that was sizeable.

Iris Flory, the Principal, doubled as the children's
governess and took care of their lessons after school hours.
She helped to shop for their daily requirements, organise
their birthday parties, take them on picnics and oversee
all the activities that were organised to keep them occupied. Every Christmas she set up a tall tree in her own
home, decorated with brightly coloured bonbons and
streamers, and gave each child a beautifully wrapped little
gift to take home. She also taught them how to sit at the
table, use knives and forks, speak correct English, and
groomed them into ladies and gentlemen with a fashionably Anglicised finesse. The children just adored her.

Everything ran as smoothly as it could. After some
time Dalmia in his generosity gifted a small van to the
school so that transport could be provided for the children
at a nominal cost. A year later he gave them two more
slightly bigger ones. The strength of the teaching staff and
clerical workers swelled and within a few years, the school
was running packed classes upto the fifth grade.

It was Iris Flory who first discovered that both Padma
and Babu were lagging behind in their class. Padma
seemed to have some difficulty in learning her lessons.

Whatever she learned by rote she could recite perfectly, but when it came to examinations she just would not write. Iris Flory forever complained that Padma was bone-lazy. No one suspected that there could have been a deeper underlying problem. She trudged along from class to class, year after year with the help of her teacher and a shove from her mother who made sure she was promoted to the next grade each time.

After years of intensive physiotherapy and months of plaster encasing, Babu's club-feet had reached a near-normal condition. No residual effect of his congenital deformity was visible except that the soles of his feet had disproportionately high arches and his shoes had to be fitted with specially designed insoles for support. He could not run very fast but most people attributed that to his obesity.

Babu's lessons were a different story altogether. Every afternoon at study time, he sat staring at Teacher Flory, noisily chewing gum. The study room had a wide, low, eight-seater table with matching cane and wood chairs, on which all seven sat with Teacher Flory at the head. Each time she asked Babu a question he waited till one of the others would reply—always out of turn. Exasperated she would throw the rest of them out of the room but Babu just would not learn. He had mastered the technique. He only had to linger on and pretend to think—when pat came the reply from one of the others. The result: Laxmana knew at one-and-a-half all the alphabets and the count of one to hundred that Babu took more than four years to master. This prepared the ground for the need of another tutor's entry into *Teen Number.*

Raj Narain, a postgraduate in Mathematics, was twenty-three years old. The eldest in a family of a widowed mother, two younger brothers and two sisters who were under eighteen, he was studying for a Law degree. His brother was employed as an accounts clerk in a cement agency owned by Dineshnandini's brothers in Agra.

Raj Narain needed a job and he fit the requirement of a Mathematics tutor for the children of *Teen Number*. He accepted the post for a salary of one hundred and fifty rupees without any fuss, because food and accommodation were free, and his work would leave him enough time to pursue his studies alongside.

At the time that Raj Narain stepped into the household, things were bad. The Bharat Insurance Company trial which had been carrying on for nearly six years was coming to an end. The dismal outcome was a foregone conclusion. Dineshnandini still grieved the loss of her mother who had died a few years ago due to cardiac failure. The day-to-day problems of running the school was becoming difficult for her. There was a certain discrepancy in the accounts that she could not understand. Babu and Padma's studies were a source of constant distress to her. The running of the home was far from satisfactory. Financial problems for Dalmia had escalated due to the demands of the long-drawn-out lawsuit. The cost of running three homes and vast business overheads was exorbitant. The brunt of this was being felt by all. His disenchantment with Dineshnandini and her own disillusionment with him were a stark reality.

That is when Raj Narain arrived. Five foot eleven inches tall, he had an athletic body and a slight Bombay-filmstar-like manner. He spoke good Hindi and mildly accented English. His almond-shaped eyes and acned skin imparted to him an earnest, soulful and boyish look. He wore clothes that were a take-off from the attire of a popular movie star of the '60s. On request he spouted Hindi film songs of the same era in a reasonably tuneful voice, without reservation. His spanking new gramophone that had to be wound up to play back 78 rpm records blared music all day from his room in the outhouse. His room overlooked a garden across which you could see a long tin cowshed that housed eight milch cows and buffaloes which were an essential feature of all the Dalmia homes.

Raj Narain had a way with the children because he could connect, and he was lapped up by all seven of them, including Padma who was usually shy with strangers. He could sing, dance, play the guitar, paint, drive, teach sums and was interesting enough for them to want to be in his company all the time. Dalmia too, was touched by the sincerity and devotion he showed. Raj Narain soon took over the nightly routine of singing verses from the *Ramayana* to Dalmia as he slept, a bed-time habit that he had maintained for many years. The tune in which he sang those verses parodied a popular number from a Dev Anand film of those days. The seven often stood hiding behind the door, conducting an invisible orchestra, or giggling and making funny faces in an attempt to make him laugh.

Dalmia administered his morning office from his bedroom, where he lay bare-bodied, wearing only his loincloth on a thick mattress spread on the floor, lined with white cotton sheets. Two men sat on either side of him massaging him with generous amounts of sesame oil, mechanically synchronised as if they were rowing a boat—an exercise that lasted for over two hours. His two phones lay on either side, and a stream of officers and staff members carried on their job of daily reporting, consulting and discussing with him as if he were sitting at the head of an austere and formal conference table. Even high dignitaries and visitors were ushered into the same massage-room nonchalantly, where he received them, half-clad, reclining and dripping with oodles of oil, with aplomb. Raj Narain sometimes substituted for the masseur if the latter was on leave, or at times even when he was not.

Raj Narain made his presence felt everywhere. He fixed the wooden doors and mended the fuse. He painted the school fence in two days single-handedly without any fuss. He found a contact with the transport authorities and obtained a road-worthy certificate for the school buses—something that was both mandatory and extremely difficult. He drove the children wherever they needed to go and chaperoned them to movies and other outdoor trips. He picked up imported and almost new electronic goods, alongwith a truckload of furniture from an auction at the American Embassy at incredible prices. He located a wholesale fruit and vegetable market that slashed the entire month's expenditure budget by half. He was everywhere and because he was handy he became indispensable. Not surprisingly, Dineshnandini's dependence on him grew. He was a super-efficient household manager and her most reliable troubleshooter.

Raj Narain, on his part, worshipped her like a goddess. He followed her around in body and soul as if he were her shadow, his own routine entirely concurring with hers. If she ate, he ate. If she fasted, he fasted too. Only when she slept did he retire to his room. His actions matched her moods in perfect synchrony.

In May the final judgement from the Supreme Court in the Bharat Insurance Company trial was pronounced, and Dalmia was awarded an imprisonment sentence for two years that entailed a confinement in the Tihar Jail. Life came to a grinding halt for Dineshnandini. She was left feeling defeated and forlorn, to fend for herself and her seven, none of whom had crossed their eighteen-year mark into adulthood. Just before that, her father, who had been living in Bombay had taken seriously ill, and nervous as she was about facing death and disease she had brought him to convalesce at her home in Delhi. Raj Narain was immediately deputed to nurse and tend him which he did to perfection effortlessly.

Dineshnandini's emotional dependence on him grew to pathological proportions. As she sank deep into the sea of mourning that engulfed her, she thrust the same solemnity onto her young seven, whom she believed ought to respect the absence of their father with similar despondency. They could only meet him once a week on Saturdays in Tihar Jail, but for them it was an irritating and unnecessary restriction. In any case they had never known their father to be with them all the time. Her hard stand suspended all their enjoyment-related activities indefinitely, with the result that no parties, picnics, movies nor visits to friends were allowed and even laughing loudly was looked upon as a grave irreverence.

A mantle of gloom descended heavily on their shoulders. They could not, for the life of them, comprehend their mother's inbuilt and chronic romanticism of melancholia that had turned her into a suffering tragedy queen. It portrayed the deep-rooted masochism that had never left her since her childhood. She wallowed in her misfortune only trying to think of ways and means of how to get her husband out of jail before the two long years elapsed.

By now the school was fraught with its own set of problems. One of the buses had met with a serious accident in which luckily there had been no casualties but twenty-three children had been injured, five of them seriously. Dineshnandini's nerves were frayed and she was under pressure from Dalmia to wind it up. That brought into focus another crucial problem. The seven children needed to be admitted into other schools and true to form, Raj Narain moved heaven and earth to meet the challenge. With his dogged perseverance, and at the risk of annoying their father, he first managed to get Laxmana into Mater Dei Convent where Saraswati's daughter

Vasudha, who was a few months older than her, studied. A little later, both Neelima and Dolly were admitted to the highly acclaimed and much coveted Convent of Jesus and Mary School which was the *alma mater* of Yashodhara and Sheela, Saraswati's other two daughters. This was in violation of Dalmia's unwritten diktat that the children of one wife could not come in close contact with those of another. Dineshnandini had no idea that this would spark off another controversy a year later, when Yashodhara would be detained in her eight grade due to poor performance in her examinations, and Dineshnandini would get the blame for orchestrating a vicious act of vendetta against Saraswati.

Padma was packed off to a reputed and established boarding school in Jaipur under the management of the Royal Trust of Maharani Gayatri Devi, where her mother erroneously thought she would grow up and become independent. The three boys also secured seats in the prestigious Modern School after an interim gap of six months. For the moment all her problems were taken care of and she felt comforted and secure. Raj Narain, without doubt, was the most unfailing and trustworthy Man Friday she could have found.

Life became a little easier for the seven as the days passed and the initial austerity accompanying their father's imprisonment started to fade. They often played in the garden that faced Raj Narain's room, watching him sit theatrically by his window, listening to him singing songs from box-office hits or karaoking the loud numbers that belted out of his HMV gramophone. They flocked to his room whenever they got the chance, and delighted in the quaint, inexpensive collectibles he meticulously displayed on a teak-wood cabinet that he had assembled with his amateur carpentry skills.

This obvious shift in power equations set off another chain reaction. The other staff members became covertly hostile to Raj Narain's extraneous authority. The newcomer had scuttled their plans by blocking the sources of all surreptitious pilfering. Under his strict vigil the cook Dhannalal could no longer siphon out his sly earnings from the daily fruit and vegetables purchase. Petrol expenses dropped considerably. No one could demand undue overheads for contingencies or wear and tear. Even the irregularities in the school accounts were detected and set right in good time.

The household manager Bharadwaj and the PBX telephone operator Ram Swarup suddenly found themselves divested of all their power and their hitherto fringe skimmings. Raj Narain was the sole decision-maker and final authority on who went where and what was to be spent on whom. This gave Dineshnandini a sense of control that made her atypically bold and, at times, even rash. She exercised her right but could not handle the accompanying responsibility that followed. She tasted the freedom that confidence brings after a long period of self-imposed repression. Throwing all caution to the wind, she made Raj Narain accompany her like a loyal ADC wherever she went, including the Tihar Jail every Saturday. He drove her in the school van along with the seven children and the painstakingly cooked food that she carried for her husband.

This was the chance that all the others had been waiting for and Dineshnandini handed it to them unsuspectingly and foolishly on a platter. Her adversaries not least of whom were Saraswati's cheering-squad and Raj Narain's hate-brigade, closed in on her like a pack of hungry wolves. She was flung deep into a thick web of conspiracy and intrigue that was to leave her badly tarnished and permanently alienated from her antagonised and incarcerated husband.

It had the perfect ingredients of a racy potboiler!

Meanwhile, owing to poor living conditions, continuously failing health and an ardent appeal to the authorities, Dalmia secured an order by which he was shifted from Tihar Jail to a small nurse station near the emergency ward of Irwin Hospital. It had been converted into a makeshift cell.

His 8 x 10 x 10 feet room was divided by a partition made of ply board, so that he could have a hospital bed on one side and four cane chairs for visitors on the other. His food that came from *Teen Number* was, as earlier, cooked by Dineshnandini, since she had perfected the art of putting together tasty and varied recipes made from products of milk or vegetables and fruit, in the eleven years that he had given up eating cereals for the cause of anti-cow slaughter.

The small area near his bed had a narrow *takht* that the attendant who stayed the night, slept on. This was to be used by Dineshnandini or Saraswati when they were on duty every alternate night. On the wall on one side of the inner room was placed a gold-framed picture of

Ma Durga in front of which Dalmia did his daily puja, lighting an oil-lamp with extreme reverence and sincerity. Outside the room four policemen from the Delhi Armed Constabulary sat on vigil, sticking out incongruously in the unclean hospital corridor that reeked of a strong disinfectant so characteristic of government hospitals. Red stains of chewed paan and tobacco could be seen splattered on the walls here and there and half-smoked cigarette and bidi butts littered the place as if they were part of the decor. A misleading 'NO VISITORS ALLOWED' sign hung outside on the knob of the door that led into the room. The corridor was a passage for the hundreds of patients with all kinds of infectious diseases, to pass through. Adjoining it was a small open courtyard where some people freely defecated and urinated, causing an unbearable stench to permeate the courtyard which became the breeding ground for millions of flies and mosquitoes.

Dalmia bore it heroically without fuss. After all, the prison sentence was a welcome opportunity to rid himself of his karmic burden of many lifetimes, and he imagined that he was in a fast-forward mode. He had read out a touching speech to his grieving wives on the day he had left, telling them that he was embarking on a pilgrimage of soul-cleansing and penitence. His nerves of steel had never been more transparent and the words were in keeping with his spirit of undaunted fearlessness and in a sense, his cold detachment from all earthly things.

At the hospital life became considerably easier for Dalmia and marginally better for his family. The routine of sending him food still remained part of Dineshnandini's duty and by that analogy, made her the more elevated of the two wives. It allowed access for the office staff to consult with and apprise him of the developments at work. It also gave an opportunity for the servants of the two homes who carried food and other conveniences to the hospital, to meet with him more freely.

Ram Dev, a personal valet of old standing from *Nau Number,* took charge of looking after all his personal needs along with Dewan Singh and Dhannalal, the bearer and the cook, who were employed by *Teen Number* to serve him in between. This opened a flow of information and people and enabled a direct interaction between him and the staff without the interference or knowledge of Dineshnandini, who only arrived every evening with his dinner and stayed on alternate nights attending to the high-profile prisoner.

Meanwhile, unbeknown to her, another sordid tale of intrigue was brewing right under her nose. Raj Narain with his extra-constitutional powers had turned into everyone's pet hate. They despised him for his proximity to and the power he held over her. The only one who stood steadfastly by her side was her loyal friend-turned-personal-secretary Sitara Devi, who had earlier accompanied her to Benaras for her mother-in-law's funeral. Sitara was a young childless widow who had survived a sordid tale of conspiracy within her marriage. Her husband had been the victim of a brutal homicide in a murky and complicated property dispute. Without claiming anything, she had returned to her parents who had sent her to work in a charity Ayurveda clinic quite near her home in Chandni Chowk. It was here that Dineshnandini had first met her. Sitara's family comprised novice jewellers who were striving to make it big. Seeing this as a good opportunity to climb socially, they allowed her to move into Dineshnandini's home to live as her personal assistant and full-time companion. In a sense Dineshnandini adopted her. Her morbid fear of living alone was temporarily allayed because Sitara took over the role of her assistant and she was educated enough to take her calls, conduct her visitors and look after all her personal needs. Since Dineshnandini was a fussy eater, Sitara even took charge of her meals and very often cooked them herself.

In the narrow and crowded lanes of Old Delhi quite close to where Sitara lived, another woman was also trying to climb the social ladder, though not quite in the same way.

She was known within the local circles to be a proven clairvoyant who possessed an uncanny insight into past lives. This had been authenticated by a surprisingly factual revelation of her own previous life that was testified by some people whom she claimed had been her family members in her previous birth.

Shanti Devi was a short, plump, boxish-looking woman of thirty-five years. She was single and her antecedents vague. Her round moon-face had a prominent and hairy double chin and was pigmented around her forehead. Her small beady eyes looked even smaller behind a pair of spectacles that resembled a giant moth with pointed wings sitting on her nose. She wore garish red lipstick and equally garish saris of artificial silk that rustled inelegantly as she walked. She exuded a stale and fishy odour when she opened her mouth to speak in her loud and harsh voice that had a distinct Old Delhi accent.

Dineshnandini met her by chance. Given her own fascination for mystics and seers, she fell headlong into the clutches of this wily con woman. Weak and vulnerable as she was, her search for someone who could ease the undefined turmoil that had set in deep within her mind, particularly after the imprisonment of her husband, had ended. Directed by Shanti Devi, she embarked on a mindless course of quick-fix remedies to precipitate his release from jail. A hundred caged parrots were purchased from illegal bird-sellers who sat outside the Jama Masjid, and set free every Saturday. She kneaded thousands of small balls of *jau* flour into which she rolled tiny square pieces of paper inscribed with the word *Ram* in red ink, to feed to the fish in the Jamuna. Shanti Devi had promised that these acts would catalyse the early release of her husband from jail and Dineshnandini performed them with absolute sincerity and blind conviction.

As wheels turned within wheels other acts of the drama unfolded. Both Sitara and Raj Narain began to resent the trespassing of the sinister Shanti Devi into the secluded territory of *Teen Number*. It was evident to them that Dineshnandini was totally taken in by the fraud and even though she did every little thing according to Shanti Devi's decree, no reprieve seemed forthcoming. Sitara and Raj Narain faithfully accompanied her on her crazy jaunts but their resentment mounted. Shanti Devi's newly acquired status made her arrogant and pompous, and this only aggravated their hostility.

The picture, as it emerged, was of Dineshnandini in the centre, surrounded by her close but not mutually harmonious inner-circle that consisted of Shanti Devi, Sitara and Man Friday, Raj Narain. Outside them was the bigger and more vicious circle that included Dhannalal the cook, Bharadwaj the household manager, Niranjan Singh the driver, Dewan Singh the bearer, and to some extent the nurse-turned-maid Sunder Bai. On the periphery were the two chowkidars, two gardeners and strangely, Iris Flory!

The die was caste and a calamity just waited to happen!

On a cold winter Saturday evening, a heavy mist hung low in the air, partially impairing visibility. Dineshnandini was to be driven by Raj Narain in her blue Chrysler to an ancient Hanuman Temple situated on the banks of the Jamuna near Kashmere Gate in Old Delhi. It was a weekly ritual she followed after someone had told her that the temple-deity had miraculous powers and granted the wishes of all those who worshipped it. She sat brooding quietly, in the back seat, when she heard the door on the other side click open. She saw the intimidating frame of Shanti Devi who slipped into the car, close beside her. Shanti Devi's appearance annoyed her. Of late she had sensed that Shanti Devi always held her hands tight while speaking to her and was unnecessarily physical whenever she got the chance. Dineshnandini fidgeted nervously trying to avoid the stale smell from her hot breath as she greeted her. Shanti Devi's wide smile showed all her decaying and yellowed teeth.

She rolled down the glass window to allow some fresh air into the car. The familiar fishy odour permeating the car nauseated her. She wished she had the courage to ask Shanti Devi not to accompany them. The car rolled out and as it picked up speed, the sound of the engine drowned her thoughts. She felt something touch the side of her arm and she heard Shanti Devi's voice very close near her ear.

'Do you know Baisahab, I want to tell you something. You are always lost in your own thoughts and you look so sad. Do not worry. Everything will be okay for you. Sethji will be back next month. Our pujas have ensured that. But what I want to tell you is that you need not worry about anything. You have me with you. I'll tell you a secret—keep it to yourself...'

Shanti's hand trailed deliberately down Dineshnandini's back and using the other hand, she pulled up her palm casually, brushing against her breast. Squinting at her palm from behind her glasses, she said,

'*Dekhiye,* it's all written here, and I can clearly see it. I was your husband some lifetimes ago. You were my wife.'

The car, which was moving at a high speed, suddenly swerved to the left to avoid another car that was trying to overtake it. Shanti Devi was flung roughly to the opposite side, her sentence cut short midway.

'What are you doing, you fool?' she shouted at Raj Narain. 'Why don't you watch where you are going? You have been looking back at us in the rear-view mirror all this while. You could have killed us! Who are you looking at *bewaquoof?*'

Raj Narain shot back at her spouting anger and venom, 'Not at you woman, certainly not. Who would want to look at your ugly face!'

Shanti cursed inaudibly under her breath smarting with the insult but was silenced by the rude snub.

Dineshnandini witnessed the whole drama in stunned silence. She was greatly disconcerted. She despised the way Shanti Devi touched her body on the slightest pretext and the stench was getting unbearable. She wanted to push her out of the car that instant, but prudence and fear got the better of her. She would talk about it to Raj Narain and Sitara later. The sinister woman petrified her!

In an age where sexuality was a highly puritanical and extremely private affair, and lesbianism rarely acknowledged in civilised circles, it took some time for Dineshnandini to understand that Shanti Devi's conduct was unquestionably prurient and perverse.

The undercurrents of Shanti Devi's sexual overtures were becoming stronger as she got closer to Dineshnandini mistaking her reticence for manoeuvrability. By now Dineshnandini was also frustrated by her failed attempts to secure the early release of her husband. She definitely wanted to rid herself of this rude and verbose intrusion into her privacy or whatever was left of it.

Both Raj Narain and Sitara offered to assist her. Raj Narain characteristically swore he would bodily throw her out of the home the next time she tried to enter it.

More temperately Sitara took it upon herself not to let Shanti Devi meet her suffering and tormented mistress by telling her that her mistress was indisposed and did not want any visitors.

Later as Dineshnandini sat in her room waiting in nervous anticipation for the intruder, the events that had transpired some days ago came back to her.

It had been a long day and she was tired.

Sunder Bai as usual was in her place at the foot of her bed pressing her legs. Her rough and heavy hands moved up and down kneading the soles of her feet. She felt drowsy and the pressure relieved her aching and weary limbs. The hands moved rhythmically up and down from her knees to her ankles. Then she felt them on her knees…lingering there just a wee bit longer than they ought. She could hear the strains of a song playing in the distance. It lulled her to sleep the hands kept kneading and massaging her legs. She felt like telling Sunder Bai to go…to leave her and go, but a dull inertia had overtaken her…and then the hand brushed the inside of her thigh…She held back her breath…She felt it again…not knowing how to tell her to stop…She felt afraid. The hand slid up again brushing the fold of her groin. The fingers lightly trailed over her pubis for a fleeting second. She jumped up in a jerk and yanked the edge of her sari that had climbed upto her knees down to her toes. She saw her two sons sleeping undisturbed on either side of her. Instead of Sunder Bai, Shanti Devi stared into her face and even in the diffused light of the bedroom lamp she could see her yellowed teeth through her lips, parted in a fixed smile.

'Got to sleep, Baisahab, Sunder Bai has gone to have her dinner. I'll press your legs for you. I've sent her off. You should not allow your children to sleep in your bed. It is not good for them.' Dineshnandini angrily shoved off her hand and raced to open the bathroom door. She closed it behind her and locked the latch tightly as if she were afraid the woman would follow her in. She could still near her muffled voice through the closed door.

'If you are afraid of the dark, I can sleep near you...'

She plugged both her ears with her index fingers to block out the sound of Shanti Devi's words. She felt sick. Without taking off her clothes she entered the shower-cabin. She turned the knob fully onto high heat. The sharp, steaming, shrapnels of water came gushing out, stinging her from head to toe. She let the water fall on her body till it burned. Then she scrubbed herself savagely with the loofah that lay near her soap-dish. Again and again she scrubbed trying to wash out the invisible stains of the fiendish outrage that had been committed on her. After a long time she turned off the water feeling slightly eased but not entirely cleansed. When she came back to her room, the faint, stale and fishy odour was still there but Shanti Devi had gone.

Loud arguing voices from outside brought her back to the present. She could hear Shanti Devi and Raj Narain loudly hurling obscenities at each other. Sitara's softer voice was trying to moderate. Dineshnandini trembled at the morbid prospect of facing the evil woman again. She ran into the bathroom to lock herself in and the sounds out. When the sounds finally died down she stepped out diffidently. She sat down only when Sitara entered her room to inform her that Shanti Devi had been turned out and would never try to come back.

The scorned Shanti Devi left cursing and shouting, swearing to avenge the insult. The inferno of unrequited lust and the humiliation was not to die down quite so easily!

The two self-appointed bodyguards were triumphant, erroneously believing that the transgressor had been rendered powerless and that they were finally at peace.

The servants of any household constitute an amorphous body that has the ability to infiltrate into and seep out of people's lives, becoming thereby the most dangerous carriers of information. Shanti Devi, the erstwhile member of Dineshnandini's inner circle and in a sense, one of her dismissed staff, was licking her wounds. Also raging with anger and humiliation was the cook Dhannalal who harboured a simmering need for revenge. Dhannalal had been brought up by Dineshnandini's mother since he had been a boy of ten in Udaipur. He had mastered Rajasthani cooking while he was in her care. When he came to *Teen Number* he was a slightly stooped weather-beaten fifty-eight-year-old man, seasoned and mature enough to handle the responsibility of a quality cook who would be loyal to her. He had abnormally thickset brows, small eyes, a bulbous nose and a pitted and scarred face. A large ugly mole high on his cheek bobbed menacingly up and down when he spoke. His uneven teeth showed the tell-tale signs of tobacco abuse. He spoke in his Mewari dialect in a voice that sounded like a piece of metal being rubbed with sandpaper. He had a deceptive manner of bending over from his waist right down to the floor with folded hands which was reminiscent of the feudal ages. He was rumoured to have eloped with a nubile fourteen-year-old girl who died in childbirth, leaving behind a daughter.

The existent staff of *Teen Number* where he took up the job of head *maharaj* had over thirty members. They soon constituted his personal fiefdom and he rose to the top of the hierarchy ranking only below Bharadwaj—the household manager. Dhannalal was put in charge of the daily purchases for the kitchen, and as his personal assets swelled from the unnoticed pilferings, the comforts grew in proportion. In his quarters, quite in glaring contrast with the others, was a new three-band transistor, a wooden double-bed and a bright framed picture of his dead wife adorning the wall near the window with a garland of bright plastic flowers around it.

In the cobbled courtyard behind the kitchen that did not form part of the main home, he conducted his cabinet till the late hours of the night, gossiping and plotting against all the potential threats to his supremacy.

Among those in regular attendance were Dewan Singh, Sunder Bai, Niranjan Singh and occasionally Bharadwaj, Kali Charan the *mali* and the Gurkha chowki-dar for chance entertainment or juicy leftovers from his cooking. Dhannalal wielded an invisible power. The staff feared him and he never let them forget that he was in total control. Like most men who have access to power and the resultant capacity to exploit it, he resented his inability to bring Sitara into his ambit. She enticed him—always standing by *Sethani's* side, and it irked him to see the control she had over the latter's purse. The young and widowed Sitara became his personal encumbrance and the object of his unfading carnality and criminal lust. His depravity and base animal instinct was playing up again, reinforced by her presence. He eyed her hungrily as she scurried back and forth from the kitchen doing her regular duties. He leched at her while she helped to cook meals that were being sent to the hospital. At times he furtively stood outside the bathroom door, craning his neck, peeping in through the crack in the window to catch a glimpse of her bathing. All this did not go unnoticed by Sitara, but silenced by good breeding and a sense of embarrassment, she said nothing to anyone.

One late evening while she was walking out of the kitchen on the secluded vine-covered, red sandstone path that led to the main home, she saw Dhannalal loom large in front of her, blocking her path with his hands stretched out wide. She stumbled backwards to avoid being touched by him. She looked around dumbfounded, not knowing what to do. There was no one in sight. The servants had retired to their respective quarters after the day's work. She moved helplessly away from his outstretched arms but he did not budge. In fact, he moved closer as if to pin her down in his embrace.

She mustered up all her strength and roughly pushed him aside. 'Let me go,' she said angrily, 'What do you want?'

Without saying anything, he pulled out a neatly folded piece of paper and thrust it into her palm. He exuded a distinct kitchen smell mixed with his own stale body odour.

'I'll let you go, but I have to tell you this. Please read my letter—it says it all. You have driven me mad and are always in my thoughts. I cannot live without you, please believe me…'

Furious with his audacity and blinded by tears of rage that welled up in her eyes, Sitara crushed the paper into her tightly closed fist and ran into the home. She was gripped by an icy chill. What if someone had seen them standing like that in the dark. How dare he outrage her modesty. She stormed into Dineshnandini's room and fell into a heap on the floor at the foot of the chair where she sat. She felt vulnerable and defiled. Her stomach knotted up till it hurt. She wanted to smash that scoundrel's face to pulp, but all she could do was stare at her fist holding the crumpled paper till she poured out the details of her encounter all in one breath to the shocked and bewildered the lady of the house. After much thought and deliberation, they decided to destroy the note and say nothing to the perpetrator of the crime.

Emboldened by the absence of a reaction from the lady of the house, Dhannalal retained his job and position and got away scot-free.

Now he had the opportunity with Shanti Devi to forge together the nexus that would engineer the complete destruction of Sitara, Raj Narain and their mentor Dineshnandini. He had Sethji's ear and all he needed to do was frame the unsuspecting and weakened trio.

Just outside Dineshnandini's bedroom was a small attached utility room which led into the children's study. It was here that Sunder Bai and Dewan Singh sat every night to set out the ironed school uniforms and polish the shoes for the children. The room had a foldable ironing board in one corner and a wall cupboard that was stocked with shoe polish and other items of use. Sunder Bai would sit cross-legged on the chatai in the 'green room', a name it had acquired owing to its green-coloured walls, carefully polishing the canvas shoes with white liquid chalk. Dewan Singh did the boys' black leather ones with Cherry Blossom boot polish from a small, flat round tin that had a smiling joker on its cover. The exercise usually lasted an hour as the two gossiped and recounted the day's events to each other!

The door that led into the master bedroom afforded a full view of the occupant Dineshnandini, sitting most often on her wing-chair by the fireplace reading intently by the light of the tall pedestal lamp that illumined her from over her shoulder. Raj Narain could be spotted frequently standing at ease, leaning against the wall, listening attentively to her lectures. Sometimes Sitara sat pressing her legs, while she lay on her bed orating her long-winded speeches for the benefit of both. One wall of the room was lined with a cabinet that was filled with books and some odd curios here and there.

One uneventful evening as darkness crept up slowly enveloping everything in its mysterious eerie mantle, and all the inhabitants with the exception of Sunder Bai and Dewan Singh had retired for the day, Raj Narain stood in Dineshnandini's room discussing the following morning's routine. All of a sudden the home was plunged into total darkness as the lights went out due to an apparent power failure or a blown fuse. Dewan Singh rose from the 'green-room', groping his way in the dark. Holding the walls, he inched his way into the door leading to the master bedroom to reach for the candle stand on the mantel shelf. Dineshnandini had also risen in the confusion, but even before she took a few steps, she tripped on the telephone wire and fell forward with her arms outstretched, trying to cushion her fall. Hearing her shout for help Raj Narain rushed forward to try to prevent her from falling but she had already landed hard on her knees that had hit the ground. Raj Narain held her arms trying to hoist her up onto the bed, but she could not move as the unbearable pain from her left knee shot right down to her ankle. She sat groaning on the floor while Raj Narain tried again to pull her up, holding her waist with both his hands. When the lights came on thirty seconds had elapsed. She saw Dewan Singh frozen in the doorway watching them fixedly as if he had caught a pupil cheating inside an examination hall red-handed. He spun around and left the room with his head lowered shame-facedly. Sunder Bai sat outside on the floor polishing the shoes as usual, as if nothing had happened.

Dineshnandini was in agony. The pain from her badly swollen knee felt as though hot molten metal had been poured into it. Raj Narain brought an ice-pack from somewhere and placed it on her inflamed joint to ease the pain. She prised herself up onto the bed with some help and lay down on it staring vacuously at the ceiling. She would need an X-Ray in the morning. She hoped there was no broken bone for that would incapacitate her for long. Sleep did not come to her even though she shut her eyes. She was aware of Raj Narain turning the lights off and slowly tip-toeing out of the room. The throbbing pain kept her awake all night.

Out in the courtyard behind the kitchen, a very crucial meeting had been convened. Summoned by Dewan Singh, Sunder Bai, Dhannalal and Bharadwaj assembled to discuss the delectable morsel of gossip that had fallen their way perchance. It would be carried to the incarcerated Master of the house with the necessary embellishments the next day. This was to be the first in a series of proofs that were being accumulated to establish an undeniable, indisputable case of adultery. Dhannalal wrote out a detailed and exaggerated first information report dictated by Dewan Singh which was signed by the other three in earnest.

The following morning after the requisite X-Rays and tests were completed, it was concluded that there had been no fracture on Dineshnandini's knee, but there was a badly torn ligament that would take at least six weeks to heal. She was prescribed the usual anti-inflammatory painkillers, and rest. Heat from an infra-red lamp was to be administered daily to encourage early repair. Expectedly Raj Narain assumed the duty of acquiring the lamp and giving the therapy with the requisite precaution and care.

Sexuality is not merely an expression of the genitals; it suffuses the body and takes on varied and covert forms of expression. Strictly speaking, behaviour can only be termed sexual when there is an interchange of energy between two living beings regardless of their gender.

A relationship that is devoid of an overt physical contact and determined by only a constant flow of emotional energy between two minds can also, strictly speaking, be termed as sexual. In most instances such equations will be condemned in the eyes of parochial judges as sinful.

In a sense the relationship that existed between Dineshnandini and Raj Narain when viewed narrow-mindedly from the periphery, was in defiance of the sanctity of a marriage. More so, to a man who was crossing over from his sixties onto the threshold of the debilitating seventies, and who was also her husband. Bred in an illiberal and unforgiving society where caressing one's own child or embracing one's own sibling was frowned upon, though incestuous liaisons were secretly rampant, it was not surprising that Dalmia was convinced that his wife was having a brazen and illicit affair with a man who was twenty years younger than her. Fuelled by the stories being fed to him by her household staff and a vindictive Shanti Devi, he felt cheated and incensed. The lofty precedents set by his *pativrata* wives Narbada and Durga made Dineshnandini appear loathsome and depraved and he decided that she was indeed worthy of being shunned without any delay. He ordered that every action of hers be monitored by his spies who constituted almost all her personal staff, for extra cash bonuses that were paid to them for this purpose apart from their fixed salaries. Encouraged by this they conferred from time to time with their Master to discuss the progress made in the collection of evidence that would finally nail her down.

Unbeknown to him they even engineered a grisly plot to poison the food being cooked by her to establish the intent on her part to murder him. The plan was executed soon enough and smoothly.

Dineshnandini had not been to the hospital for over a week because of her sprained knee and the doctor's advice. Unsuspectingly, when she arrived at the hospital after a gap of seven days having resumed her movements, she noticed an unnerving calm outside the room. The policemen on duty parted without greeting her as she approached and let her in. Inside too, she sensed an unnatural air of solemnity. Her husband slept on his bed with his face to the wall and Ram Dev stood near his pillow with his head bent down in serious contemplation. Her heart lurched up into her mouth. The crepe bandage she wore felt tight and constricting on her aching knee. She looked at Ram Dev questioningly. Through a half-opened mouth he whispered, '*Seth Saab* is not feeling well since he ate his food yesterday. He was unconscious for more than twelve hours. Maji was very worried so she called the doctor. He has done some blood tests but the reports have not come. Maji has said that no one should be allowed to disturb him, and he will not eat any food.

Something happened to him as soon as he ate the rasgullas that came from *Teen Number*...'

Dineshnandini dropped heavily onto the settee near his bed and the *Bhagwad Gita* she carried in her hand fell to the floor with a noisy thud. She held her husband's feet in her customary greeting—with trembling hands. They felt ice-cold. She watched him turn around painfully as he tried to speak, roused by her touch. '*Kya tha tere khane mein...kya dala tha tune....itti garam cheez kya thi...baarah ghante behosh rahe hum...kyoon Ram Dev...batah isko...kaise sar ghoom raha thaa hamaara....nurse nurse ko dek kar man chalta thaa....bolti kyoon nahin...kya thaa khaane mein* (What was there in your food...what did you put in it...what was that hot substance...I was unconscious for twelve hours...why Ram Dev...tell her...how my head was spinning...even the sight of the nurses is arousing me...why don't you say something...what was there in the food)?'

The words kept coming in broken sentences but the import was clear to her. She felt the ceiling of the room turn in fast-moving concentric circles and the ground from under her feet give way. She rose from her place, steadied herself against the wall, and in measured steps limped out of the room into the messy and stinking corridor for the last time. She would never return to the hospital or see her husband till he completed his term and came to *Teen Number* in the August of '64, an angry, bitter and unforgiving man. A macabre crime that she could not have even conceived of had been executed. The proof had been put together perfectly; the evidence was indisputable; the witnesses were competent to stand trial; the accused and her accomplice had been caught red-handed, and the motive had been clearly established. It was an open and shut case that left very little scope for clemency of any kind. The frame-up was complete!

In the days that followed, an angry and aged man—the victim of a brutal treachery—sat on his hospital bed painstakingly studying a dossier that contained over thirty documents. In it was a note written in Dhannalal's hand that had been signed alongside by Sunder Bai and Dewan Singh. There was a detailed record of the incoming and outgoing calls to and from the three telephone lines of *Teen Number* compiled by Bharadwaj. There was a testimonial by Shanti Devi that declared that she had seen enough with her own eyes to believe that there was an amorous and growing involvement between the two main accused—his wife and her children's tutor. She had added a footnote that said that her loyalties to the Master of the house, whose salt she had partaken of, compelled her to bring to his notice the murky developments that were taking place behind his back. A similar written statement signed by the driver Niranjan Singh was also documented in the file. A copy of the pathology report of the blood analysis of the victim along with a laboratory analysis of some specific food samples was included in the set. It showed an abnormal presence of *dhatura* in the blood and traces of the same hallucinogen in the food.

Attached alongside was an opinion of a biochemist on the nature and toxicity of the substance that was found from the adulterated food sample taken from the rasgullas. It specified that the drug which had its origin in natural sources could damage the body organs and impair mental faculties if administered in large doses. There were transcripts of conversations between Dineshnandini and some outsiders who had been named. Similar written statements from all the outside staff members, excluding Iris Flory, were also gathered.

There was also a letter written and signed by the Maharani of Doongarpur that detailed her association with Dineshnandini some twenty-five years ago. It stated that both the accused and her father had executed a near-perfect plan to con her and fleece her of a large sum of money by posing to be a bal-yogini with supernatural healing powers and clairvoyance.

The fact-finding exercise was well underway. A lawyer had been consulted on the prospective course of action and the repercussions of the matter, and it was arrived upon that if adultery was proven, the erring wife would forfeit all her rights to her husband's wealth and would lose even the right to a maintenance. Her children who were under eighteen years were, however, entitled to a maintenance in keeping with the capacity and status of their father, only till such time that they became adults.

The victim believed that the accused, his youngest wife, the mother of seven children whose paternity was also now in doubt, had slyly amassed a huge fortune from him, without his consent or knowledge and had enough lucre stashed away to take care of herself and her seven, so no guilt burdened his conscience. She also had a sizeable income from the school which had been closed down by his decree only recently. Conveniently he chose to ignore the number of times he had, on some pretext or other, taken away her paltry earnings of a couple of lakhs, and how willingly and innocently, she had given them to him.

He decided that it was time to take matters into his own hands. First and foremost the monthly allowance was to be scaled down to a mere six thousand rupees which was to be handed to the household manager to run the home and not to the Lady of the home. Then Raj Narain and Sitara, her two accomplices, had to be sacked. The school had already been closed down so that would pose no problems of putting him back in control. The honour of cooking his meals had been restored to Saraswati and he finally made up his mind to restrict his interaction with *Teen Number* to occasional visits that could be kept to the bare minimum.

Oblivious of the thick web of intrigue that was closing in around her, Dineshnandini sadly resigned herself to nursing her injured knee and wounded heart. She suspended her visits to the hospital, and forced her reluctant seven to meet him during the stipulated visiting hours. She would interrogate them thoroughly again and again when they returned, weighing each word they said regarding his health and mood, to try and unravel the mystery on the other side, wallowing helplessly in her own predicament. It was not the first time in her life that she felt disrobed and alone.

Sitara's feeble attempts to comfort her and Raj Narain's hitherto reassuring presence did nothing to relieve the sharp gnawing pain she felt deep within her. She tried to alleviate her distress by writing, but her fingers felt as if they had been buried under an avalanche of ice and snow—frozen and numb.

The poet in her had receded into an inaccessible corner of her psyche.

She reflected on her pathetic state wondering where she could take her seven minor children and escape this humiliation. She was watching a noose that she had willingly slipped around her neck, slowly tighten and asphyxiate her. Caught in the vortex of the worst turmoil that life presented to her, she questioned herself again and again, trying to isolate the unknown forces that had pushed her on the wrong turn at the crossroads of her life a decade and a half ago. She could no longer moderate the role that had been assigned to her. She was on a death-defying free fall into a deep pit where no one would hear the thud when she hit the bottom, or pick up the pieces when she disintegrated with the impact. The blood-curdling scream that left her lips was audible only to her inner ear.

She wondered why her innocent seven had been made to bear the brunt of what were allegedly her deeds. The hairline fracture in the bony structure of her life had turned into a formidable and unbridgeable chasm. She locked herself into her room to shut out the ghouls that came knocking at her door. Life had still not doled out its final tragedy. It was to turn another hundred and eighty degrees for her when her husband returned from hospital after completing the last few months of his detention.

At nine o'clock on the morning of 16 February the same year, an urgent closed-door meeting was called at the hospital. The agenda was to discuss the plan to be executed for settling a crisis that was threatening to get out of hand. Those who attended it were Ram Dev, Dhannalal, Dewan Singh, Bharadwaj and Raj Eshwar, who had an unchallenged track record of loyalty to Dalmia. All of whom stood in solemn silence in front of their master waiting for his orders.

It was vested upon Bharadwaj to convey to Dineshnandini that his master desired the dismissal of Raj Narain and Sitara from their service with immediate effect. Raj Eshwar was given a free hand and the authority to deal with Raj Narain as he deemed fit, and to get him to sign a confession of his vile misconduct after which he could be left dead or alive, but never to be seen in the vicinity of Delhi. The rest were told to continue their reconnaissance with alacrity and precision.

Dineshnandini who was mentally incapacitated, was too numb to react. Deeply perturbed by the developments she lacked the courage or confidence to retaliate. The preposterous allegations against her did not in her mind even warrant a denial. It would debase her in her own eyes, so she sealed her lips and in mute silence that was taken as acceptance, watched the turn of events like a cold and impassive entity. The seven children who were visibly unsettled by their mother's state, got no answers or sympathy from their father. They wrote emotional and touching farewell notes to Sitara and Raj Narain whom they had grown to adore and who had become more than just constant companions to them.

As Raj Narain, with swollen red eyes, laboriously packed a large metal trunk with his belongings to leave the home that had been his haven for longer than he could remember, they hovered around him, holding his hands, sharing his grief, wiping his tears, promising him that they would bring him back. Both Sitara and he departed separately on a dreary, bleak and windy February afternoon, the forbidding iron gates shutting out the home that they would never see again. Raj Narain looked back at the crescent figure made by the seven assembled in the distance waving their hands in a final goodbye.

The taxi sped away towards the railway station from where he was to board a train to Agra, and get back to the place where he belonged.

The journey to the station seemed to be taking longer than he had imagined. He looked out of the window and noticed that the taxi was speeding on a highway that led past the Delhi border. Only when he tapped the driver's shoulder to enquire why they were on an unfamiliar route nowhere near the station, and the driver ignored him, did he realise that he was being abducted. He settled back nervously in the seat, not knowing what to do. It was pointless to try to jump out of the speeding taxi. The driver pulled up almost forty-five minutes later in front of an iron gate over which a signboard with 'Bhagwati Glass Works Private Limited' inscribed in bold letters stared down at him. He knew he was in Ghaziabad, the industrial town on the outskirts of Delhi, at the premises of Dalmia's sixty-four acre glass factory. There was no one in sight as he entered. He was without fear or panic for he was prepared for any eventuality. His life was meaningless and he was quite prepared to surrender it...

No one knows what happened to Raj Narain thereafter, but a detailed and signed confession of sorts did find its way into the dossier sometime later. His mother, after frantic appeals to his employers and futile attempts to trace him for a year, gave him up for dead!

In August 1964 when Dalmia returned from prison, he pronounced his final judgement to an already intimidated Dineshnandini. He announced that he would not conduct any of his activities from *Teen Number,* he would never eat anything in her home, and never spend the nights with her. He also told the bewildered seven that he would come to visit them sometimes—perhaps once in two or three days for a couple of hours, a pattern that he maintained for a while after which even his occasional visits completely stopped. The finality and cruelty of his words struck a hard blow to the wounded subconscious of his dependants who were sensitive enough to perceive the repercussions of his avowal but not bold enough to question it!

Padma had returned after her unsuccessful stint at the Jaipur boarding school where she had been sent and was studying privately to appear for her Intermediate examinations. After some setbacks, Babu was studying in one grade below his level. Laxmana had shown the academic brilliance that was expected of her and never stood second in her class. Neelima's progress, although not as outstanding as Laxmana's, was satisfactory. The younger three were no trouble or, to an extent, inconsequential.

Dineshnandini was saddled with the arduous task of single-parenting her brood in whom she saw streaks of their father's eccentricities in some form or another. It terrified her. She also felt terribly demeaned because the rumour that Dalmia had separated from his youngest wife, fuelled by Dalmia himself was rife, and this only added to her feebleness.

Time heals, but it also hardens! The scabs that formed on the wounds of the tender minds of the seven fell off, but not without taking their toll on each one them. The seven revolted against the treatment being meted out to their mother and become an umbrella of protection around her instead of it being the other way round. When their father visited them, they were coerced into sitting in awkward silence on the gol gadda with both parents, who either exchanged no words with each other or if at all, it was only ugly slander in unstoppable torrents from their father. Those couple of hours spent perforce with their father every other day became the most wretched experience of their lives, resulting in a systematic destruction of their psyches. After their father left, they huddled together on the gol gadda with their distraught mother like frightened sheep for hours. No one spoke or protested because they had been forbidden to do so by her. They would never forgive their father, the self-proclaimed re-incarnation of an entity who was greater than Christ in his qualities of forgiveness, for subjecting them to this unending misery. The great man, who at one time was at the zenith of his fame due to his unequalled contribution to the progress of industry in independent India, whose Midas touch had turned him into a legend, had reduced himself to the size of a midget who was persecuting a tiny, five-foot high, frail and helpless woman, the mother of his seven children at *Teen Number*.

Despite the rumours of the other scandalous lifestyles from the *Nau Number* and *Pandrah Number* homes nothing changed for them. The *Nau Number* lot, significantly due to the favoured position of their mother, continued to enjoy their father's patronage. Everything the others did was condoned. Everything the *Teen Number* lot did was condemnable. When Ila cut her hair, despite knowing that her father strongly disapproved of short hair, he said she had burnt it while doing an *arti*. When Yashodhara was caught scaling the walls of her home it did not warrant her a punishment. When Meera was on the verge of converting to Christianity at a nun's boarding school, he was very sympathetic to her and blamed himself. When Dhruv tried to attack the security guards appointed for him by his father, he proudly spoke of Dhruv's fearlessness and temper like a doting father would of a spoilt child! But none of this was extended to the *Teen-Number* lot who were always treated by him in a stepfatherly manner. They ached to be loved by him and resorted to the most obvious methods of retaliation by making sneaky complaints to him about the others, based on whatever scraps of information they obtained from their grapevine!

Dineshnandini was a worried woman. She needed her husband's support to get her girls married and boys settled professionally. Padma had to complete her studies and then a suitable match was to be found for her. She needed his support to reign in Babu who had become rude and obnoxious. Instead, their father made it a point to let it be known that he had nothing to do with the *Teen Number* lot and his only family was with him in Nau *Number.*

In the three difficult years that followed, the older four went to colleges—some by merit and the others with a push from their mother. The immediate problems were ostensibly solved but other related ones cropped up.

The monthly allowance was barely enough to cover the kitchen costs and Dineshnandini was always short of money though she never dared to ask for more. With Sitara gone the home was being run by fourteen-year-old Laxmana who often stole a few hundred rupees to buy comics. She would account for it under the miscellaneous expenditure head. That way she had all the others toeing the line to be in her good books. The overall expenditure was monitored by the household secretary, which was a constant source of bickering between him and the children and also an easy way for him to feather his own nest. The situation was at most times volatile!

Saraswati had finally got him where she wanted. Back after his two-year term in jail, Dalmia was completely disillusioned with her sole adversary Dineshnandini. Her debilitated and weary husband was finally back in her fold after a sixteen-year exile, as it were. Asha was relegated to the forgotten chapters of history and posed no threat. Dineshnandini had been reduced to being a loathsome, degraded, condemned and separated wife. Saraswati feared no competition from her anymore. The *Nau Number* children were in overt control and her husband's physical and emotional dependence on her had assumed manic proportions. His inflamed paranoia and sharpened complex of persecution had compelled him to detest Dineshnandini. Saraswati had despised her for foisting herself on her husband and for imposing her own family on his business. It was just as well that they had proved to be utter disasters. Dineshnandini had produced seven children to compete with hers for a share in his life and wealth, but now she was permanently out in the cold and her family had been irreversibly eliminated. It was time for her to consolidate her position.

Saraswati was not happy with the conduct of Vasudha who wanted to marry a boy of German origin, or of Yashodhara who flouted all rules of conventional behaviour. But all this did not rattle her anymore. She had the rock-solid support of her husband. She knew he would never waver in his commitment to her since his disenchantment with Dineshnandini was complete. She had forgiven him for the mental and physical cruelties that he had heaped on her in all the years she had been married to him. She forgave him the breach of promise he had made to her father when he had asked for her hand in marriage—the promise that there would be no further marriages, that he had broken twice afterwards! Her memory selectively erased all the painful experiences that she had been through, and the agony that had driven her to the doors of the Home Minister to complain about her husband's atrocities. She was sure that in the last lap of his life she was in the driving seat and nothing troubled her any longer because she had regained her man whom she nearly lost to an avaricious and calculating woman whose cover had finally been blown. The task had taken long but destiny was on her side. It helped to have the full-fledged support of her brother-in-law Jaidayal, who exerted the strongest influence on Dalmia's life. It was a position that would remain intact till the day Dalmia died.

Dineshnandini had been rendered powerless. Contrary to what everyone believed, she had no amassed wealth, no place where she could take her unsettled seven, and no one willing to take their responsibility. Neither her father nor her brothers were in a position to stand up against Dalmia to fight for her rights.

On a cold dreary morning on 11 January 1967, Dineshnandini's father died in a hospital in Agra of complications that arose from a perforated ulcer. In a tough battle for life that lasted for over three weeks, he breathed his last, an unhappy and worried man. Just a few hours earlier in a cruel telephonic message, Dalmia had directed someone to tell his half-conscious father-in-law that it was a good day to die as Lal Bahadur Shastri had departed for his heavily abode on the same day in Tashkent some years before. The dying man followed his instructions, leaving behind a crestfallen Dineshnandini. Dalmia never came to the funeral nor did he bother to console her.

If the time that Dalmia spent in prison was bad for *Teen Number,* then the next five years after his return were much worse. Financial constraints condemned Dineshnandini and her seven children to a life of penury. The household allowance did not even cover their basic needs. Their unfulfilled demands and heavy peer pressure made them bitter and rebellious. Their mother would start her daily morning routine by either lecturing whoever she could get hold of on the sins of marrying wealthy men or women; about the misery that money brings with it, and about the need to get their acts together and wake up to reality because they would be getting nothing from their father. She harped on her liberal thinking and emphasised that she would be quite happy to marry off her girls to good, educated boys from reasonably well-to-do homes if they so desired—with the proviso that they could be neither Christians nor Muslims. She would have to swallow her words not too long after.

The impressionable ones would listen to her rhetoric, sometimes with boredom, sometimes with interest, taking it all in, never for a moment suspecting that all her life, she did not have the courage or clarity to either say what she meant or mean what she said. The polarities within which the framework of her thought existed made her believe one thing, say another, and think something quite different. Not realising that such contradictions send confusing signals to tender minds and can trigger aberrant behaviour, she carried on. Padma posed specific problems. She was unable to relate to her brothers and sisters and take on the role of the eldest. She usually locked herself up in her own room where she spent hours playing with stray cats and dogs. She could never share anything of hers with anyone and there was constant friction between her and the rest. Since children can be insensitive and even cruel, they ganged up against her and made fun of her, pushing her further away into a shell. Their mother was in a sense unfit to deal with this. With Babu she was over-indulgent. Her approach quite strangely smacked of a strong gender bias in sharp contrast with the persona that had interacted with Jawaharlal Nehru and written firebrand pieces on women's empowerment and against male domination. Due to her constant pampering and partiality, by the time Babu turned fifteen, he became obnoxious. He beat up all the youngsters and bullied Padma. He spent all his time in the servants' quarters playing with their children. He roamed aimlessly back and forth from his private tutors' homes, equipped neither with his books nor stationery. Complaints about him kept pouring in but no one took any action. It only became a major problem when every year Dineshnandini would have to cultivate and bribe his teachers to make sure that they did not detain him in the same grade. Babu's personal grooming, however, did not improve, nor did his lackadaisical manner change. He continued to visit the strictly-out-of-bounds *jamadars'* quarters, squat on the floor with them, and eat the food they cooked in their utensils. He drank cheap liquor, started to eat meat and even smoke bidis in their company, in exchange for which they fleeced him of whatever money they could grab and hand-me-down clothes that were almost new.

When Dineshnandini heard of this, all hell broke loose. Instead of handling it maturely with patience and understanding—the two qualities she lacked—she raved and ranted like a lunatic till she made him cry. He pleaded and begged for forgiveness and swore that he would never do those things again but his had become an 'unpardonable offence.' She, of course, felt too cheated to listen to him. And a deep new discord set in.

His father too, instead of being sympathetic with his not-uncommonly wayward teenaged son dealt them another blow. He told Dineshnandini that he had learnt that Babu was afflicted with a terrible venereal disease and needed strict handling and reforming. On the other hand, he told Babu that he did not have to study because 'a son of Dalmia would never need to work'. Due to the complete mishandling of a minor crisis that most adolescent boys undergo, his natural sexual stirrings were perceived by his enraged father as something sinful. This was to have long term consequences on Babu's life.

Iris Flory's daughter Joan, who was targeted as the culprit along with Babu in his crime, was banished from

Teen Number. It left behind an ugly festering wound on Babu's mind that his mother would learn of only many years later.

Then it was Laxmana. Since all telephone calls were monitored by the PBX operators employed in *Teen Number* and a daily report of incoming and outgoing calls was sent to her father, it was quite easy for him to find some pretext to shout and scream about everyday.

The next casualty was Baba Mitera, the Hindi teacher's son, also a permanent fixture in *Teen Number* and of the same age as Laxmana. Dalmia alerted by his loyal PBX operator Bharadwaj, looked upon Baba as Laxmana's lover or more aptly, corrupter. The unsuspecting and innocent fourteen-year-old who had just about begun to menstruate was viciously defamed.

'She's going to bring disaster to the family. I'm warning you. Just stop that Mitera boy from coming here.'

The 'Mitera boy' was summarily dismissed and was never seen again, as was his mother—the Hindi teacher.

Then it was Neelima's turn.

'Everyone is talking about how bad she is. She is always sandwiched between two boys on the front seat, driving around at crazy speeds in the city. God knows where she will take us. Tell her to be patient. Her sexual development is beyond her years... We'll get her married soon. She should be patient.'

The outbursts were unstoppable. If it wasn't one thing it was another. He was perverse and bizarre—but only to the inmates of *Teen Number.* Saraswati's children never seemed to be criticised or castigated by him. They remained his favourites and were showered with love and attention despite all their impropriety.

In *Teen Number* the fallout of these daily hammerings was two-fold. A deep rancour against their father was breeding within the seven, and Dineshnandini's own frustrations made her cantankerous, and an ill-tempered nag. All she did was let out dirty, street invectives in her daily diatribe to Laxmana who retaliated occasionally. After a prolonged spell of endurance, Neelima decided it was more satisfying to scream back at her like a banshee or switch off when provoked by the gutter language that had become so much a part of her. To escape, she ran away from home to spend the whole day with one friend or another or secretly remain in the company of the several male friends that she had acquired. This gave her temporary respite, and with them she felt beautiful, desired and feminine. So against all odds, she persisted with her defiant getaways.

Dineshnandini had made a grave miscalculation. Her behaviour alienated her even further from her children barring Raja, from whom she sought moral support. In him she created a full-time watchdog who was vested with the authority to attack anyone who made her cry. Thereby, she made him her favourite child and everyone else's pet anathema. Unmindful of the age difference and spurred by his mother's tears, he, the self-appointed protector, resorted to slapping, kicking, spitting on and even locking up his sisters if they disobeyed or were offensive to their mother.

It was hell on earth! The once heavenly home became a ruinous battleground of bad blood, with the growing monsters hating each other. Even the youngest were not spared and got dragged into insane controversies or scraps that made them all miserable.

The parenting had been disastrous. A pack of highly maladjusted, half humans that were being pulled in two opposite directions by their mother and father, and many conflicting directions by other forces. Governed by the natural law of the jungle, all of them, freaky products of the accident of their birth, their genetic pool and their uncaring environment tied tightly to their karmic vicissitudes, were waiting for their own holocausts!

It was the seventy-sixth year in the life of a controversial, infamous septuagenarian. Mortality and fatigue stared him in his face. He was reading a draft, the first, in a series of three wills that would bequeath his estate or whatever remained of it, his life's possessions, his assets and his liabilities to his wives and his dependants after his death. The division of his wealth was in keeping with the magnanimous spirit of justice and equality that was deeply ingrained in his perception of himself. Even though Asha was his now-forgotten spouse, her children—Dhruv Hari, Meera and Alka—were dealt with fairly, and despite his aversion for his wife Dineshnandini, she and her seven children had been treated with the same impartiality.

In his mind, he had chosen to forgive the woman whom he perceived as an adulteress and a sorceress who had impersonated his beloved Narbada to wilfully deceive him, the woman who had illicitly amassed vast riches from him, who had tried to poison him with the intent to murder him, whom a lesser mortal would have ostracised and shunned beyond human redemption. It made him feel grandiose. He was the embodiment of mercy, taller than the Lord Christ himself, and the veritable reincarnation of Rishi Bhrigu.

In a single stroke he had pardoned Dineshnandini for her treachery and sins and accorded himself the status of Divinity.

'I hate the sin and not the sinner,' he had repeated to her many times—but what he preached and practised rarely matched! That he hated the sin was never in doubt but that he despised the sinner and her progeny was also never more evident from his actions. However, to delude himself with the grandeur of an angel of mercy and to relieve the pain of a pricking conscience, he absolved himself by drawing up an equal and fair distribution of his wealth to be executed in a will after his death.

Oblivious of the drafting of this document and terrified of the impending mortality of her aging husband, Dineshnandini was in a hurry to discharge her responsibilities towards her children. She managed to get Padma engaged to her husband-to-be after a few extremely attractive proposals for her were scuttled by her father.

Laxmana had already met the Muslim boy with whom she would begin an intense and romantic relationship that was to survive vitriolic opposition and last for over two decades but not culminate in marriage. Neelima was seeing the man that she was to marry after a long stormy affair, and several minor aborted ones, six years later.

After feeble protests and great reluctance, on Dineshnandini's insistence Babu too was to marry a seemingly innocent woman from a neo-political family belonging to the backwaters of Bihar. Her entry into *Teen Number* was to portend an upheaval of an unimaginable kind.

Padma was married exactly six months after Dalmia made his first will.

The will was followed by an amendment in a codicil that was drawn up in '73, a year before Babu was married. Dalmia's final will documented and registered in '77, two years and five months before he died, and was to be fiercely contested after his death.

Both Padma's and Neelima's *kanyadaan* ceremonies were performed by their father and the expenses borne by him albeit grudgingly. In between the two, Dineshnandini got Babu married and acquired a new member in her home, a beautiful, virgin bride over whom she felt she had complete authority and control. This calmed her temporarily.

The woman in the guise of a *Bhabhi* Ma, however, would resort to every ploy in the book to survive. So perfect was to be her con game, and so foolproof her deception that even if she were to be tried before an unbiased, independent jury, she would only come across as someone incapable of carrying on a thirteen-year-long incestuous affair.

Laxmana as such had been written off. Her involvement with Aziz Quraishi, a Muslim boy who was her colleague from her post-graduate class at the university, was a reality that she worried about but did not want to remember. She buried her head in the sand like an ostrich each time anyone brought it up, hoping and praying fervently that Dalmia would never find out and Laxmana would never have the nerve to tell him.

Just as walking around a fire does not entail betrothal of souls, minds and bodies, none of the three marriages of her children were complete unions of those three elements. Their inherent, though entirely dissimilar inadequacies, were to lead to a complete break-up of two marriages, and a partial but not-so-visible disintegration of the third.

The other siblings from *Nau Number,* Sheela and Vasudha were also married off as Dalmia discharged his duties towards his beloved Saraswati with great enthusiasm and fanfare. That was scaled down for Asha's daughter Meera, who married a handsome Bengali boy of her choice. Dhruv Hari, meanwhile, had eloped in a Mills & Boon type of runaway romance with a gorgeous Muslim model who was under eighteen, in a daring act of defiance against his father in particular, and against society in general. With some anger and a lot of hidden admiration for his son's recklessness and fearlessness—in whom he saw a mirror-image of himself—Dalmia melted when he set eyes on the doe-eyed beauty. Ayesha's child-like innocence, fairest of skins and disarming and limpid eyes captivated him, and his rage gave way to tenderness and a perverse pride.

Unfortunately, as if they were jinxed, none of the marriages worked. Barring two, none of them lasted. The overt reason was of course incompatibility. Deep down and closer to the truth, however was the common inability to relate to other human beings maturely—an enviro-genetic dysfunction that bound all eighteen of them!

The dismembering of the *Teen Number* lot was more or less complete after '74. In the year preceding his death Dalmia ceased to visit *Teen Number* and gave very little money for the upkeep of his wife, home or children. Unbeknown to Dineshnandini, this was in accordance with his brother's advice, and supported by a lawyer's counsel that since his wealth was self-earned, there was no liability on him and he was not obligated to maintain his children who had all attained the age of eighteen. He firmly believed that their mother had secretly stashed away sizeable funds and was in a comfortable position to look after them; therefore his act of omission was no injustice. The measure of his anger could be gauged from the fact that before Padma was married, he had offered to hand over the paltry one and a half lakh rupees to be spent at her wedding to her prospective father-in-law because he did not trust Dineshnandini to give it all to her! What an irony! All her life Dineshnandini had fought to wash off the slur on her—she had married the man only for his money. In fact, in keeping with an eccentric pledge, she had never even touched a currency-note with her hands! Who was to tell him that she and her children lived in abject penury, counting each penny saved from the paltry earnings of Raja's potato crop that he planted on the front lawns, or the puny returns from the sale of the gladioli he grew in the backyard. Since Dalmia's visits to Teen

Number had completely stopped and no calls of theirs were put through to him by the *Nau Number* operators, there was an impenetrable Iron Curtain around him. His failing health and the anxiety it caused Dineshnandini, along with the uncertainty of her unsettled children, impelled her into unfailing but futile attempts to get through. She would beg, beseech or nag any one of the seven that she could get hold of to make phone calls to him on some pretext or another so that she could get some sliver of information about him. Her neurosis was playing havoc with her sanity. The once-in an-odd call that was put through was met with the same response.

'I will come when I can…You cannot come here to see me…Tell your mother I am well…' or more cruelly at times—'Tell her that I am not going to die so soon!'

All letters and written pleas fell on deaf ears, and as the seven suspected, were probably never even shown to him.

Thoroughly frustrated, one day, prompted by Dhruv Hari, Neelima, Raja and Laxmana landed up at the gates of *Nau Number* and were ushered into their father's room as if they were criminals on death-row being granted a last wish of mercy before being hanged.

He was frail and wasting. His hearing was severely impaired. His left ventricle had failed and he was completely bedridden. He could barely speak and was too weak to sit up. Saraswati shouted in his ear.

'*Teen number ke bacche aaye hain…uthiye…yeh aapko pranam kar rahe hain* (The children from *Teen Number* are here…get up…they are greeting you).'

Opening his eyes he looked at Raja and then the other two, and wept. He was joined in silent tears that poured down the faces of the three visitors.

'*Kharcha kaise chalta hai Raja … Aamdani ka kya zaria hai* (How do you manage your expenses, Raja? What is the source of income)?' he mumbled, then he said something in Saraswati's ear after which he lay back on his pillow and shut his eyes tight, the pain and anguish visible on his face.

Raja spoke up, 'Don't worry Papa … You do not get disturbed … We are all right and can manage …' The lie in his voice was not camouflaged by the tremor.

That was exactly six months before the day their father died a helpless, solitary man, captive of his circumstances, who had to a large extent become desensitised, perhaps to block out the pain of what troubled him. He would finally leave behind three shattered women and seventeen children, most of whom were not settled. Even in death there would be no peace on his face, and his brows would be etched with a deep frown.

Total secrecy was maintained about Dalmia's failing health and no one was permitted to meet him. His impregnable fortress was guarded by security personnel who took orders only from Saraswati or her sons. Saraswati's two boys were working in their father's companies, both separately controlling the functioning of his offices, and in the last two years of his life, had taken over the entire decision-making of his business.

Dineshnandini had finally given up. Divested of all hope of ever seeing her husband again, she would wake up sweating in the middle of the night, fearing the news of his death as one fears a living ghost! She knew it was coming but she did not have the courage to face it when it did. In her mind she was living his death every waking moment of her life and suffering her worst nightmares when she slept.

Late one night in September, an inebriated stranger tottered in through the open gates of *Teen Number*. He arrived on the front verandah demanding to meet Dineshnandini. The chowkidar came in to tell her that a man calling himself Harish was asking to see her. A frightened Dineshnandini clutching Raja's hand went out nervously and found herself face-to-face with the unfamiliar Guru Harishwar Prasad, the counterpart of Haveli Ram, who had been housed in *Nau Number* for over twenty-five years—the dreaded tantric who had turned everything against her. She trembled with the panic that gripped her, expecting to hear the doomsayer utter something dreadful. Her mind raced ahead as she tried to read his thoughts before he opened his mouth to speak.

The rotund, debauched looking man with an obscene belly that depicted years of abuse of food and alcohol and a degenerate lifestyle, was wearing large diamond solitaires in his ears. In a visible state of unrest he was reeking of a strong, cheap liquor, and trembled with anger as he spoke. 'Dineshnandiniji, Sethji is dying...He is lying unconscious...You and your children will get nothing...His will has been changed by Gun Nidhi and his mother…Grave injustice has been done to you…Do something if you can…You have very little time…It is already too late…' Harish sat down on the shoddy sofa that lay on the front verandah, surrounded by seven anxious faces as he slurred incoherently.

'I have sinned…I poisoned Sethji against you and your children…I have made a grave mistake…God is going to punish me for my deeds…But you should know that the will has been changed by them…Sethji is helpless and his mind is paralysed…He is almost dead…All is lost…'

Like shards of glass his words penetrated Dineshnandini's pained soul. She was not thinking of the will. She was thinking of the dying man and began to cry. The rest of the children who had gathered around her, wept in chorus. Afraid and helpless they knew death was imminent, but this messenger was not what they had expected. Someone brought him a glass of cold water and they watched him in glum silence as he drank it, mopping his brows with a crumpled hand towel that he pulled out of his pocket.

It was only later that they learned that Gun Nidhi had thrown Harish out of the home that night in a bid to break out of his wicked stranglehold. Harish's subsequent visit to *Teen Number* was not a charitable one for an altruistic cause, but more to avenge his insulted pride. He was violently angry that his control was being vanquished and that the single source of his enormous funds was going to be permanently choked.

Harish the powerful insider, the carrier of the most vital clues to the mystery behind the closed walls of *Nau*

Number was sitting in a posture of surrender at the doorstep of his benefactor's greatest foe, willing to tell all. The prospect was attractive but the fear psychosis was deep and the news of Dalmia's rapidly ebbing life was even more unnerving, so no one had the desire to 'reign in' the renegade. Moreover, with her husband dead, Dineshnandini thought that all links with the other home would be broken and with him gone, all animosities would be neutralised. How naive she was?

After a two-hour long dramatic tell-all, Harish left, leaving behind an intimidated and demoralised bunch of half-humans who knew neither how to react nor how to protest—virtually a curtains-down scenario.

A sudden crack of thunder and a flash of lightning reminded them that a squall was brewing. With some help Harish staggered up, leaving a damp stain of sweat on the cracked, wrinkled Rexine sofa where he had sat. The nauseating smell of cheap liquor stayed suspended in the air. The slow incessant drizzle in the background did not prevent him from walking the red sandstone path for the last time, never to be seen again.

Devastated and defenceless the children and their mother stayed awake that whole night, desperately attempting to get through to the telephone line of *Nau Number.* They sat around the instrument waiting for it to ring—to hear the dreaded news of the death of their father. It was only a matter of time. It would come in the next seventy-two hours but three of them would get a glimpse of him, lying comatose, before he died.

At 5 a.m. on the morning of 26 September the shrill ringing of the phone pierced through the still sleeping world of the *Teen Number* home—menacing in its tone like a trumpet of doom. The sound startled Dineshnandini, the only one who was not asleep. She had been jolted out of her light slumber by a loud cackle of laughter from her thirteen-year-old maid who slept on the carpet in her room. The laughing banshee did not augur well. It chilled her to the bone. She was expecting something terrible when she heard the loud, unbroken, urgent ring of the telephone. She knew by instinct it was the message that she had feared every moment of her life. With shivering hands she lifted the receiver and handed it to Raja who stood beside her for she did not have the courage to put it to her ear. The voice on the other end spoke in Marwari.

'*Khel khatam ho go Babu…They athe aa jao…Sethji ko sarir saant ho go* (The game is over Master…come here…Sethji's body lies in peace)!' It was the cook Hanuman who had worked in *Teen Number* briefly before he was whisked away to *Nau Number* some years ago. His words hung in the air like a fearful apparition as the line went dead, leaving Raja too numb to react and his mother in a devastated heap.

The anxiety felt in anticipation of a disaster is far more disturbing than the actual encounter of the disaster itself for the human mind can insulate itself from shock or pain when faced with a real assault. With surprising com-posure Raja collected all the others, bundled them into the car and drove off towards the forbidden fortress. The one call he made before leaving was to Neelima telling her to reach *Nau Number* without delay. He did not need to tell her anything more.

They arrived on the deserted, tree-lined road that led to the home where their father lay lifeless, in his mortal shell, on a mattress on the floor. Their car slowed down as it entered the formidable gates that they would drive through for the last but one time. They would come there once more thirteen days later, but without their mother.

The body was kept in a stark room that had been cleared of the little furniture it had. The bare walls showed cracks in the plaster here and there and a large cobweb hung from the ceiling on one side. The emaciated figure lay on the floor on top of a crumpled sheet that was spread out on a mattress that had seen better days.

They filed into the room holding back their tears, their hearts pounding hard. No one looked up at them. Saraswati sat at his feet holding his lifeless ankles tightly in her grasp, pinning him down with both hands as if she were afraid that he would get up and walk away. She held him down in death as she had held him in life. Without lifting her head she waved one hand gesturing to them to sit far away from her in one corner of the room. Ila, Sheela, Vasudha, Yashodhara, Gun Nidhi, Vidya Nidhi and some other unrecognisable but familiar faces sat in concentric circles around him. Sitting close to Saraswati was her dear friend and long-time associate Lalita Shastri, the widow of the late Prime Minister Lal Bahadur Shastri—as if she symbolised power and clout. Dineshnandini and her seven sat far away huddled together—all eyes fixed on the dead man. His death was now a stark reality. They looked absurd crying and wailing, for not a sound came from anyone else. Raja was regurgitating his memories of the last few days.

Just after Harish left the *Teen Number* premises that fateful night, Raja made a frantic call to the operator declaring that they would storm the gates of *Nau Number* if they were not allowed to see their father. He was possessed by a demonic energy that had temporarily overcome his natural fears. He assumed, perhaps, that being on his lowest ground nothing could make him any worse off.

Whether it was the threat in his voice or pity in her heart or some unknown fear in her mind, Saraswati allowed them to see their father that night. Accompanied by Laxmana and Neelima, Raja entered silently and intrepidly into the morose, dark premises of Saraswati's fort that few had dared to trespass in recent years. They saw their father lying still and supine on a hard wooden bed that had no bedhead or footboard. His breathing was arrhythmic and his defibrillated chest moved up and down in noisy jerks. Incense sticks were lit in a bunch in one corner of the room from where wisps of smoke rose up in the air and clouded the familiar picture of Ma Durga smiling benevolently down at them. Saraswati sat on a wicker mat reading loudly from a *Ramayana* that rested on a carved bookstand on the floor. The pallu of her sari covered her head halfway down to her eyes. Her large red bindi was visible through the weave of her white muslin-cotton.

On seeing them enter, she purposefully stopped, closed the book and looked up at them as each one filed up to touch her feet, before they settled on the odd cane chairs that were placed randomly in the room around the bed.

Neelima's muffled sobs broke the silence and were followed by the sounds of suppressed weeping from the other two.

Saraswati sat unmoved. Ila appeared from somewhere and put her hand into Raja's saying matter-of-factly, 'Send positive thoughts.' She was telling them not to intrude on the peaceful vibrations of the room that was to home the life of the wasting mortal for merely seventy-two hours more.

Raja's thoughts came back to the room where his father lay dead before him, and he saw Dhruv Hari standing in the doorway. Tall and fierce in his manner, no one dared to stop him as he approached the body and lay prostrate at his father's feet. Saraswati did not move from her position—symbolically and overtly one of supremacy and control. Not a shred of anguish or pain, or even a tear was seen on her face or on the faces of her children.

Dineshnandini's dual mind was on its own racetrack. Before her lay the forgotten and frozen history of a life of thirty-two years of her marriage. She saw the glorious man who had been her husband when he was at the pinnacle of his fame. She had fantasised about him being another Jawaharlal Nehru–like grand political luminary. For him she had envisaged a nationwide mourning and an ostentatious funeral like that of a world leader. On his death the entire country should have been plunged into grief and all flags lowered to half-mast, and millions of women should have felt widowed and children orphaned. Here he lay lifeless like an utterly forlorn, ordinary mortal before he began his last journey to Nigambodh Ghat— the ground where half a dozen unknown and unclaimed bodies would be burning alongside his. He would not even merit the easily obtainable honour of a cremation on the banks of the Ganga where, as per Hindu belief, his soul would attain instant nirvana! He would soon be reduced to a handful of ashes and dust and then be relegated to obscurity like any other creature who lived and died as an ordinary man. She searched her mind and juggled her thoughts to precipitate the grief that she should have felt but she was numb! No twenty-one gun salute, no royal bedecked gun carriage and no tricolour wrapped around the body.

She was oblivious of the several pairs of eyes that viewed her with contempt and repugnance, as the con woman who was enacting the last lap of her life's drama on a platform that she would never be allowed to visit again. Every move of hers was perceived as an act of duplicity by those who believed that it was she who had perpetrated an unsuccessful plan to do him to death by poisoning only twelve years ago, and that his exit was the fruition of her innermost desire, albeit much later than she had wanted.

It was only when she saw Dhruv Hari bent over double to touch her feet that she realised that his mother was not present in the room. She looked around checking to see if Asha was sitting innocuously in some corner, unnoticed by the rest but she was nowhere to be seen. She leaned towards Raja and whispered in his ear, 'Go and get Asha, maybe she has not even been informed.'

Raja waited a while before he left. In abject silence he drove the five-minute distance to *Pandrah Number* with his mind on fire and limbs feeling like lead. Raja had a hard time trying to persuade his distant and detached stepmother to come to *Nau Number* for the last *darshan* of her estranged but now dead husband.

'*Ab matti ko kya karna hai dekhkar* (Now what is the point in seeing the dust)?' she said. He held her feet reverently and pleaded with tears in his eyes, more out of insecurity and fear for himself than compassion for her.

'Please Maji,' he implored, 'I will not leave without you.' His earnest plea expressed his subliminal need to clutch on to anything for support. They were the persecuted ones—the ones who were more orphaned than the favoured and controlling Saraswati faction. They could commiserate and empathise better with each other.

Raja came back to *Nau Number* with Asha, her face ashen and movements robotic.

He led her by her trembling hand into the room where the unbathed and spiritless body of her husband lay. She sat down on the floor close to Raja who did not let go of her hand, fearing that she would leave abruptly. When she saw Jaidayal, she frowned distastefully and stood up in a huff, brushing aside Raja's arm.

She looked at Dhruv Hari, her only son, the eldest male child of the dead man lying before her, in whom Hindu religion vests the right to light a funeral pyre and commence the last rites of death deemed to liberate the soul from the body—the cardinal reason for which humans have coveted male offspring from times immemorial—and she voiced her fears.

'They will not let him give the *mukhagni* to his father. What is happening here is all wrong. I am going. I can take this farce no more. For me the man had died much earlier, but if you Raja, have any sense of *kartavya* towards your ancestors and any loyalty to your dead father, if you are his seed and feel some shred of emotions for me, make sure that Dhruv Hari, his eldest son—no power on earth can challenge that—is not divested of his right to set his father's mortal remains on fire ... .'

Dineshnandini sat unmoved with her head bent down as Asha's words fell on her ears. She did not see Asha leave the room or Dhruv Hari's cheeks flex as he gritted his jaws in a tight spasm that stayed on his face. Nor did she see the fire in his eyes as he stared at the man who lay before him.

All she could hear was the sounds of the inconsolable sobs that came in waves from her children and that echoed the cries of her own heart. She sat alone, surrounded by her seven, each one individually experiencing his or her own pain. No one came to give them a shoulder to cry on or wipe their tears! A short while later Ila came and announced matter-of-factly, 'You can go home to freshen up if you want. We will not be taking the body for cremation till twelve.' Her words fell unregistered and her syrupy voice evoked no response.

How eerie it is that merely by the cessation of a beating heart or a contracting diaphragm a being turns into a body.

The ice blocks stacked alongside the corpse were melting rapidly on that hot September day, tracing irregular streams of water around the room. A soiled and yellowed sheet that was frayed at the edges covered the body. It flapped now and again with the movement of the air from the fan that whirred noisily from the ceiling. Saraswati did not move from her position as if she were rooted to the ground. Two men who looked like members of her staff approached the body. They applied black soot on the soles of his feet and pressed two white sheets of paper separately on the left and right one to take the impressions. No one moved or questioned the bizarre necromantic deed. Only Dineshnandini and her seven had a bewildered look on their faces but this bewilderment too was to remain unaddressed forever like many earlier ones.

The sheet on the corpse moved up and down deceptively, making it appear like the man who was lying dead for over twelve hours, was taking a sporadic, laboured breath, but that was only an illusion—an illusion very much like the one his entire life had been, the enactment of a soap opera that had come to its natural end after eighty-four years, but would give way to yet other dramas before his remains would return to dust. The survivors would witness another lurid tale of ill-will, hypocrisy and discrimination, much to their horror and indignation, that would bring into sharp focus their impotence once again.

His body was bathed with *Ganga jal* and a sandal paste tilak traced on his forehead. Signs of the swastika were drawn in sandal paste on his bare upper rib-cage. A *tulsi* leaf was placed inside his mouth, and wreaths of roses and marigolds were placed on the body. All his descendants queued up one by one, and knelt down and touched their foreheads to his feet to bid him farewell, the youngest one being Babu's two-year-old boy.

When Dineshnandini approached the corpse she faltered. She feared that her husband would sit up any minute to shout abuses at her, spout the venom that he had held inside him and pull his feet away from her, not wanting her to touch them. She knelt down and took off the red glass bangles from her wrists, placed them on his knees before she touched her feverish brow to his feet. Her faint red bindi got wiped out leaving a mark on the dried skin of his feet. She stayed in that position for what seemed like an unending moment of agony, till someone pulled her up and led her away to make way for the others who were standing behind her. She turned back to look at him and heard his voice echoing loudly in her ears…

'I came to this earth with my fists closed but shall leave with open palms and a smile on my face to unite with the Param Brahma. *There is no death of the soul… Only the body perishes…'*

She turned her gaze again to his face, but saw no smile on it; his hands lay open by his sides lifelessly.

Indeed facts are stranger than fiction, as fiction is but an imitation of facts. What was to unfold was an absurd charade that would have been comical had it not been so tragic.

Nigambodh Ghat is one of the oldest cremation grounds on the banks of the Jamuna in what used to be the outskirts of ancient Delhi, but with the expanding metropolis, the city has spread on either side of it enclosing it in its populace. Dalmia had accorded all his kin who pre-deceased him a ritualistic funeral on the banks of the Ganga and might have desired a similar one for himself, but his surviving sons chose to perform a hasty cremation at the Nigambodh Ghat instead.

Once a man dies, whether his body is fed to the vultures as Parsis do in their Tower of Silence, or interred into the bowels of the earth as Christians and Muslims do, or burnt on a pyre of wood like Hindus do, makes no difference to the imperishable soul that has left it to return to dust. However, the Hindu religion decrees that the human body be disposed off in a prescribed manner—by being set alight by the eldest male child on a pyre made of wooden logs on the banks of the holy Ganga to attain salvation. This constitutes the penultimate purpose of all life on earth.

For Dalmia his wishes in death were ignored as were most of his wishes in life, particularly in the last years when he became captive to his ailing body and powerless mind. It was decided by those in control to cremate him in Delhi as it was more practical and less time-consuming.

The bier bedecked with roses and marigolds was hoisted onto the shoulders of his sons on all four sides, and amidst loud wails of the lamenting women, placed inside a hearse where many ordinary mortals must have lain before him.

The three factions, distinctly separate in their identities, assembled in their own vehicles to reach the ghat.

In contravention of the set norms of Marwari society, all the women with the exception of Asha, accompanied the body in the irregular, disjointed entourage to perform the last rites of this man who had been the monarch of the Indian industry in his heyday and who had engaged in a self-destructive epic combat with the highest powers of his time!

At the cremation ground the body was placed on a pyre of a few sandalwood logs scattered carelessly on top of ordinary ones. His brother and sons circumambulated his pyre barefoot, in descending order of their ages. The women stood huddled on one side in three distinct groups, vying for vantage positions away from the harsh rays of the afternoon sun that shone cruelly overhead. As the priest began to chant some slokas, each one of those present on the ground was charged with the kind of energy that Vedic incantations suffuse in human minds.

Jaidayal stepped forward, followed by Gun Nidhi, a lighted log of wood in his hand, to enable and guide Gun Nidhi to set the pyre alight, when a minor scuffle drew their attention away from the body. They stopped. A loud argument ensued from behind. It was coming from a group of people who were holding back a man who was shouting something. His voice drowned in the loud sounds of *Om* that reverberated around the ghat dotted with some freshly lit, some half-burnt and some cold *chitahs* of unknown men.

Some voices could be heard.

'How can Jaidayal light his pyre?...He has six sons...Gun Nidhi should not either...He is not the eldest...Where is

Dhruv Hari?...He is the eldest...If he does not perform the *kriya* his father's soul will not be at peace...Call Dhruv Hari...'

Loud voices could be heard from all sides. Raja, Babu and Bunny stood stone-like watching the happenings helplessly. Gun Nidhi and Vidya Nidhi assumed a more aggressive posture taking position on either side of Jaidayal. The wailing women cried out louder, not in symphony with the sounds of *Hari Bol, Hari Bol* that were coming from the side where Jaidayal's family stood. Possessed by some superhuman energy a lean, tall man with fire in his eyes broke out of the human cordon that enclosed him. He snatched the burning log of wood from Jaidayal's hand and surged ahead like a relay runner sprinting forward to set the pyre alight. This sparked off loud murmurs of protest from the far side.

'*Yeh kaise agni dega...yeh to Mussalman hai...isne janeu nahin pehan rakhi hai...koi roko ise...roko is paagal ko...koi roko* (How will he light the pyre...he is a Muslim...he is not wearing the sacred thread...someone stop him...stop this mad man...someone stop him).'

By now the dissenter had reached the head of the body and was just about to touch the wildly dancing flame to it when a group of men led by Vishnu Hari, the eldest son of Jaidayal rushed forward. They roughly shoved him aside sending the lighted *mashaal* rolling to the ground. He was punched in the face and roughed up and then his hands were held in a tight pinion behind his back. They dragged him away as he shouted, kicking and convulsing wildly. Blood trickled down his left brow into his eye and fell in drops on his white khadi kurta.

'*Mein Mussalman nahin hoon* (I am not a Muslim). This is my right. Nobody can stop me. I will set the pyre alight. It is my birthright and I will give the *mukhagni* no matter what...!' A sharp punch in his ribs silenced him as he doubled over with pain, just managing to break his fall.

Suddenly a young woman in her twenties, wearing a white cotton *shalwar-suit* ran out from a group of people, her hair blowing in untidy wisps around her face as she charged towards the loner. All the rest stared at them in utter disbelief that soon turned into rage and indignation. She ran forward blindly upto the man who was being held back hard by seven men, who were far greater in number than in strength. She tried to hold onto the hands that were raining blows on him. She clung to him sobbing loudly, '*Mat maaro...mat maaro...chod do inhe...please mat maaro* (Don't hit...don't hit...leave him alone...please don't hit him).'

The blows stopped and their hold slackened, and then, as if in a melodramatic climax of a film, the camera placed on a circular trolley panned a final shot of a distraught pair clinging tightly to each other, crying inconsolably—tears mixed with tears and blood. Locked in an embrace that dented two bodies and souls, ignoring the whispering voices, sobs, and shocked countenances around them, they stood oblivious as Vishnu Hari lit the pyre.

Vishnu Hari, son of Jaidayal and the upholder of the *Hindu Dharma* in his own right, the future founder of the *Vishva Hindu Parishad*—the organisation that would protect the tenets of the Hindu religion, had displaced the natural rights of an outnumbered solitary male in the most blatant manner.

The pyre burst into flames as the woman mopped the brow of the man with her hands and his blood stained her fingers in a bond that sealed the common pathos of two suffering souls. An empathy drew them together, unmindful of the peril that could re-confirm their incestuous liaison in the eyes of all those who stared at them in shock or were too terrified to react.

As the flames rose high engulfing the body, through the rising smoke from the half-burnt wood and flesh, their silhouettes in the distance made time stand still. The touch of their bodies and the exchange of energy from their aching souls did little to relieve the frustration and sorrow that bound them together at that moment. They stayed etched in the memory of all those who witnessed the last act in the drama of the life of the man who would hardly rise from the ashes to alleviate their agony—he had never done that during his life of eighty-four years.

The woman clinging to the wounded and bleeding man was Neelima and the man, her stepbrother Dhruv Hari.

Exactly twenty-four hours after my father died, the meagre monthly allowance that was being sent to my mother was stopped. Six months later a document purporting to be his will was read out in the Registrar's office at the Tees Hazari Court by his lawyer R.S. Sharma in the presence of Raj Eshwar, T.K. Menon and the other concerned parties namely the three factions headed by Saraswati, Asha and Dineshnandini.

All those who wanted to know the details of his last will and testament presented themselves at the ceremonial reading to acknowledge, rejoice at or express grief over what had been bequeathed to them from my father's combust estate. My mother was reluctant to let us go to the reading of the final legacy, so only Raja and Babu presented themselves there.

Later, despite having suffered very trying times during which she had exhausted all her resources to support the family and run the enormous household with its grossly exaggerated overheads, my mother just would not agree to let us challenge the main beneficiaries in court, namely, Saraswati and her children.

The circumstances that culminated in the filing of a petition challenging the will were as dramatic as the life of the testator had been. After much deliberation a suit was filed in the High Court that granted an *ex-parte* stay on the estate to the petitioner's group.

It was an eerie and unexpected victory. Unlike the defendants, we had no money to fight, no documents to support our hunches and no skill to tackle their might. The only thing we did have was a deep conviction and the potential power of truth.

The bitter battle carried on for a period of three long years. In the end following an out-of-court settlement, my mother had a roof over her head and we, some semblance of the justice that we had sought!

Epilogue

Many characters in this saga have died—my father, Jaidayal, Shanti Prasad Jain, his wife Rama, her son Ashok. And those who live continue to suffer or enjoy (as the case may be) the effects of their own accumulated karmas, the karmas that have woven them into this complex tapestry that depicts the history of an era gone by.

Birth is not the beginning of life nor death the end!

The millennium has ended. The 1900s have given way to the 2000s on a continuum that stretches from *aadi* to *ant,* a beginning that I did not see and an end that I shall not know, a line of continuity that spans a space and time incomprehensible to the limitations of the human mind.

From the moment of a single cell's fusion inside the womb during that divine miracle of conception, through the indefinable pattern of growth uptil the complete cessation of it all in death, on an uninterrupted journey that encompasses the past, present and future...what is life?

Who am I? Where did I begin? Where will I go from here? What is my mission on earth? Why was I chosen at this point of my life to document this history? A history that is so challenging and vast that words hopelessly limit its power and enormity.

In the timeless expanse of the universe, I am first a minuscule spark of energy that was perhaps at some-time contained in a seed, or in the droppings of a bird, or the ashes of the dead, dancing on the waves of the Ganga along a predetermined path as compelling as it was unchangeable.

Where is Narbada—the single entity who dogged and affected the lives and consciousness of twenty-four individuals intertwining their existences in these pages of love and hate? Her soul traverses the span of the mil-lennium gone by into the womb of endless time. Has she become someone I know, or is she me? I can see none of her in myself—no rusticity, no simplicity, no devo-tion, no self-effacing sacrifice, no martyrdom. Yet I was chosen to write! Chosen from a recognised family fabric of established writers; chosen over some who shared the life and emotions much longer and more extensively of the larger-than-life entity Ramkrishna Dalmia—the man whose middle-name spelt 'controversy' and who was the greatest anachronism of his time.

What is the reason for me to be essaying this script with an alien energy that has totally possessed me? The answers will come...but when and to whom?

I look back at the events of life gone by. We shall all be gone, one by one like leaves falling off a tree in autumn to make way for new ones to grow in spring—just like Narbada, with her sweet tinkling laughter and some fairy's song. But the notes of her melody like those of Matthew Arnold's *Scholar Gypsy* will remain suspended in the air this millennium and the next and the next... till another spark of energy shall take her life form before she returns to finally unite with the original energy source in the mightiest fusion that the cosmos knows!

Where is Narbada and to which dust has she returned? Birth is not the beginning, nor death the end...

Who Lives Where

Saraswati: The seniormost of the three wives of R.K. Dalmia who were alive at the time of the writing of the book, Saraswati lived at Akbar Road in New Delhi with her two sons Gun Nidhi and Vidya Nidhi, their wives and children, and her daughter Vasudha and her children. She died in 2010.

Ila: Saraswati's eldest daughter Ila suffered from cancer. She lived in the annexe of a property that appends Ms Edward Keventers at Sardar Patel Road, in Chanakyapuri, New Delhi with her husband Niranjan Koirala. The property was bequeathed to her by her father. She died in 2003.

Sheela: She lives with her husband Rajesh Aggarwal in another annexe on the same premises on Sardar Patel Road, New Delhi, also bequeathed to her by her father.

Gun Nidhi: Married to Manju Kapoor, the writer, he lives at 27 Akbar Road, New Delhi. He owned and managed the property of over seventeen acres of Ms Edward Keventers in Chanakyapuri, which was sold to a real estate giant over a decade ago.

Vasudha: She married and divorced a man of German origin, Purushottam Schmook. She lives at 27 Akbar Road, New Delhi, with her children.

Yashodhara: An art critic and historian, after moving to Delhi from Bombay, she lives with her husband Masih Rehman. He is a senior correspondent with a foreign journal.

Shakti: She divides her time between Delhi and Bangalore for medical reasons. She is single.

Vidya Nidhi: He runs an olive oil business. He no longer lives with his wife Nilanjana who is a school teacher. His two children live with their mother at 27 Akbar Road, New Delhi.

Asha: The second in seniority of R.K. Dalmia's wives, she lived with her daughter Alka Pereira in Hauz Khas in New Delhi. She died a few years ago in Delhi.

Dhruv Hari: He lives off a part of a settlement from an eviction in Goa. He changes homes, travels around from city to city, country to country. He divorced his wife Ayesha Sayani. They have one child—a daughter who studies in the United States. His natural talent as a brilliant photographer has never been realised.

Meera: Dhruv's twin sister is married to Solil Chatterjee, the son of Late Lt. Gen. S.N. Chatterjee. She lives in Vasant Vihar, New Delhi.

Alka: She was married to and then divorced Michael Pereira. They had one son, Anand. She died some years ago in New Delhi.

Dineshnandini: The youngest of R.K. Dalmia's wives, Dineshnandini lived at 3 Sikandra Road, in New

Delhi, with two of her sons, Shiv Nidhi (Babu) and Vishva Nidhi (Raja), their wives and children, and two of her unmarried daughters, Laxmana and Archana. She continued her literary pursuits and headed an association for women writers. She has written four autobiographical novels and several anthologies of poetry that have been widely acclaimed. She was the recipient of the prestigious Maithili Sharan Gupt Award for the year 2001, and the Sahitya Academy Award for 2001–2002 in the Year of Empowerment for Women. She was awarded the Padma Bhushan in February 2006 for her contribution to Hindi Literature. She died on October 7, 2006.

Padma: Dineshnandini's eldest daughter was diabetic. She had a multiple bypass heart surgery at the age of 40. Her husband Chandra Shekhar Seth who died in 2015 lived in Meerut. She has two sons, Vineet and Gaurav. She lived with her mother and younger son at Sikandra Road in New Delhi since the year of her surgery. She died on 23–11–2010.

Shiv Nidhi (Babu): He lives at Sikandra Road with his estranged wife Mridula and their son Rudra. He spends his time listening to bhajans or music and attending religious discourses.

Laxmana: She lives at Sikandra Road in New Delhi, and is involved in making video-films and documentaries with her partner Aziz Quraishi.

Neelima: She lives with her husband Amitabh Adhar in Delhi. Her daughter Mrinali and spouse Nishant live in Delhi. They have two children. Her son Yameer and spouse Sharnamli live in Dubai with their two sons.

Vishva Nidhi (Raja): He lives at Sikandra Road in New Delhi with his wife Ritu and their two children, Vinayak and Shreya. He is an exporter-cum-commodities trader.

Karuna Nidhi (Bunny): He lives in Pune. He is divorced from his wife Nidhi. They have one son, Ruchir. He is married to Gauri Bapat. They have a son Aarav.

Archana (Dolly): She lives at Sikandra Road in New Delhi. An elected member of the All India Congress Committee, she works with the Congress President Sonia Gandhi, and heads the Grievance Cell. She is single.

Glossary

aadi	beginning
achkan	long coat worn by men
Adi Shakti	Divine Mother
anaj	cereal
ant	end
arthi	bier
arti	devotional ritual
Arun Sanghita	ancient writings on palm leaves believed to spell out the past and future of every human being on earth
azadi	freedom
baaraat	bridegroom's entourage
bachiya	child
bahu	daughter-in-law
baisa/baisahab	elder sister; term also used to designate the lady of the house
bal yogini	female child-saint
bechari	poor thing

bewaquoof	fool
Bhabhi Ma	sister-in-law accorded the status of a mother
Bharatiya Hindu naari	Indian Hindu wife, an epitome of devotion
bhoga	free meal; prasad
bhoot-ki-kahani	ghost stories
binnie	term used to designate daughter-in-law
bitiya	daughter
chaadar	shawl
Chandra Lok	abode of the Moon God
charkha	spinning wheel
chatai	grass mat
chhatrapti	ruler of the universe
chitah	funeral pyre
choora	set of ivory bangles worn by newly married women
chor	thief
churail	female malefic spirit
dadi	grandmother (paternal)
dai	midwife
devta	god
dhatura	hallucinogenic substance obtained from a plant
dulha	bridegroom
dupatta	long scarf
gajra	string of flowers
Ganga jal	holy water of the Ganga

Ganga Ma	Mother Ganga
ganja	bald
Gayatri jaap	repetitive incantation of the Gayatri Mantra
Gayatri Mantra	a sacred verse in Sanskrit; an incantation to the Goddess Gayatri
ghunghat	loose end of the sari used to cover the head
girgit	garden lizard
godhuli	dusk
gol gadda	round mattress
gola	ball
goli-raand	slave widow
gopi	cowherd and Lord Krishna's playmate
gorkha	Nepali watchman
Griha Laxmi	Goddess of Home
gyaana	knowledge
haldi	turmeric
havan-kund	pit for the sacred fire ritual
head maharaj	head chef
Hokum	Yes Master/Madame
imli	tamarind
jagir	land-holding
jagirdar	land-holder
jamadar	low-caste sweeper
janeu	sacred thread worn by upper-caste Hindus

jau	barley
jee-huzoor	yes-master
jeewan mukta	free from the material world
jharoka	window
kabar	grave
kanyadaan	giving away of the daughter in marriage
karela	bitter gourd
kartavya	duty
kathal	jackfruit
kirtan mandli	group of hymn singers
kurta-pajama	Indian dress comprising a loose shirt and trousers
Ma Jagdamba	Goddess Durga
Maha Chandi Path	a form of Durga worship
majli	middle
mali	gardener
mama	uncle (maternal)
mashaal	torch
mogra	jasmine
motu	fatso
mukhagni	lighting of a funeral pyre
munim	clerk
nag shaiyya	the mythological serpent bed
naliya	child
nana	grandfather (maternal)
nani	grandmother (maternal)
nath	nose ring
nivar	bed

odhni	long scarf draped over the head and shoulders by women
paigamber	divine incarnation
pajeb	anklet
pallu	loose end of a sari
panda	priest
pankha	fan
parikrama	circumvention
pati parmeshwar	Husband-God
pati seva	service of the husband
pativrata	devoted to the husband
pilia	long yellow scarf given to the mother of a son to be worn for all ceremonies
pitthoo	street game played with stones and a ball
pranam	greeting; salutation
purohit	priest
Raj Mata	Queen Mother
riyasat	estate
roudra mudra	pose of destruction
Sahasra Chandi Yagya	a fire-based Hindu ritual comprising the incantation of Durga's name 1,25,000 times
samrat	emperor
sandhya	prayer
sanskar	value
saptrishis	the seven saints
sasural	in-laws' home

satta	gambling; speculation
satya graha	fight for truth
satya, ahimsa, swadeshi	truth, non-violence, usage of all things Indian
saut	co-wife
sethani	Lady of the house
sewa	service
shabad	sacred verse from the *Guru Granth Sahib*
shalwar-suit	Punjabi dress
shehnai	Indian musical instrument usually played at weddings
shesh-nag	the mythological serpent on which Lord Vishnu reclines
shraddh	prayer service for the dead
sindoor	red-coloured powder worn by married women
Surya Lok	abode of the Sun God
Surya Pujan	worship of the Sun God, usually 40 days after the birth of a child
takht	wide flat bed without headboard or footboard
tapasya	meditation
tarpan	act of satisfying through oblation of water
tezaab	hydrochloric acid
thali	plate
tinda	vegetable of the gourd family
tongawala	person plying a tonga

tulsi	basil
udan khatola	mythological aircraft
vaidya	Indian doctor
vairagya	detachement
Vishnu Lok	abode of Lord Vishnu
yagya	a fire-based Hindu ritual
Yaksha, Yakshi	guardians of Kuber's wealth

Bibliography

A *Short Sketch of My Life* Ramkrishna Dalmia.

A *Short Sketch of My Life and A Guide to Bliss* Ramkrishna Dalmia, January 1962.

Karma Veer Yogi: Shri Ramkrishna Dalmia Smriti Granth compiled by Harishankar Divedi and Jaidayal Dalmia.

Sant Shri Jaidayal Dalmia: Smriti Granth compiled by Harishankar Divedi and Vishnu Hari Dalmia.

Freedom at Midnight Larry Collins and Dominique Lapierre, Simon & Schuster London 1975.

Indira: The Life of Indira Gandhi Katherine Frank, Harper Collins 2001.

Mahatma Gandhi and His Apostles Ved Mehta, India Book Company & Andre Deutsche Ltd. 1977.

Before Freedom—Nehru's Letters to His Sister Ed. Nayantara Sahgal, Harper Collins, New Delhi 2000.

Newspaper clippings, Nehru Memorial Museum and Library, Teen Murti House, New Delhi.

Vivian Bose Commission Report, 1955.

Dineshnandini Dalmia, *Kandeel Ka Dhuan,* National Publishing House, Delhi 1980.

Dineshnandini Dalmia, *Aahon Ki Baisakhiyan*, National Publishing House, Delhi 1989.

——*Mujhe Maaf Karna*, National Publishing House, Delhi 1985.

——*Yeh Bhi Jhoot Hai*, Radha Krishna Prakashan Pvt. Ltd., Delhi 1993.

www.ingramcontent.com/pod-product-compliance
Lightning Source LLC
LaVergne TN
LVHW020313200726
843507LV00012B/2082